Essays
Catholic and Missionary

Essays
Catholic and Missionary

EDITED BY THE REV.

E. R. MORGAN, M.A.

WARDEN, COLLEGE OF THE ASCENSION,
SELLY OAK

LONDON
SOCIETY FOR PROMOTING
CHRISTIAN KNOWLEDGE
NEW YORK AND TORONTO: THE MACMILLAN CO.
1928

Printed in Great Britain

PREFACE

THE vastness of the missionary task to which God is calling His Church is being revealed to those of our generation who have eyes to see and ears to hear, with a vividness and urgency that are as splendid as they are bewildering.

The response of the Church must be not only of the heart and will, but of the mind. Enthusiasm will fail unless it is tempered and directed by hard thinking; resolve will be impotent until the imagination is stimulated by great ideas.

Every branch of the Church and all religious bodies have alike fallen short in their missionary duty. All have made mistakes in method. Lamentation over past neglect and error is fruitless and paralysing, but a new vision of God's purpose through the Church will bring that true repentance which by the grace of God makes prompt recovery.

It is in a spirit of humble gratitude for the apostolic labours of other Christians that the writers of these essays venture to express their deep conviction that the Catholic witness of the Anglican Communion is something real, distinctive, and effective in the whole purpose of God.

The Catholic presentation of Christianity, while it embodies and gives expression and effect to the unique and final revelation of God in Jesus Christ can yet absorb and transmute all that is good and of permanent value in other religions, cultures, and institutions. It bears witness to the living transcendent God at work in history, to the need of the worshipful life, to sacraments as necessary to a sacramental view of the world, to the unity and continuity of the Church as guaranteed by Apostolic Scriptures, Creeds, and Successions.

Anglican Catholicism by claiming the Creeds as a sufficient doctrinal basis for unity is free from the restrictions of elaborate Tridentine definitions, and thereby

v

affords opportunities in the younger Churches for indigenous theological expression. Its theory of Catholic Order ensures unity without endangering initiative.

There are certain inevitable limitations about a volume of this kind. The writers live and work in different parts of the world. Most of them are not personally known to each other, and it has been impossible to read each other's essays.

Some are in a better position than others to make a survey of principles : some have vivid experience of one aspect of the missionary task and intimate acquaintance with the people of a particular country or district. All, however geographically limited their sphere of work, have tried to develop ideas which apply at least in some measure to the whole Church.

While each contributor must be held responsible for his or her own opinions, we trust that our common loyalty and obedience to the Living Christ in His Church has given a certain unity of aim and character to our work.

The late Dr. Burn threw himself enthusiastically into our project in its early stages, and undertook to act as editor. Though he has not lived to see the task completed, the inspiration of his wisdom and scholarship remains.

Thanks are due to Canon E. F. Spanton, Secretary of the U.M.C.A., and the Rev. G. G. S. Gillett, Editorial Secretary of S.P.G., who have virtually been co-editors with myself; to Miss Letitia Kettlewell for reading the proofs; and to many others who have made valuable criticisms and suggestions.

E. R. MORGAN.

COLLEGE OF THE ASCENSION,
   SELLY OAK.
  MICHAELMAS, 1928.

CONTENTS

vii

I

CHRISTIANITY AND THE CLAIMS OF OTHER RELIGIONS

BY EVELYN UNDERHILL

B

SYNOPSIS

Christians can only make good their claim that Christianity is *the* world-religion by proving it to be distinct in kind and superior in effect as compared with other systems.

Three possible attitudes to other systems :

(a) To dismiss them as wholly false.
(b) To regard them as imperfect revelations of the one true God.
(c) To maintain that the Gospel does not merely crown but rather cuts across them.

The purpose of this essay to recommend (c).

Similarities in doctrine and experience between Christianity and the great religions of the East incline modern missionaries to base their appeal on the inclusiveness rather than the uniqueness of the Gospel.

Difficulties in the way of establishing the true distinctiveness of Christian theism by this method discussed.

The claim of Christianity to be unique must be justified in respect of its conceptions : (1) of God, (2) of religious experience and (3) obligation.

(1) THE CONCEPTION OF GOD.

Ideas of transcendence and immanence present in all greater religions.

But the religious soul needs a *personal* God.

Only Christianity through its doctrine of the Incarnation brings the " numinous " into relation with the actualities of human life.

Again, in the deeps of reality revealed by the Cross, Christianity stands alone.

Apart from special revelation the Christian view of God is superior in three points : (a) Holiness, (b) Redemption, (c) Grace.

(2) EXPERIENCE AND (3) OBLIGATION.

It is in personal religious experience that other faiths are most closely akin to Christianity. Examples of this affinity. But whereas there is in non-Christian experience a cleavage between the individual experience and the general outlook and practice of the official religion, Christian experience is the flower of a fully articulated system of creed and life, having value not for itself alone but for the Church.

Christianity is supreme in that Christian experience has as its fruit a vigorous co-operation with the divine love in every department of life, and this co-operation is asked from all.

Christianity faces the claims of other systems of belief, not as a creed, but as a living church, a Mystical Body.

CHRISTIANITY AND THE CLAIMS OF OTHER RELIGIONS

SEEN from without by a dispassionate observer, Christianity appears in the world as merely one among several great theistic systems which declare the reality of God ; offer an exclusive and authoritative explanation of His nature and man's relation to Him ; and lay down the rules which shall govern this relationship. The chief of these religions are, of course, Hinduism, Buddhism, Islam, and the religious philosophies of China. These, at their best, do offer to their adherents well-articulated theological systems, a real conception of God, a real interpretation of human life. Therefore the Christian claim to be in a unique sense *the* world-religion can only be justified in so far as Christians can prove their possession of a Gospel which is not only distinct in origin, but also distinct in kind and superior in effect from these its great theistic rivals.

There seem to be three attitudes which missionary Christianity can adopt towards these rival faiths :

(*a*) It may dismiss them with contempt, as wholly false and " devil-inspired."

(*b*) It may regard them with respect, as partial and imperfect revelations of the one True God who gives His light to every man : preparations for the Gospel, which contain a spiritual promise that this Gospel will not destroy but fulfil, and much material which it can utilise.

(*c*) Avoiding the dangerous " either—or " of (*a*) and (*b*), Christianity may allow that the position (*b*) does witness to a limited truth ; whilst claiming that the Gospel nevertheless brings in a wholly new revelation of the supernatural, a fresh dynamic, which does not merely crown but rather cuts across all other forms of theism, as the primitive Gospel cut across the religious culture of the Graeco-Roman world. As that primitive Gospel accepted from Hellenism both philosophic conceptions and religious practices, but only under conditions which safeguard its peculiar claim to a spiritual and ethical uniqueness, so modern Christianity may act towards the philosophy and religious practice of the East. But this position, requiring as it does most delicate discriminations, can only be adopted with safety by those who have fully explored the facts supporting (*b*) ; and this in the most generous and docile spirit. It is the position which I desire in this essay to recommend.

Enlightened missionaries can no longer claim to be the proclaimers of the one and only divine revelation over against the wholly false religions of the " heathen world." It is now more than a century since Henry Martyn discovered that the Sūfis were " quite the Methodists of the East," and had many points of contact with evangelical piety. Since that time, the study of comparative religion and the publication of Oriental texts have more and more brought into prominence similarities both in doctrine and experience between Christianity and the great religions of the East ; and placed beyond denial the fact that holiness, Union with God, can be had and is discovered outside the Christian fold. This changed situation means, of course, that Christian theology must now take its place in the arena, and there demonstrate its superiority over its great rivals. Only in so far as it can prove its possession of a richer, deeper, more inclusive conception of God, and a more adequate and life-giving means of communion with Him than they are able to offer, can it justify its claim to be in a peculiar sense His saving revelation to men.

Nor can the missionary lightly assume that this will be an easy task. He cannot base his claim on the manifest superiority of Christianity at all levels to any and every non-Christian creed. The cruder products of Christian iconography and devotion should warn him against ill-considered criticisms of non-Christian " idolatry," " formalism," and " magic " : nor will he find it safe to rely on the supposed uniqueness of any one Christian characteristic. Arguments of this kind are always open to the attack of well-informed opponents, and become increasingly dangerous as the study of comparative religion proceeds. A careful and sympathetic inspection seems to reveal more and more " Christian " qualities and insights among faithful theists outside the Christian fold. Thus Christianity subordinates all things to the will of the Eternal and Infinite God : but so does Islam. She offers a sublime vision of the relation of that infinite yet immanent God to the world : so do the Vedantists. She declares God's accessibility to man's love, His delight in meekness, His demand for entire surrender : so do the Sūtras and the Sūfi mystics. She proclaims a historic incarnation of Deity, and offers men a personal object of devotion and love : so does Hinduism. She sets a lofty ethical standard : so do Buddhism and the religions of China. Her call for renunciation, her offer of salvation from the world, her claim to be a religion of redemption through sacrifice, all have their parallels in the story and doctrine of the Buddha, who ministered to mankind in a spirit of love for forty years; and in that doctrine of the Buddha-Saviour, which is the strength of Mahayana Buddhism. Her offer of forgiveness and restitution is stated in other terms in the Buddhist doctrine that the working of the law of Karma may be modified or transcended by deeds of love. Christian asceticism and mystical experience, too, have their close parallels among the Hindu and Sūfi saints ; and in these we sometimes observe that same transfiguration of personality, that enhancement of spiritual power, which so deeply impress us in the records of Christian sanctity.

These discoveries, reinforced by a general willingness to apply the doctrine of development to the religious constructions of men, have brought a violent reaction. Missionaries of the modern type often seem inclined to recommend their faith on account of its likeness to that which it supersedes. They explore similarities between Christian and non-Christian piety, treat with the utmost reverence the spiritual riches of India and of Islam, and accept from non-Christian mystics a witness which is, as a matter of fact, given with far more depth and splendour by the great Catholic saints. Their appeal is based less on the unique character of the Gospel than on its inclusiveness ; its power of unifying and explaining a larger area of religious experience than its great competitors. Admitting the claims of these competing systems to be real means of communion between man and God, they chiefly emphasise the richer, deeper conception of His nature, the more adequate and life-giving communion with Him which Christianity offers the world. As the early Fathers found in Platonism a preparation for the Gospel, so the philosophy of the Upanishads, the morals of Lao Tsi, the charity of Buddha, and the fervours of Bhakti Marga are all persuaded to witness to Christ.

This attractive line of apologetic, however, has its own dangers. Those who adopt it will find an increasing difficulty in establishing the true distinctiveness of Christian theism. Necessarily dwelling exclusively on the best and highest spiritual developments, and emphasising the mystical and personal aspect of religion as expressed in the lives of individual men of prayer, they easily lose sight of the great and fundamental differences which show themselves—not in the transcendent experiences of the occasional saints who reach those summits where " all lovers lose themselves," but in the action of religion upon the mass of ordinary men. They forget, too, to ask what is the relation between the experiences of these saints and the religious system out of which they arise. Spiritual genius will everywhere attain its goal : but those who can venerate both George Fox and St. Teresa, while remaining in the Anglican fold, have every reason to remember that sanctity does not guarantee the particular doctrinal scheme accepted by the saint. Moreover, these apologists seldom allow for the reflex action of Christian culture on the religions which they see in so benevolent a light : for whilst many profound truths harmonious with Christian teaching have certainly been extracted from the Upanishads and the Buddhist and Taoist Scriptures, this has most often been done by persons who have been influenced by Western philosophy and thought. Nor does a method which goes to the utmost lengths in toleration provide the incentive required for a vigorous pushing of the Christian claim. For all these reasons it seems that a very careful review of first principles, and a critical sifting of material in their light, is now required from those who are called upon to put the Christian case over against non-Christian theism.

In all full religion we find three factors present in various degrees of vividness. There is first the religious fact, the Reality over against the human soul : God, however crudely or even wrongly conceived. There is next the religious experience, corporate or individual, of men's souls —prayer and worship of all sorts, from its primitive beginning to its consummation in the saint. Last, issuing

from this, there is the religious obligation and performance
—duty, in its vast range from the merely ritual to the
most purely ethical demands. In the religious evolution
of humanity these three factors seem to ascend together.
Obligation only reaches the level of self-sacrifice, where the
conception of God reaches the level of spirituality, and the
experience of God reaches the level of surrendered love.
The claim of Christianity as a world-religion must therefore be justified by its life-enhancing power in each of
these three respects. If it be indeed God's supreme self-
revelation to humanity, it must give humanity not only the
best conception, but the fullest and most fruitful experience
of Him ; and must demand and support a life harmonious
on all levels with the Reality that it reveals. By its
proven superiority in these respects it conquered the
Roman world. Only thus will it now conquer in the East.

(1) **The Conception of God.**—What is the central claim
of religion ? It is, to reveal God, Reality, to man ; and
teach man how to live rightly in relation to that God, that
Reality. " What art Thou ? What am I ? " said St.
Francis. All doctrinal religions stand or fall by the
answer they give to this question.

Now since for the Christian the supreme attribute of
God, the face He turns towards men, is self-giving Love,
we must surely believe that He gives some knowledge of
His nature, some dower of supernatural grace, to all who
truly crave for Him and seek Him. Even in view of the
worst perversions of the religious sense, Christians cannot
logically deny this. They must acknowledge with St. Paul
that the revelation of the Gospel is a fuller revelation of
that same God who transcends all our definitions, but is
known in some degree in all the genuine spiritual experiences
of man. These religious experiences, as soon as they touch
spiritual levels, affirm in various ways one truth : that of a
God who is both utterly transcendent to His creation and
fully immanent in it, who is perceived to uphold the
universe He has brought into being, yet is not identified
with it. This conception informs both Moslem theology
and the deepest passages of the Bhagavad Gita. It is true
that the Semitic mind seems always more profoundly
aware of transcendence ; whilst Aryan religion in its
highest and purest developments tends towards a pantheistic immanence, which ultimately involves the identity

of Creator and Creation. Nevertheless both these types
of theism, in the experience of genuinely religious souls,
escape the logic of their own doctrines. Islam, with its
solemn insistence on the overruling power and will of
Allah, yet knows the " inner light " and the personal
raptures of the union of love ; whilst Bhakti devotion
affirms the distinctness and personality of God, " all-
powerful, all-knowing and all-merciful," the Master and
Lover of the soul, in a way that is consistent with
Christianity. To this extent, then, non-Christian theism
bears an involuntary witness to Catholic truth ; whilst
disclosing under analysis needs and cravings in the religious
soul which it can only satisfy by a departure from its own
metaphysical principles.

The chief of these needs is that of a personal God. For
the religious philosophies of China, for Hinduism and for
Buddhism, the Ultimate is strictly impersonal. There may
be personal embodiments, " bridges " which witness to the
hunger of man for communion with God ; but the Absolute
One cannot be conceived in personal terms. The final
stage in religious evolution, the discovery of " God the
Companion," is not reached by theology ; [1] though it may
be reached in the secret experience of personal sanctity.
As against this, Christianity comes to the world as a
revelation of the Absolute God, made through man to men,
which discloses in the essential nature of the very Godhead
the perfection of all that we mean by personality. The
declarations of the great Christian mystics are here
unequalled in their combination of a vast metaphysical
sweep with the tenderest intimacy. They offer to humanity
the one profound reading of the Universe which escapes
pantheistic monism on one hand and arid transcendental-
ism on the other, whilst conserving and harmonising the
complementary truths contained in each. Non-Christian
theism may, and at its best does, give us the "numinous";
which will break through somewhere, whenever human souls
direct their desire to the Unseen. But it fails to bring
that " numinous " into close relation with the actualities
of human life. It is noticeable that the efforts of the great

---

[1] " Religion . . . runs through three stages, if it evolves to its final
satisfaction. It is the transition from God the void to God the enemy,
and from God the enemy to God the companion " (A. N. Whitehead,
Religion in the Making, p. 16).

mediaeval reformers of Hinduism—Ramanuja, Nanak, and Kabir—were mainly directed to this end. Here is the point in which Catholic Christianity fulfils the world's religious need, and can meet its rivals without fear on their own ground. For the truly distinctive Christian conviction, and the necessary sequel to belief in the Incarnation, is the threefold sense of a God who is Infinite yet Personal, utterly transcendent yet completely immanent ; an Eternal Reality " wholly other " than the world He creates and upholds, yet self-revealed within history in terms of human nature, and within each soul in terms of sanctifying grace.

The Christian revelation of God, as One who enters the faulty and half-developed life of mankind in order to redeem it by love, here cuts right across the Brahman conception of a God already equally immanent in the whole world, and the Moslem conception of prophecy as the supreme means by which the Divine is disclosed to men.

This conviction of the Christian theist, that the transcendent God of the supernatural and eternal world, to which the soul has access in contemplation, is the indwelling God of nature and of history too, floods the whole of existence with new light; and gives religious worth both to the spirit's loftiest speculations, and to the body's humblest deeds and pains. The Christian cannot endorse the Buddhist's pessimistic rejection of the here-and-now : because the Incarnate finds the material of redemption in the here-and-now, and comes to men along the channels of sense. He cannot regard the material world as *maya* : because the sacraments guarantee the material world as a means through which God is self-given to the soul. He cannot conceive of the spiritual life as a solitary adventure, a laborious ascent out of nature to a transcendent One : because he knows he is a cell of the mystical body indwelt by the Holy Spirit of Love. Hence where the purest and most fervent non-Christian devotion offers a way of escape from the world, Christian devotion at its noblest always seeks to penetrate and redeem the world. It proclaims the ethical transcendence of pity ; and aims at that perfect balance of eternal love and temporal duty in which, as St. Teresa says, " Martha and Mary combine." Only Christianity has given to men a conception of God which has as its corollary this rich and fruitful ideal for human

life, and gives that ideal concrete expression in constructive works of charity and reform.

For Christianity reveals the very character of God and
the classic standard for man in one figure, that of the
historic Jesus ; and sets forth as the object of God and
objective for man, the bringing in of the Kingdom by the
Christ-like method of sacrificial love. True, other incarnational faiths claim to bring God, or a god, on to the human
stage ; and thus witness to the soul's conviction that He
does reveal Himself to man within the world of the senses,
disclosing in terms of mortal life truths deeper than we can
discover by the paths of abstract contemplation. But
even cursory comparison, for example, of the story of
Krishna with the story of the Cross, shows how strong is the
Christian position here ; so concrete and historical, yet so
unearthly in its transcendental beauty, is the figure it
presents to the devotion of men.

In the deeps of reality revealed by the Cross Christianity
stands alone. However noble as far as they go the
teachings of Taoist or Buddhist ethics may be, they stop
short here. Far more is involved than the negative
renunciations and moral disciplines of the Eight-fold Path,
or those fervours of self-immolation which are found among
the devotees of all creeds. Christianity offers, in this one
symbol, an interpretation of human life and a revelation of
the nature of God so profound and yet so simple that, in
the Augustinian image, " an elephant can swim in it and a
lamb can wade." It is a revelation which has been proved
in the experience of the saints to be inexhaustible in
significance and energising power. Rightly understood, it
is the principle of the Cross, with all that is implied by it,
which sets the Christian conception of divine Reality over
against even the noblest lights of non-Christian theism.
On the other hand, nothing that the East, with its
inborn sense of the Infinite, has to tell us about the space-
less splendour, the living joy of Brahma, the soul's thirst
for self-loss in Nirvana, or the limitless regnancy of Allah,
adds anything of value to the metaphysical side of Christian
theism as we find it in St. Augustine, Dionysius, and St.
Thomas. Theosophists and other advocates of " Eastern
wisdom " often seem to argue as though Christianity had
no religious philosophy at all. But the Church, if she will
but bring out her old and new treasures, can meet all the

philosophical claims of her great opponents on their own grounds; even where that claim is presented, as so often, in a dress borrowed without acknowledgment from the wardrobe of Christianity.

Apart from all claim to a special revelation, the Christian view of God possesses three points of manifest superiority over its rivals—namely, its conception of holiness, of redemption, and of grace. (a) First, for Christian theism the inmost reality of the universe is fundamentally ethical. The holiness of Deity consists not in unspeakable majesty, knowledge and power, but in the absolute fullness of righteousness, mercy, and love; that untouched moral perfection from which man's nascent virtues come and towards which they aspire as their goal. Hence, though Catholic Christianity can well afford to smile upon the child-like superstitions and literalisms of humble and primitive minds, it can never tolerate any type of worship, any form of fervour, any ritual observance of law, which is consistent with immoral, cruel, or unjust conceptions of God's demands and man's behaviour : or admit the claim of a religion which permits the survival of obscene or barbarous rites. The lofty claims of Hinduism to be a genuine spiritual culture, which reveals the Being of God, and teaches a way of attaining Him, crumble when we consider that the religious system of which this is the apex still supports not merely barbaric sacrifices and other gross and primitive types of idolatry, but the horrors of temple prostitution, child marriage, and the caste system; and offers divine honours to such figures as Kali and Shaiva. So, too, with the Moslem attitude to womanhood, and the dubious raptures of certain Sūfi " saints."

(b) Secondly, in the conception of God as truly working within His world, and working through men, to redeem from sin and incarnate the Eternal within the historic scene, Christianity brings the world a fresh dynamic, a " good news " about reality. This gospel acknowledges that there is something wrong with the world and with man, which God desires to set right : not by a rejection, but by a transfiguration of material life. The implicit pessimism of Indian thought, shown in its determined aloofness from practical life, is replaced by a convinced optimism that gives to every soul its place and task within the redemptive scheme, and hence an incentive to action which immanental monism and Bhakti devotion cannot provide. It is true that Christian theology does not " explain " the mystery of evil and suffering, or claim that it can make all the pieces of the cosmic puzzle fit. But in its deepest reaches it can show the religious soul how to make of suffering a means of redemption and of union with God.

(c) Last, in the vivid realisation of grace, as the active love and power of that one Infinite God, working within every soul ; in the transfiguration of man achieved by a generous dower of life given to him from above, not laborously achieved from below—Christianity brings in and accounts for a wider range of spiritual facts, establishing a dearer and more intimate relation between the ineffable God and the spirit of man, than non-Christian theism can do, if it remains true to its own principles.

For Christianity religion is a free gift, not an achievement. All its speculation about the nature of Divine Reality is coloured by this fundamental quality of self-imparting love. This gives an ethical character to its metaphysic, and a metaphysical character to its ethic. The " machinery of grace "—the Incarnation, with its continuance in the sacraments—describes the manner in which this infinite love is applied to the finite soul. This profound Christian paradox, cutting deeper than any monistic theology—the sense of the small and creaturely status of man, the immense transcendence of God, yet the loving and cherishing communion of that Holy God with this little creature, His saving, " supernaturalizing " action within the world of souls—is implicit in the doctrine of the Trinity. It has nowhere been better stated than by von Hügel :

" This poor little shelter of reeds, with the Absolute ever burning down upon it ; this poor little paper boat, on the sea of the Infinite—God took pity upon them quite apart from sin and the Fall—God wanted to give their relative independence a quite absolute worth, He took as it were sides with His own handiwork against Himself and gave us the rampart of His tender strong humanity, against the crushing opposition of the pure time- and space-less Eternal and Absolute of Himself." [1]

There is here given by Christianity something which

[1] *Selected Letters*, p. 93.

no other theistic system can give, yet which finds room
for all the best things these religions have to tell us about
Divine Reality.   For the Christian can say, as against the
intense intellectualism of Vedanta religion, "of God
Himself can no man think," and yet, as against the theological agnosticism of the Buddha, "God so loved the
world that He *gave*." [1]   It is really from its ability to hold
together and express in its concept of the Divine Nature
this intense otherness, yet personal and cherishing intimacy,
that the unique richness of Christian experience and unique
power of Christian action spring.

   (2) **Experience and** (3) **Obligation.**—It is probably in
the region of personal religious experience that Christianity
now finds it most difficult to meet the claims of other
religions, and establish her own superiority.   On the one
hand, our knowledge of the evolution of cultus forces us
to recognise primitive survivals in the Church as well as
the temple, and to acknowledge in the one as in the other
the power of appropriate symbols to stimulate religious
love and awe.   The "heathen," if religiously awakened,
no more "bows down to wood and stone" when he
venerates his religious objects, than does the Catholic
Christian who finds devotional stimulus in the Crucifix.
On the other hand, modern exploration of the psychology
and history of Mysticism and comparative study of its
documents has made it impossible to set up a sharp opposition between the Christian and non-Christian life of prayer.
Much in Christian experience has its parallels—encouraging
or disconcerting according to our point of view—among
the Hindu, Buddhist, and Sūfi contemplatives.   The great
devotional passages of the Bhagavad Gita and the psalms
of the Bhakti poets must be accepted by any unbiassed
student as genuine accounts of communion with God, and
given a high place among the religious classics of the world.
Hindu and Moslem methods of meditation, carefully
analysed, are seen to aim at, and in a measure to attain,
the same results as the disciplines described by Ruysbroeck
or St. Teresa.   The two main paths followed by contemplative souls in their response to the attraction of God—

---

   [1] "Primitive Buddhism," says Dr. McGovern, "is psychological
agnosticism, in which no attempt is made to explore the recesses of the
noumenal world, and no theories concerning ultimate reality are
postulated" (*Introduction to Mahayana Buddhism*, p. 54).

the way of abstraction and the way of personal communion —have been known and explored by Hinduism and by Islam. If we confine ourselves to examples of high spiritual attainment, it is often impossible to distinguish between the experiences of the Sūfi and the Christian contemplative, so similar is the language in which they describe their union with God : whilst much in the literature of Bhakti might come from the records of Christo-centric mysticism.

1. Heaven and earth cannot contain Thee—and yet Thou sayest " Come ye all unto Me."
2. I dreamed that I loved Him, but when I considered, I knew that His Love was before mine.
3. Our soul is so fully united to God of His own good-ness, that between God and our soul may be right nought.
4. He who doth My work, who is surrendered to Me, devoted to Me, void of attachment, who hateth nothing that is made—he cometh to Me.
5. Thou hast bound my heart in thought of Thy Name, and now I cannot but sing it ; therefore have mercy upon me, making perfect that Thou hast ordained !
6. What a day of gladness is that day in which my Beloved, who is my Treasure, comes to my house ! All evils fly from my heart when I see my Lord ! [1]

Would anyone undertake, without previous knowledge, to divide those sayings according to their Christian and non-Christian origin ; or deny to any of their authors a share in the knowledge of God's love ?

The best modern apologists of Hinduism have taken full advantage of this manifest identity of feeling, and, by the use of religious language evolved under Christian influence, have heightened the apparent similarity between the mystical experience of east and west. Thus Professor Radhakrishnan, one of the ablest of these writers, observes that " Bhakti, or true devotion, according to the Gita, is to believe in God, to love Him, to be devoted to Him and to enter into Him " ; and further that " True devotion

[1] (1) Thomas à Kempis ; (2) the Sūfi mystic, Bayazid ; (3) Julian of Norwich ; (4) the Bhagavad Gita ; (5) Richard Rolle ; (6) the Bhakti poet, Kabir.

issues in unselfish conduct. The devotee is consumed by an all-embracing beneficent love that seeks not its own." [1] These propositions could hardly have assumed this precise form without the help of the New Testament : and it is above all when its texts are thus interpreted in the light of Christian thought, when its mystical fervour is emphasised and its less desirable elements are ignored, that Bhakti religion seems so rich in spirituality. [2]

But the point to be noted here is the cleavage between the individual experience of the mystic who has " chosen the way of love," and the general outlook and practice of that official religion which now seeks to recommend itself in the person of its saints. Whilst Christians can afford to admit the valid experiences of special minds who are called to such an immediate communion with God, and whose asking, seeking, and knocking have received their reward, they should observe how often these natural mystics are compelled in obedience to their inner light to overpass the limitations, or ignore the special doctrines, of the systems within which they arise. Thus the despairing pessimism—indeed virtual atheism—of Buddhist philosophy falls away from that Buddhist contemplative for whom Nirvana becomes fullness of joy. Thus the Hindu mystic, philosophically committed to a monism which leaves no room for a personal God, can only express his communion in personal terms—" Thou art my Lord, and I am thy servant ! " Thus Hallaj, greatest of Sūfi Mystics, is also greatest of Sūfi heretics, and draws from Christianity some of his most characteristic ideas. [3]

The loftiest Christian mysticism, on the other hand, implies and is harmonious with the whole Christian creed and life. The contemplative and the charcoal burner feed on the same Scriptures, and gaze on the same ideal— Christian experience on all its levels is " all of a piece." But the love and joy, the intimate tenderness of Bhakti and Sūfi devotion are often irreconcilable with much in the official creed. Thus, while the mystical sayings ascribed to Krishna can be so translated that they evoke

[1] S. Radhakrishnan, *Indian Philosophy*, pp. 562–64.
[2] The coincidences and distinctions between Bhakti and Christian mysticism have been excellently worked out by Dr. Appasamy (*Christianity as Bhakti Marga*).
[3] *Cf.* L. Massignan, *La Passion d'al Hosayn ibn Mansour al Hallaj*, pp. 501 ff.

memories of the Fourth Gospel, and hymns written in his honour have an almost evangelical tone, nothing can make the life of Krishna, regarded as an incarnation of God, even tolerable to the Christian consciousness. So, too, the Koran declares that there are certain souls " pleasing to God " to whom He communicates inwardly " His essential mystery," giving to them by His Spirit the grace of an interior and tranquil communion with Him.[1] But by this concession it introduces into its system a dangerous dualism between binding law and free grace, and admits an ideal of sanctity hopelessly at variance with the moral standard required of the average adherent.

Yet Bhakti and Sūfi religious experience do at their best witness to the universal invitation of divine love to the soul, and that soul's power of effective response. They show us the joy and liberation which this simple and loving practice of the Presence of God brings to the human spirit, even under the most unlikely conditions, and by means of the least adequate symbolic forms. Therefore it seems that Christian teachers would do well to emphasise this aspect of Christian experience, and use to the utmost the attractive power of that Eucharistic and Christo-centric devotion, in which the longings of Bhakti and Sūfi piety are so amply fulfilled. In the best expressions of this piety —in the Gita or the Songs of Kabir, the sayings of Hallaj or of Al Ghazzali—we find most of the essential factors of personal religion : the paradoxical strivings and sur-renders, the passionate longing for holiness, the sense of an immanent yet unachieved divine companionship :

" O Holy Rama, all blessed and all merciful, fulfiller of every desire of the soul ! Bestow on us the gift of constant love and devotion." [2]

" Is it I that am here, O God ? or is it Thou ? If it be I indeed, whence doth this knowledge and power soar up in me ? and if it be Thou, whence comes this powerlessness, this weakness ? " [3]

In such prayers as these Christian and non-Christian are indeed at one. But here Bhakti and Moslem experi-ence stop, and genuine Christian experience begins. For Christian experience is the flower of a fully articulated

[1] *Cf.* L. Massignan, *La Passion d'al Hosayn ibn Mansour al Hallaj*, pp. 501 ff.
[2] Bhakti prayer.   [3] Jāmi, *Salāmān and Absāl*.

system, and a flower which is the earnest of fertility. For it sanctity is not a personal rapture, but a life-giving state ; having value not for itself alone, but for the community, the Church, within which it arises, and which gives it nurture and support. We here touch the very genius of incarnational religion, which is centred on the loving self-giving of God to men, and not on the spiritual craving of man for God.

Thus the non-Christian saint is usually a lonely soul, neither getting much support from the religious system in which he is born, nor contributing much to it. Those who seem to the Christian most truly marked with the seal of holiness are also most withdrawn from the general religious life. The Sūfi is always aloof, and often unorthodox. The Hindu saint is a hermit ; Buddhist sanctity is monastic.

Moreover, all these mystical schools are, without exception, orientated towards a personal experience and satisfaction. Therefore they teach the deliberate production of ecstasy as a means of attaining God, and usually have a technique adapted to this purpose. Here the opposition between the Christian and non-Christian mystic is complete. " Christian asceticism," says Dr. Maréchal most justly, " is not directly ordered to the attainment of mystical states. It has as its end the perfection of super-natural charity . . . the Church knows of methods and schools for the attainment of spiritual perfection, but not, properly speaking, of schools or methods for procuring the mystical states, far less of procuring ecstasy." [1]

Thus it is that while the best and deepest in all the great forms of theism already puts before the soul the love of God, the craving for God, as the earnest of man's true end, only Christianity establishes that dual and organic relation-ship between the soul and God, and between soul and soul, which is implied by these partial yet persistent lights. Even Bhakti religion at its best, which seems so rich in spirituality, so homely in its appeal to simple souls, fails in experience to transcend the self-regarding stage of devotion.   It is not creative ; never achieves that " divine fecundity " which is the goal of the supernatural life for the Christian saints.   We may safely assume that Professor

[1] J. Maréchal, S.J., *Studies in the Psychology of the Mystics*, pp. 324, 325.

Radhakrishnan is giving the most favourable account of it when he says :

" When devotion is perfected, then the individual and his God become suffused into one spiritual ecstasy, and reveal themselves as aspects of one life.   Absolute monism is therefore the completion of the dualism with which the devotional consciousness starts." [1]

And, we may add, a lonely satisfaction, an essentially aristocratic type of spirituality, is the ideal to which that devotional consciousness tends.

In strong contrast to this is the whole Christian conception of the experience and obligation of the supernatural life, as at once intensely personal and richly social.   This conception transmutes the arid and really self-centred asceticism, into which man's secret instinct of renunciation degenerates if left alone, into warm and love-impelled self-sacrifice, and replaces the sterile emotions of monistic ecstasy by the " transforming union " of the soul with Christ.   It is here, where Christianity is strongest, that Bhakti and Sūfi experience are weakest.   For Christianity refuses to rest in emotional experiences.   It links fervour with service, and conceives of men as tools of God called to work for the redemption of the world.   The Christian mystics have always known that the experience of God and the emotion resulting from that experience are not the same. The immense claims made for Oriental mysticism of the affective type are found under analysis to be, very largely, descriptions of religious emotion :   and religious emotion as such is much the same in devotee and in saint.   It is not here, but in the enhancement of life and sublimation of desire—the call to heroic virtue and the grace which supports the response—that the Christian discovers the genuine experience of God.   The Oriental mystic abandons the world and accepts painful discipline in order to gain the satisfaction of union with the Supreme.   The Christian mystic, as the fruit of that union, is impelled for love's sake to return to the world and there do hard and painful things. This difference is implicit in the organic and creative character of the Christian life.   Whilst the personal element in Catholicism, the developed and deeply felt communion with God, as explored in prayer and expressed

----

[1] *Indian Philosophy*, i. 565.

in the sacraments, fulfils the wistful hints and cravings, the isolated achievements of non-Christian theism, this personal experience derives its sanction from the strength and reality of that corporate life to which it contributes and of which it is a part. At the very heart of the Christian society is the adoring self-surrender of the saints ; consciously abandoned to the purposes of God, and indwelt by the Spirit of Christ. And, sharing this life of consecration in innumerable ways, all the lives, hopes, sufferings, works, of every kind of man and woman, contributing to the one life of the Mystical Body—the true and invisible Church. Cardinal Mercier surely marked the deepest distinction between the Christian and non-Christian conception of the spiritual life when he said :

" The interests of a Christian are not a private matter. They are the interests of the whole community. All that you do, for good or for evil, either benefits or damages the whole society of souls. By your work, your purity of life, your participation in the common suffering, you can intensify and extend the Kingdom of Love." [1]

In such a vision of the whole Supernatural Society, as the agent through which God's active love works within the world of time for the bringing forth of Eternal Life, the rich character of Christian experience and the vast span of Christian obligation are seen at their best. The experience in its wholeness is both individual and social ; the resulting duty is a ceaseless vigorous co-operation with the Divine love in every department of life—the faithful carrying through of the fruits of contemplation into action. Though non-Christian theism might acknowledge this principle, in practice the difference between the demand made on the average Christian and that made on the average Moslem or Hindu is nowhere so striking as here. Christian love is asked from all ; and Christian love, whether fulfilled in prayer or action, is always apostolic and creative—it seeks to renew and transform the world.

This does not mean that the Christian claim, as against its rivals can be expressed in the crude terms of practical philanthropy, whether medical missions, schools, or other " corporal works " ; or that this claim may ever be supposed to rest on the civilising power of Christian ethics,

---

[1] *Lettre sur l'Unité Catholique*, Mai 1922.

or any other utilitarian consideration. But it does mean that the realistic Christian sense of being part of a dedicated society, which is committed to the heroic task of transforming the world of succession—not merely to helping souls to escape from it—is irreconcilable with the declared aims of Hindu, Buddhist, and Moslem piety. Christian obligation —that call to a wide and world-embracing love which applies the living Spirit of Jesus to the whole of life— cannot be satisfied by that negative morality and obedience to ritual law which fill so large a place in other religions. Thus of the five " pillars," or essential duties of Islam,[1] four are ritual obligations, whilst Hinduism is even more completely enslaved by ceremonial rules. Even the most convinced admirer of Eastern Wisdom must concede a certain difference between the Christian *viaticum* and the obligation which rests on the pious Hindu to pass from this world holding on to the cow's tail. It is true that the atavistic tendency to emphasise ritual observance dogs all organised religion, Christianity included.[2] But the heart of Christianity is not ritual obligation. It is dynamic love —the loving movement of God to man, inciting the return movement of man to God. This return movement is not achieved by an abstraction from the world and bodily life; as in the inherently pessimistic systems of Brahmanism and Buddhism. It involves the transfiguration of the whole of life, the penetration of every moment of the day by the Spirit of Christ. The true peculiarity of Christianity is the fullness and richness with which the Unchanging God is thus brought to growing souls of every type ; and these souls are awakened to a limitless obligation of service, which can yet be fulfilled within the common life.

Thus Christian ethic is not a code, but results from the free application of a principle. Certainly the non-Christian religions at their best set a high ethical standard, and demand many virtues we are accustomed to regard as particularly " Christian," *e.g.* truthfulness, humility, mercy, self-denial, adoring love—even kindness to animals, which Mohammed taught in almost Franciscan terms.[3] Yet the

[1] Repetition of the Creed, Obligatory Prayers, Fasting, the Mecca Pilgrimage, Almsgiving.
[2] *E.g.* the slum priest who observed of his flock : " My people are savages, and I *prefer* them to be savages, so long as they come to Sunday Mass."
[3] *Cf.* Ameer Ali, *The Spirit of Islam*, p. 157.

ultimate appeal in every case is found to be to a sublimated self-interest. Moslem morality rests on law, and is recommended by rewards and punishments. Hindu and Buddhist ethics are controlled by the widespread doctrine of Karma ; but Karma is merely a drastic application of the law of consequence to human conduct—it is implicitly self-regarding. There is no obligation here, merely prudence. The " holy life " for the non-Christian is nearly always a negative way of deliverance by means of obedience to law. For the Christian it is the living fruit of deliverance, the self-oblivious life of supernatural charity. This is the only free, dynamic morality which has yet been given to the world.

The witness of all the saints, of all whose lives lie in the direction of God, is to an ideal of human existence which Christianity alone is able to fulfil. They all speak in various tones of a life which cuts right across the natural scene, and has an objective often incompatible with merely " natural " good. Christianity lays hold of this " other " life, this nascent supernatural impulse, and calls it to fulfil its destiny within the natural scene, not apart from it. It shows this other life as the means by which the Eternal shall be incarnated within the time-world, and that world be transformed into the sacramental expression of His will. The heroic careers of all the apostolic saints, from St. Paul to Henry Martyn, the creative sufferings of those who have carried through history the mysterious principle of the Cross, the Christian power of accepting and sublimating every temperament and every gift, using for the purposes of Eternity all the aspects of man's many-sided life—these constitute the Church's real answer to the claims of other faiths. For she can match and transcend in the realm of experience that which these other religions claim, and can offer souls the food they need in order to carry out all that religion demands.

Taking all this together, we begin to see that the strength of the Christian position does not lie in any explanation of the world which it may offer, or any " way of escape " from its duties and trials, but in its organic character. Its vision of God, experience of God, obligation towards God, form *one* thing. It is as a living church, a Mystical Body, capable of dealing with the world and with life, and not as a creed, that it faces the claims of other systems of belief. We have here, as nowhere else, the coincidence of philosophy, experience, and ethics, each explicating the other, and together fulfilling all the needs of the mind, the heart, and the will of man.

But Christianity will only establish this, its full claim to be regarded as the peculiar self-revelation of God to men, by using the whole of itself and living up to its own best lights. It must develop depth as well as width; once more rooting its charity and activity in the supernatural love of God in and for Himself, once more fully thinking out and fearlessly expressing its own philosophical foundations. It must balance expansion by inwardness and recollection, and orthodoxy by vigorous initiative. At present the contempt of the Eastern mind for our shallowness and lack of quietude on the one hand, our cowardly failure to apply Christian ethic to public life on the other, is too often justified. The path of penitence must be the path to power.

II

THE PRESENTATION OF THE GOSPEL
TO THE GREATER RELIGIONS

BY LAURENCE E. BROWNE

SYNOPSIS

In the approach of Christianity to the greater non-Christian religions an attitude of intolerance on the one hand and the idea that all religions are more or less equally true on the other are alike impossible.

The superiority of Christianity cannot be established by claiming it to be original or to contain a greater measure of truth than other religions.

Its claim to finality lies in the fact that it alone among religions is an organically compacted synthesis.

Christianity embodies the elements of truth in the other religions and they are in a position of unstable equilibrium.

Yet it must be admitted that historic Christianity has often failed to represent the organic wholeness of Christ. Causes of this : Nestorian Christianity as an illustration.

Leading elements in the Gospel considered in relation to the teaching of the greater religions. The idea of salvation—Christ the Way, the Truth, and the Life—The Incarnation—Mysticism and service—The Cross—The Church—The sacramental principle—Eternal Life.

The Christian Faith in its fullness satisfies the human heart : it is a synthesis fitted for all men, all places, and all times.

THE PRESENTATION OF THE GOSPEL TO THE GREATER RELIGIONS

DURING the Apostolic Age Christians were in no doubt how they ought to present the Gospel to the nations. They held aloft the light of revealed truth before a world in darkness, before people led astray by the devil into all manner of errors. The witness borne by St. Paul at Lystra and at Athens to some gleams of earlier light among the Gentiles scarcely affected his general attitude, which was to see in Judaism alone a preparation for Christianity. With the rise of the Apologists in the second and third centuries a change of attitude was inevitable. The very fact that they entered into discussion forced them to seek common ground with their opponents so as to lessen their opposition. When Greek Apologists found things they could admire in Plato, or Roman Apologists in Seneca, they were ready enough to acknowledge it. Justin Martyr could even claim that the truths imperfectly apprehended by the ancients were perfected in Christ, and Tertullian could speak of the *anima naturaliter Christiana* bearing witness to Christianity. The recognition of the good points in other religions is more widespread in our own days, and is carried much further than the Apologists could have understood or approved. While there may be here and there a thoughtful Christian who can still say with St. Paul, " the things that they sacrifice, they sacrifice to devils and not to God," the general tendency is to lay the stress on the good points in other religions, and to recognise in them the workings of the Holy Spirit. The early Christians had not sufficiently thought out the doctrine of the Holy Spirit to be able to apply to other religions the rule of charity which " rejoiceth not in unrighteousness but rejoiceth with the truth." The motive behind the modern attitude is certainly more Christian, and therefore the attitude is to be commended. But there is a great need for thought and discretion, for there can be no doubt that a superficial comparative study of religions has led many people to an unjustifiable tolerance, a refusal to condemn where condemnation is due, and to a facile acquiescence in the dictum that all religions are more or less equally true. It is highly important that all missionaries to people of the greater religions should face seriously the question of the nature of the truth that those religions contain. For while on the one hand it is unchristian to deny truth wherever it may be found, it would on the other hand take away all the motive for aggressive missionary work if faith in Christ were no longer regarded as the unique and final religion for all mankind.

Some Christian writers have laid stress on the obvious originality of Christianity as compared with other religions, and this particularly in dealing with Islam, because it can be so readily proved that Mohammed gained from many sources, mainly Christian and Jewish, the ideas incorporated in the Koran, and that the developed Islam of a century or two later was indebted further to Christianity and also to Hellenistic thought. The weakness of the argument is seen when one turns to apply it to religions earlier than Christianity, in which there can be no question of any true elements having been borrowed from Christianity. But even in the case of Islam one can hardly imagine oneself saying to a Moslem, " Many of the things you say are true enough, but they will do you no good because the founder of your religion borrowed them from others." If the rule of life by which one walks is good, it cannot be made bad by historical research showing it to have originated elsewhere than the worshipper supposed.

Other Christian writers have admitted that non-Christian religions contain many elements of truth, but assert the superiority of Christianity as containing a greater measure of truth. In a sense this answer to the problem is more subtly dangerous because it is so near to being correct. The error in it is twofold : first that truth is not a commodity which can be measured in units. It is not possible for the elements of truth and error in a religion to be computed after the manner of book-keeping, so as to show a greater or less balance to the credit of the religion. Secondly, the very suggestion of adopting this method of computation prejudges the result, for however much greater the credit balance of Christianity proved to be, the result could only be to place Christianity as superior in degree to other religions. And we must again emphasise the fact that unless Christianity is different in kind from other religions, in fact the only religion fitted to be the final religion for the whole of mankind, we have no justification for the missionary enterprise.

Is it then conceivable that in this world of human beings with limited intelligence there should exist a religion which can be spoken of as final ? Obviously no religion can be regarded as complete, in the sense that any body of finite beings can know all truth ; but we can speak of a religion as final for all time if the various elements composing its body of truth are so organically compacted that no fresh element of truth can be found which is alien to it. It is in this sense that we claim that Christianity is true and final for all time ; and by Christianity we mean not merely its body of doctrines, but also its manner of life and fellowship. We make this claim because Christianity is the attempt to understand Christ, the attempt to live the life of Christ, because Christ is incarnate in the body of His disciples, and because He is the Truth itself in all its fullness. We do not claim that the Christian Church at any time or place, or any part of it, has fully understood Christ, or has fully succeeded in living the Christ life ; and in what follows it will be necessary to bear in mind that distinction be- tween " Christianity " as here defined and " the Christian Church "—that is the body of Christian people who have lived at any time or place upon earth.

Let us then consider the way in which the elements composing the body of truth of the perfect religion are organically compacted. There are religions in which the various elements are in no sense compacted at all, but are rather placed side by side without being brought into any organic relation with one another. Such a religion is spoken of as a syncretism ; while a religion whose compo- nent elements form a consistent and organic whole may be spoken of as a synthesis. Most religions on examination will be found to fall between these two, the elements having been partially brought into relationship ; and such religions we shall speak of as imperfect syntheses.

We shall see as we proceed that this definition of a

religion as a perfect synthesis is the true criterion of the perfect and final religion. Before proceeding further to examine Christianity from this point of view, we must notice that the perfect religion will not be marked off from others by the originality of all its doctrines. We should rather expect to find in it many parallels with other religions, for every good thought that man is capable of thinking must either form part of the perfect religion already, or at any rate be assimilable without any strain on the system. Nor is the final and perfect religion merely marked off as such by its imposing array of true doctrines. For if it is the true religion for all mankind it must be possible for it to be held by a man of low intellectual power. We readily acknowledge some such persons as good Christians when they are quite incapable of understanding a complex body of doctrines ; and we can imagine a race of men in that low stage of intellectual development, who were undoubtedly to be reckoned as Christian by their fidelity to the full extent of their powers to the person of Christ.

Turning then to examine Christianity as a synthesis, we see that in its beginning it borrowed only from certain departments of human thought, mainly Jewish and Hellenistic. Before Christianity, Philo had attempted to bring these two departments of thought together, but had only succeeded in making a syncretism of them. Our Lord was able to make a synthesis of the two because He went back behind the ordinances of the Law to the underlying principles, as, for instance, when He went behind the Sixth Commandment to the underlying principle of brotherly love. Actually the only really " original " thing in Christianity was Christ Himself. It is the person of Christ which is the means of synthesising the various truths because, as He Himself claimed, He is the Truth itself. It has often been mentioned that the two conceptions of the Messiah and the Suffering Servant were never brought together until Christ was seen reigning from the tree. But more than that, His perfect manhood was the means of showing forth in one synthesis such varied conceptions as sacrifice, prophecy, and priesthood. While the varied conceptions of God, such as His holiness and His mercy which were known to the Hebrews, and His wisdom which was known to the Greeks, found their synthesis in the person of Christ by reason of His divinity. Further, it was the conjunction in one person of Godhead and Manhood that brought into synthesis such apparently opposing ideas as humility and almightiness. The fact that Christianity was thus initially successful in being a synthesis of all that was best in Judaism and Hellenism would not prove it to be the perfect and final religion. The claim of Christ to be the Truth was to be tested again and again. In the early centuries of our era the great opponent of Christianity in Europe was a medley of Oriental and Egyptian beliefs and practices, mostly of the mystic type, which pass under the general name of the Greek Mystery Religions. Looking back on that great conflict, we can see how the Christian synthesis was able, without any alteration of its structure, to take into itself all that was best in these Mystery Religions ; and succeeding ages have shown, and are showing, that the Christian synthesis is fitted to receive all that is best from every quarter. It is striking to find the following statement from a part of the world where the Church is face to face with the three great religions of Hinduism, Islam, and Buddhism : " We have inherited the riches of the nations which have before us been gathered into the Church, the riches of wisdom and knowledge which they had from the Light that lighteth every man, and look to discern other rays of that same Light in the high thoughts and aspirations of the nations which are yet to be gathered in." [1] " This capacity of absorbing into itself elements of spiritual life, which were originally independent of it is not a defect of historical Christianity, but one of its qualifications for being accepted by the modern world as a universal, an absolute, a final Religion." [2]

Let us now contrast this stability of the perfect religion with the instability of others. Religions which are a mere syncretism cannot last as such, because reason will eventually rebel against them. For instance, when the Israelites who worshipped Yahweh as their tribal God entered Palestine, they learnt from the Canaanites to worship the Baalim or local land-owning gods. The inconsistency of these two beliefs was so patent that the syncretism could not last indefinitely. What happened was that the idea of the Baalim as the givers of all good gifts was taken over into

[1] Prefatory Statement, Indian Church Constitution.
[2] Rashdall, *Philosophy and Religion*, p. 165.

the religion of Yahweh, while the unworthy conception of the plurality of gods was cast off. Perhaps more instructive is the fate of the Mystery Religions. They tried their best to assimilate Christianity, and adopted a good deal of Christian nomenclature, under the name of Gnosticism. But the Christian elements could not be assimilated, and were merely tagged on to the old religions as syncretistic additions. The resultant religion, being a syncretism of diverse and partially contradictory elements, was in a state of unstable equilibrium, and was doomed sooner or later to collapse. It sometimes happens that a religion succeeds in forming a synthesis of certain elements by rigidly excluding others, thus maintaining a temporary stability. Such was the case with Islam at its first commencement, selecting only such elements from Christianity, Judaism, or elsewhere which could be combined with Mohammed's preconceived notions into a consistent whole. Mysticism did not form part of that synthesis, and the few mystical elements in the Koran were syncretistic additions. The Moslem conception of God was such as not to allow the assimilation of mysticism. When eventually mysticism forced its way into Islam it was a severe crisis for the religion, which resulted in the formation of Sūfi sects who practise mysticism and more or less ignore orthodox Islam. Although the religion of Christ is a perfect synthesis, it is possible for the Church at some particular time and place to hold a conception of Christianity which is an imperfect synthesis. This was the case with the Protestantism of the nineteenth century, which found itself nonplussed by the new truths of science, because it had accepted into its system certain notions about the Bible which were not part of the religion of Christ. The crisis was a severe one. But looking back on it now as a thing of the past, we see that the acceptance of those scientific truths has enriched our conception of Christianity.

Turning now to the great non-Christian religions of the present day, we find that each one of them is undergoing a severe crisis, with all the appearance of imminent disintegration. The influence, not only of Christianity but also of Western culture, on Islam, Hinduism, and Buddhism has broken into the imperfect syntheses of those religions. The agnosticism of many Japanese students, the neglect of caste rules by a certain section of Hindus, the growing materialism and indifference to religious practices of the educated Moslems of Cairo and Constantinople, are all signs of the break-up of imperfect syntheses. Occasionally we hear the cry " Back to the Vedas " or " Back to primitive Islam," but no stability is attained that way because there is no perfect synthesis to be found even as an ideal in these religions. The only sincere attempt to go back to primitive Islam is that of the Wahhabis, and the result, so far from being a perfect synthesis, is a religion which is only fitted for the restricted conditions of Arabia. Christian authors sometimes write as if the break-up of other religions was a thing to be welcomed ; but it must be remembered that in most cases it does not lead to Christianity, but rather to materialism, which, as we know in Western lands, is a great dead obstacle to religion. It may even be that as materialists they are more impervious to spiritual influences than they were before. In throwing off the old religion because its imperfect synthesis is found to be contrary to scientific thought and unfitted for the modern world, they are apt to throw off even those truths which the old religion contained ; and in order to accept Christianity they must needs go back and accept afresh many truths which had once been rejected. The idea, therefore, that a service is being rendered to the cause of Christianity by undermining another religion is false. If the religion is imperfect it will break down through its essential instability, and its followers will be the first to attack it when they find that it has failed them. What is needed is to undergird rather than to undermine the other religion, supporting the truths it contains and welding them into a closer synthesis by the knowledge of Christ. This the missionary will be able to do if he knows the minds of his hearers, and approaches them in the spirit of friendship and helpfulness, teaching them the positive truths which will supplement or correct what they already believe.

It is well known in mechanics that an object which is more or less unstable, when pushed out of its position, may rest in another position of unstable equilibrium, instead of undergoing a complete collapse at once. This gives a good picture of what often happens in imperfectly synthesised religions. Hinduism at the beginning of the nineteenth century did not know that there was anything amiss with its system ; and one can scarcely imagine what a blow it was when the British forbade *sati* and infanticide as flagrantly immoral. Hinduism had always regarded infanticide as permissible ; while *sati*, or the immolation of a widow on the funeral pyre of her husband, was regarded as a noble virtue and the highest expression of wifely devotion. While the majority of Hindus paid an unwilling obedience to the new law, no doubt the conscience of many responded to the morality underlying it, and accepted it as true ; but the acceptance broke into the imperfect synthesis of Hinduism. Other blows to the synthesis came from other Western influences, notably that of the missionaries who depicted before their hearers a new way of life and the new ideal of Christ. " Nor should we forget that there is much in Indian life which is neither traceable to its past nor visibly connected with either Christianity or Western culture. Deep within the inaccessible retreats of Hinduism is the welling up of a new inspiration, having no tangible connexion either with the past or the present. Now and then, without preparation or warning, the religious forces of Hinduism throw into light men of Christian heart, features and love who had no contact with the historic Jesus or the visible Church. They are silent reminders of the fact that God is working in His own way in religions." [1] One of the results of these various blows to the synthesis of Hinduism was that a certain section of the Hindus adopted a new position of temporary stability, as in our mechanical model, by forming the Brahmo Samaj which incorporated certain ideas from Christianity and Islam. At the time the Christian missionaries thought that this move was on the way to Christianity, and were surprised not to win many converts from the Brahmo Samaj. Actually the new position was rather more stable than the old one. Since its first period of development the Samaj has not grown in numbers, but the same process has been going on, without being given a name, within the fold of Hinduism, so that now all Hindus who have come much under Western influence have accepted certain elements from Christianity. Anyone who knows Hinduism will realise that these Christian elements cannot be perfectly synthesised with Hinduism. The position is different from what it was before, but it is still unstable. Missionaries

---

[1] Quoted from an important article by P. Chenchiah, " Christianity and Hinduism," in *The National Christian Council Review* for March 1928.

must pay great heed to such a change as this, or they may be simply emphasising facts already accepted or attacking errors already rejected. They must deal with the situation as it is at present, and prepare for the next move. The next move may be again a " reform " of Hinduism, that is a sliding into a new position of temporary equilibrium, or it may be a complete collapse of the system leading either to a drift into agnosticism as a counsel of despair, or to a mass movement towards Christianity.

If we admit, then, that none of the great non-Christian religions has ever been a perfect synthesis, and that their seeming stability at certain times has only been due to a rigid exclusion of unwelcome elements of truth ; and if we admit on the other hand that the religion of Christ is a perfect synthesis, it follows that Christianity must eventually prevail except where deliberate sin or refusal to face the truth block the way.

But the history of Christianity has not been an uninterrupted advance, and the cause must be sought in a failure of Christians to maintain the Christian synthesis intact. First, not because of its frequency, but because of the immense influence for evil of the sporadic cases that occur, must be placed moral failure on the part of the minister or missionary. And with it, as a companion evil, must be placed moral failure on the part of the laity. Christianity is life, and failure to live the life vitiates the synthesis in its most vital spot. A Christian missionary who does not show forth Christian virtue in his life, a Christian congregation which sinks into internal quarrels or the selfishness which does not welcome converts, are obvious causes of weakness to the Christian cause. Along with them, though not strictly speaking comparable, must be remembered faults in the example of Europeans resident in Oriental lands, or in the acts of European governments, which are laid by Orientals to the charge of Christianity.

Apart from these moral weaknesses, which have only to be mentioned to be condemned, there are more subtle causes for the failures of the Church. When two communities live side by side, the one Christian and the other non-Christian, and there is no political or social pressure for conversion either way, it often happens that the two communities remain apart, each living its own spiritual life, not attempting to understand one another, and the

D

ideal the highest Christian life was a weakness in the
Christian synthesis which might have passed unnoticed had
it not been for the rise of Islam. Islam was essentially
anti-ascetic, even though asceticism forced its way into
Islam as a syncretistic addition. The other tendency to
be referred to is the cult of images. Throughout the whole
Church, East and West, the use of images had definitely
developed into a cult or veneration of images by the sixth
century. Whether the Oriental Churches practised this
cult more than other Christians we do not know, though
this is suggested by the fact that the opponents of the
cult who met at Constantinople in A.D. 753 declared that
none but Nestorians or Monophysites could logically make
an image of Christ,[1] and also by the fact that the strongest
defence of the cult came from an Oriental, St. John of
Damascus.[2] As with asceticism, it was the rise of Islam
that drew attention to the error of image worship, and the
Caliphs of Damascus, Yazid I and II, anticipated the Roman
Emperors, Leo III and Constantine V, in persecuting
Christians for practising the cult. Thus we see that the
Christian synthesis had become weak at two points just at
the moment when Islam appeared on the stage of history.
Islam, as we have seen, was itself an imperfect synthesis,
but it was not yet proved to be such, for it seemed a complete synthesis as far as it went ; and Islam was strong in
those two points where the Christian Church was weak.
Is it not possible that the failure of the Nestorian Church
may have sprung from this cause ?

In an essay on the modern presentation of Christianity
this long digression into past history might seem out of
place, until it is seen how the same problems are recurring
to-day in India. Asceticism occupies an extraordinarily
prominent place in the religious ideal of Indians. Idolatry
is not only practised by the more ignorant Hindus, but is

---

[1] The argument was that either the artist pretended to depict the
whole Christ, God and Man, in which case he circumscribed the divinity
and confounded the natures (Monophysitism), or else he pretended only to
represent the humanity, in which case he divided that which ought to be
united (Nestorianism).

[2] " The Nestorians now have no pictures of any kind, only a plain
cross, to which they pay the greatest reverence. They alone among the
Eastern Churches make a principle of not venerating images, although
there is evidence that formerly they had them, according to the usual
Eastern custom " (Adrian Fortescue, Art. " Iconoclasm," in the
Encyclopedia of Religion and Ethics).

defended philosophically by the learned in terms almost identical with those with which St. John of Damascus defended the cult of images.

Finally, among the causes for failure we must mention heresy and schism. Heresy is of two kinds : the belief in wrong things, and the narrow-mindedness which excludes the truth held by others. If we were able to trace the results of men's thoughts in the course of history we should no doubt find that many a failure was caused ultimately by intellectual dishonesty or intellectual cowardice. Schism may be caused by heresy of either kind, or merely by political conditions and difficulty of communications ; but whatever the cause may be, schism weakens the hold of the divided body on the one synthesis of the Faith.

It remains to treat briefly some of the leading elements of the Gospel in relationship to the greater non-Christian religions of the present day.

Encouraged by the name of Jesus we preach salvation full and free. Judaism, Zoroastrianism (still existing, and making converts in Persia), and the Eastern branch of Buddhism, look forward to a Saviour ; but none of the non-Christian religions have any full conception of salvation because they are not aware of the depths from which we need to be saved. Hinduism and Buddhism lack the real sense of sin. The possibility of forgiveness is ruled out by the relentless theory of Karma. Judaism alone has an adequate sense of sin, but nothing is more pathetic than the way in which the greater sins are held in suspense annually till the Day of Atonement, and yet that day brings now no atoning sacrifice, but only the memory of how in olden days sacrifices were offered to take away sins. It needs the knowledge of the Fatherhood of God as taught in the parable of the Prodigal Son, and the knowledge of God's attitude towards sin and suffering as shown in the whole life and death of Christ, to bring assurance of salvation from sin and pain. Nothing but Christianity in its fullness can take away the sense of fear, for it needs perfect love to cast out fear. Mohammed took refuge in the Lord against the mischiefs of His creation, against jinn and men ; but, in spite of that, Moslems no less than Hindus live their lives in fear and superstition. It must be reckoned as a failure to apprehend Christ when fear is still present among Christians, as in the case of the modern

Greeks, who are in the trammels of fear of unlucky days and of the evil eye.

Other religions have nothing to offer comparable with Christ, the Way, the Truth, and the Life. What a contrast between Him who is Himself the Way, and the Mahdi of the Shiites guided in the right way ! " O Ananda," said the Buddha, " I am growing old, and my journey is drawing to its close. . . . In future be to yourselves your own light, your own refuge : seek no other refuge. Hold fast to the truth of your refuge : look not to any but yourselves as refuge." It is the experience of countless missionaries that men are drawn irresistibly to the person of Christ. Long before the Hindu will see in Christ the sole incarnation of God, before the Moslem will give Him the title of Son of God, before the Jew will accept Him as Messiah, He comes to occupy in their minds and hearts a place that none other has. The character of God, especially His moral holiness and His Fatherhood, which are new conceptions to people of most other faiths, is best presented, not as an abstract proposition, but as arising out of a study of the person and teaching of Christ.

The eternal Word of God incarnate in time as Jesus Christ is a conception which will one day find a home in the hearts of Hindus and Moslems. The great Hindu doctrine of the Upanishads that equates the human soul with the divine is a truth gone wrong by attributing to the present the future goal, asserting that men are by nature that which they can only become by adoption. Consequently the Hindus, with their thousands of *avatars*, have failed to reach the idea of an incarnation of God, and have but the pretence of it which the Docetists tried to introduce into Christianity. Moslems believe that the eternal Word of God, existing from all time with God, was revealed in time as an Arabic Koran. Eventually they will see that the living Christ is better than an infallible book, but the belief is firmly entrenched and will not too easily be corrected.

No presentation of Christ can be regarded as complete that does not adequately set forth both the way of Martha and the way of Mary. The latter is the mystic way which the East loves, and the former is social service for the Kingdom which the East needs to learn. It is the mystic way, communion with the Holy Spirit, which brings out the cosmic significance of the historical Jesus. The strength of Oriental mysticism is the strong sense of the reality of the unseen world, and the earnestness with which the mystics devote themselves to the search for union with God. Its weakness is in the imperfect conception of the moral nature of God, which betrays itself in the lack of fruits of the Spirit in the moral life of the mystics. It will be a great day for Christendom when the knowledge of the moral character of God as revealed in Christ is linked up with their sense of the nearness of the unseen and their desire to be in mystic communion with God. The missionary cannot afford to omit either the mystic way, which makes Christ a present reality to his hearers, or the way of service without which the Christian synthesis cannot be completed. For the way of service is the way of the Cross.

The Cross of Christ in the first days was to the Jews a stumbling-block and to the Gentiles foolishness. To the non-Christian world to-day it is still both a stumbling-block and foolishness. One of the weaknesses of Oriental religions is their disregard of historical fact. Fables of *avatars* that have no historical support seem to them as good foundations for a religion as facts like the life and death and resurrection of Christ. Moslems take as the perfect man an ideal Mohammed far removed from the Mohammed of history. Were it not for this indifference to historical fact it is inconceivable that Moslems through the centuries should have acquiesced in the Koranic denial of the death of Christ, a fact not only supported by the strongest literary evidence, but also borne witness to day by day throughout the world at the Holy Eucharist as clearly as Muharram year by year bears witness to the tragedy of the field of Kerbela. The death of Christ upon the cross is a demonstration of the love of God for mankind ; His resurrection is God's vindication of righteousness ; and both together have a unique significance for Christians, who, by union with Christ, die to sin and rise again unto righteousness.

An important article of the message is our belief in one Holy Catholic and Apostolic Church. This belief we set over against the racial particularism of the Jews, the partition walls of castes and sub-castes of Hinduism, and the Moslem brotherhood restricted to their co-religionists. But what we preach and believe in is contradicted before the eyes of the world by the divisions of Christendom.

For the Church, that now is, is far from having attained to that ideal in which we believe—the One Holy Catholic and Apostolic Church—which is synonymous with the Kingdom of God. And while we cease not to proclaim the Gospel of Christ's kingdom on earth, and His eventual return to receive it to Himself, we must also incessantly repent the sins that perpetuate divisions, and pray for the healing of the stricken Body.

In the great religions of the world there is a very sharp cleavage in the matter of the relationship of material and spiritual things. In practical religious life this cleavage shows itself in the attitude towards idolatry, enthusiastically observed by Hinduism and Buddhism, and whole-heartedly hated by Judaism, Islam, and Zoroastrianism. A pantheistic philosophy, such as one finds in Hinduism, gives its support to idolatry, but the two are not necessarily interdependent. On the other hand, a Manichaean belief that matter is essentially evil would of course rule out the possibility of idolatry. So sharp is the difference of opinion between the idolators and the iconoclasts that compromise is impossible. But although compromise is impossible, a synthesis of the underlying ideas of both sides is effected in Christianity. Setting aside as derogatory to God the pantheistic philosophy that all things are God, and the Manichaean philosophy that all material things are evil, we must trace the other motives underlying the practice of idolatry and the abhorrence of it. The idolator believes that God is revealed in His works, that material things may be the channel of communication with Him, that an image of God may act as an assurance of the presence of God, and that adoration intended for God should be directed towards the image which represents Him and declares His presence. Iconoclasts on the other hand show that such adoration too often rests upon the material object only and does not soar aloft to the divine. But apart from this tendency of the more thoughtless idolators, there is the more fundamental objection to idolatry that an image, which for the maker of it may represent so much of his conception of God as he can express by chisel or paint brush, becomes for succeeding worshippers not a revelation of the living God, but a limitation of Him within an exceedingly narrow compass. The localisation of God, which is also objected to, is really only a part of the limitation of Him which is inseparable from idolatry. The haters of idolatry believe that, since God is a Spirit, He must be spiritually apprehended as a living and unlimited power. Now the Christian doctrine of sacraments and the sacramental life gathers up into one these diverse aspirations. The sacramental life means the appreciation of God in His works : " The heavens declare the glory of God, and the firmament sheweth His handiwork " (Ps. xix. 1). " The invisible things of Him since the creation of the world are clearly seen, being perceived through the things that are made, even His everlasting power and divinity " (Rom. i. 20). The sacraments of Baptism and the Holy Eucharist proffer gifts of divine power through the medium of things that are seen ; but being the channels of His grace, whereby His life is imparted to His worshippers, rather than representations of His being, they do not fall under the condemnation of limiting the Infinite. In sacraments God is spiritually apprehended, and it must be remembered that while we are in the body there is no escape from the use of our senses : whether we listen to the Word of God, or read sacred writings, or even meditate in silence, our ears or eyes or brain are called into play. No one will mistake the few words said here for an attempt to explain fully sacramental doctrine. But enough has been said to show that there is no synthesis of apparently opposing truths more remarkable than this provided by the sacraments and the sacramental life. And whether we are addressing those who shed tears of love over their idols, or those whose zeal against idolatry is such that (as St. Paul said) they even desecrate temples, the doctrine of the sacraments must form an essential part of our message.

Finally, we lay before our hearers the Gospel of life eternal. Till late in Old Testament times the Jews sought righteousness without the knowledge of reward and punishment after death, and we cannot but admire them for it. But though Christianity speaks of reward and punishment, the words sink into insignificance compared with the promise, " I am come that they might have life, and that they might have it more abundantly," for life exceeds reward by so much as victory is greater than the victor's medal. The modern Moslem is inclined to allegorise the delights of heaven pictured in the Koran, and we may encourage him in so doing, for it may lead him to set less store by the future satisfaction of the appetite for pleasure, and to think more of becoming fitted for eternity in the presence of God. And who can estimate the value of the Gospel of life eternal with God when it reaches the heart of the Hindu whose hope, after an almost endless series of births, is to be engulfed in the divine as a drop of rain-water in the sea ? or of the Buddhist whose final hope is the extinction of all that can say " I am " ?

From all that has been said this fact emerges, that the Christian faith in its fullness satisfies the human heart wherever it may be found, that it is a synthesis fitted for all men, all places, and all times. The one aim above all else must be to present the whole faith. Owing to our own personal limitations, it is much easier to present a partial view of the faith. It is easier to lay stress on the views that appeal to oneself. It is easier to stir up enthusiasm for a small sect. It is easier to present the faith with that English colouring that is familiar to us. It is easier to present, wherever we go, that stage of the faith which makes its appeal to our own twentieth century. Far harder, but infinitely more worth while, is it to present the Catholic faith in its due proportions, not coloured overmuch with the peculiarities of the missionary himself, or of his homeland, or of his century. Such a presentation can scarcely be offered save by one who values his position as a member of the Great Church, feels himself in fellowship with the redeemed of past ages, and looks forward to fellowship with generations yet unborn who will bring in their new contributions to the understanding of the one Christ.

III

THE PRESENTATION OF THE GOSPEL TO NON-CIVILISED PEOPLES

BY ROBERT H. BAKER, C.R.

SYNOPSIS

Some characteristics of Bantu religion.

Belief in God—in spirits—dynamism—animism—ancestor worship.

Points of contact :

1. Belief in God.
2. Sense of need.
3. Desire for fellowship in the Church.

Hindrances to the presentation of the Gospel :

1. Language.
2. Internal opposition of individuals.
3. Social opposition.
4. Fatalism, magic, and witchcraft.
5. Failures of Europeans.
6. Other hindrances.

The Presentation of the Gospel :

Preaching and teaching.
Testing during Catechumenate.
Use of catechists.
Use of Bible.
Use of literature in the vernacular.
Pastoral dealing with souls.

Secondary means of evangelisation :

Educational work.
Industrial training.
Medical work.
Contact with European Christians

The Building of the Native Church.

1. Native ministry.
2. Liturgical worship.
3. Fellowship in service.

It is love that matters.

THE PRESENTATION OF THE GOSPEL TO NON-CIVILISED PEOPLES

Some Characteristics of Bantu Religion.—Some years ago at Bagamoyo in Central Africa, a missionary was looking on as a caravan of porters was preparing to set out for the interior of the continent. The chief porter uttered an invocation : " May God be favourable to us ! " The European in charge of the party replied in a swaggering way : " God ! We have no need of him. My god is my money and my gun." The porters put down their burdens, and began to withdraw. The European asked the missionary to use his influence with them, but they said : " No. This white man is bad : did you not hear him insult God ? With him we should be sure to have misfortune." And they all left him. Quite recently in Southern Rhodesia the present writer was passing a cemetery in company with a native who had been under Christian influence for fifteen years or more. The native, referring to the burying-ground, said : " Would you come down here at night after dark by yourself alone ? " The answer given was : " Yes ; why not ? What has a Christian to fear in so doing ? " To which the native replied : " He has not anything to fear, but I don't think those people would let you."

These anecdotes, illustrating two important features of faith in Bantu Africa—belief in a supreme God, and belief in spirits—make it quite evident that these non-civilised people have a religion of their own. Many and various are the ways in which religion has been defined, but most attempts agree in representing man as waking up to a Presence outside himself. Observation and experience suggest that the Supreme Deity is not to be confused with a deified ancestor, for the more one gets to know the people and their tribal life the more one realises that they have a belief in God who is supreme over all. It is true that they do not offer much worship to Him, but they give Him a name which shows that He is distinct from the various lesser deities and spirits in whom they believe. For example, the group of tribes popularly known as Mashona speak of Him as *Mwari*, while another though less used name is *Nyadenga*, which means " the one in heaven." In Central Africa He is known as *Leza*, because He nourishes people ; another name *Mpambe* (from *ku-pamba*, to excel) is almost the equivalent of " the Almighty " ; while yet another name is *Chiuta* (derived from *uta*, a bow, because He stretches the rainbow across the sky). *Chiuta* is thus God in space, and the rainbow is a sign of Him. Similar designations are to be found in the speech of other tribes.

The Bantu belief in God as educed from the various names and titles given Him has been thus summarised : " God is intimately associated with the sky and what comes from it. God is Creator, and the determiner of destiny. He is a Person, morality is ascribed to Him, and some idea exists of Him as a benevolent Being." The Supreme Being of the Bantu is, in fact, much like the " One Above " vaguely believed in by many English people, much aloof from most of them, little worshipped or regarded, yet turned to in times of emergency when all other sources of help have been explored in vain.

The most important factor in Bantu religion, however, is dynamism—the belief in an energy or potency immanent in all things, yet as intangible and all-pervasive as the ether. Though everywhere and flowing through all things, it draws itself to a focus in certain conspicuous objects. Doctors and diviners are believed to have the secret of controlling this energy, which they apply to the needs of everyday life by means of charms and medicines, by the practice of witchcraft and divination, and through a system of taboos which regulates the behaviour of the individual and the tribe.

Akin to this is animism—a belief in spiritual beings having a separate life of their own, yet associated for a time with material things. It is not easy for us to grasp the Bantu idea of human personality, but they do believe in a vital principle apart from the body. Their burial customs make it plain that they believe in a personality that continues after death. Even though the body decays, the man himself survives. No more than we do they believe that the dead are extinct ; though with them, as with many more civilised folk, there is some vagueness and confusion of thought as to their condition. Thus it comes to pass that ancestor-worship plays a great part in their religion. The living need the help of the departed in struggling with the evils around them, and the dead need the attention and devotion of the living to provide for their well-being. Each has need of the other. Offerings are made to the spirits, and no doubt fear has some part in the worship given to them, but filial piety has its place as well, and in a sense the attitude of the worshippers is one of reverence and awe. Other spirits, however, are believed in ; some malignant, regarded with fear and dread, who are held to seek opportunity to haunt the living, and these do much to rob life of happiness and joy. Besides these, there are nature spirits connected with hills and mountains, rivers and waterfalls, trees and pools. Each grade has its own special cultus, and the particular people concerned have their own obligations to perform. Our knowledge of all these matters is somewhat vague, but this much is abundantly clear, that in the view of the Bantu the world around them is filled with a vast number of spiritual powers.

Points of Contact.—It is thus plain that in the religion of the Bantu there are various points where the Christian teacher can make contact with their beliefs in the same way as St. Paul made his approach to the Athenians— " Whom therefore ye worship in ignorance, Him declare I unto you."

1. In the first place there is no necessity to attempt to prove the existence of God. The Old Testament prophets and writers never did so. Those whom they addressed would have thought such an effort absurd, as no one would have dreamt of denying Him. So it is with the Bantu, who are a thoroughly religious people.

2. The heathen among non-civilised people know and admit that they are in darkness. Many of them realise the dimness of the light that their religion gives and long for more. They hunger for knowledge. " We want to know ; we wish to learn " is the cry going up in many parts to-day. The missionary can teach them of the Light that lighteneth every man, by whom grace and truth are given and revealed. Their own religion tells them of God ; they

have dim inklings of Him as the Creator, as the unseen Spirit. We can add to this knowledge of His holiness and love. We can show that the end of religion is to love God and to be loved by Him. The great sign of His love is that He sent our Lord Jesus Christ to reveal to us that love, to save us from sin and Satan, to set us the example of a perfect human life, and to give us grace.

3. The Catholic Church alone can fully and effectively give them the message that they ask for. The individual missionary can do little of himself. This is not to say that individuality and personality are of no account, but they can only work fruitfully within the life of a disciplined and organised society. The social organisation of the Bantu enables them to respect a society with an agelong history and a world-wide activity. Especially can they understand the religion of such a society when it can show that it comes as the representative of a Teacher whose object was not " to destroy but to fulfil " : that this Teacher is the Son of God who inspired and commissioned His followers to convert the whole world. And the attraction of such a society is strengthened by the fact that as a fundamental principle it recognises no distinction of race or colour, while it proclaims with certainty a message which has been the same all down the long ages and will continue unchanged to the end.

Hindrances to the Presentation of the Gospel.—Certain difficulties and hindrances soon become apparent.

1. The first three may be grouped together as being closely connected—namely, language, lack of vocabulary, and differing types of thought from our own. Not only has the missionary to learn a new language, he has also most probably to learn one of a type wholly different from any he has met before. It may be quite possible for him to gain sufficient knowledge to preach in the vernacular after a few months of hard work ; at the end of some years he may even amaze some of his own fellow-countrymen with the apparent fluency of his discourse. He himself, however, is only too painfully aware of the many things he wishes to say that must perforce remain unsaid, since the divergence in ways of thought existing between himself and his flock prevents him from presenting his message in a form that will be easily grasped by them.

2. Besides this, there is the internal opposition of

individuals to be overcome. At the very beginning of missionary work in a new country the people begin by suspecting the motives of the new-comers, asking " Who are they ? What is their work ? What is their object ? " Even after the Church had been at work in her country for about thirty years, one old chieftainess asked the writer : " Have you no home and no work that you go wandering from place to place with your belongings on the pack-saddles of two donkeys ? " Most semi-civilised folk have also such a vein of untruthfulness that they rarely give a straight answer to a stranger, and in consequence seldom expect a straight answer to their own questions. Thus an attitude of suspicion exists at the beginning that it takes a considerable time to break down. Even when this has been accomplished and the people recognise one's sincerity, they will say most probably that the teaching offered is all right for white people, but not for those of their race ; or, later, again they will assert that, though most probably true, it is too difficult for them.

3. A still further hindrance is the social opposition from their fellow-countrymen, often backed up by the influence of the chiefs and elders. This obviously is the case some little time after the first contact with Christianity. At the beginning (after the first suspicion is conquered) the new teaching may begin to have some degree of popularity, but soon certain difficulties arise as it begins to dawn upon the older people that the new religion in many ways cuts across native life and institutions. Customs in regard to marriage have to be revised ; betrothals arranged years before may have to be cancelled. Sacrifices to spirits are forbidden; burial customs are interfered with ; witchcraft and divination are prohibited.

As a result of the new outlook on life individual initiative develops among the younger people and so tends to make a break with tribal tradition, the incubus of which does so much to hinder the progress of the less civilised races. Naturally the elders are suspicious of the new customs and the changes in the ways of life. The consideration of a somewhat similar state of things nowadays in England will help us to be sympathetic with grandfathers in Africa and elsewhere who also are perturbed at the vagaries (as they think them) of the young people. For they, too, shake their heads somewhat despairingly and say : " Things

E

are different now from the days when we were boys."
Yet one cannot set back the clock or put old heads on
young shoulders, and in these distant lands, as in England,
the older folk are coming to recognise and accept the
inevitable in a greater degree than many of them were doing
a generation or so ago. It is significant, for instance, that
in the Manyika district of Southern Rhodesia, the term
wakuru (the elders) is used by the younger generation in
many cases as a term equivalent to our use of the words
pagan or *heathen*.

4. Still further hindrances which have to be faced are
those connected with fatalism, magic, and witchcraft.

Fatalism, which is the belief that all events are pre-
determined by an arbitrary law, results in an attitude of
mind which regards all that happens as inevitable. This is
noticeable in many ways. M. Allier quotes the Basuto as
frequently saying to a missionary such words as " If only
God would convert me ! " and " When God speaks to me,
I shall become a convert." Nor is this attitude found only
in regard to things of the soul, it shows itself in all moments
of life. Everywhere there is a lack of strength of will.
When natives are seized with sudden cold or overpowered
by the current of a river, even though they are more robust
and physically vigorous than Europeans, they will not hold
out for so long a time, and will make less of a struggle to
save their lives. When a Mosuto is sick he lies and suffers
in silence without murmuring ; he makes no effort to
struggle against his malady, but gives himself up without
any resistance until his sickness either leaves him or else
carries him off.

Magic has its varying aspects of divination, possession,
and witchcraft, but all are so much intertwined that it is
difficult to know where distinctions are to be drawn in so
short a space as is possible here. All are connected with
the practice of " medicine." The " doctor " has to do with
all aspects, and there are few converts to Christianity in
early days who do not at some time have recourse to the
diviner, the witch-doctor, or the magician for one cause or
another. We need to try and distinguish between the
false and the true, since mixed up with a great deal of
deception (especially in the practice of the healing art)
there is a considerable knowledge of remedies of value ; so
until we are able to replace the crude ideas of the mass of

the people with knowledge of better remedies and confidence in those who administer them, we must be prepared for lapses of this kind. Far more serious are cases of resorting to divination for the purpose of locating guilt in moral cases, and it is these which are the greatest hindrance to Christian progress. Social pressure from the heathen elders often leads new converts to turn back to these evil customs ; and though such matters should not be overlooked when exercising discipline, they should not as a rule be regarded with undue severity.[1]

Lack of moral fibre is the cause of backslidings such as these, and it is in the strengthening of the will by the use of sacramental grace that the remedy will be found to cure these evils.

A few other hindrances to accepting Christianity must also be briefly mentioned.

5. A closer acquaintance with Europeans too often shows that with a large proportion the practice of the Christian religion holds little or no place in their lives. As a result, many of the native people readily copy their prevailing slackness. The recognition of this fact should do much to rouse the Church to the necessity of a vigorous campaign towards strengthening its work among settlers in distant lands, though, after all, they are to a great extent only witnessing to the weaknesses of popular religion in the homeland whence they come.

6. Polygamy also keeps some among the heathen from accepting the Faith ; customs such as the inheriting of a father's or brother's wives have their influence in retarding conversion ; while domestic quarrels culminating in divorce account for a certain amount of apostasy and backsliding. Others, again, after Baptism hold indeed to the Church, but fail to get beyond a view of the Gospel in which legalism predominates, and, remaining in the stage of a formalist morality, fail to realise the glorious liberty of the children of God.

The Presentation of the Gospel.—In passing from these difficulties, hindrances, and discouragements to the factors that make for progress, the first place must be given to the evangelical preaching to which reference has been made above. It is thus that individual conversions are brought

---

[1] They are seldom as serious as, *e.g.*, going to a European civil court to seek divorce, whence the return to penitence is much more difficult.

about, as people are led one by one to faith, repentance, and renunciation. Among the less civilised peoples there is little difficulty in understanding the meaning of " turning and becoming as little children." In most fields of work, too, the complications arising from the conflicting claims of different forms of Christianity are not very obvious. In the darker places of the earth the spaces, as a rule, are wide enough for the " churches " and the Church. It is only in the realm of the higher levels of civilisation that the diseases of Christianity become apparent. Any form of Christianity is an advance on the heathen beliefs of the non-civilised, and we must be thankful wherever Christ is preached, however inadequately. Yet, if only the Faith in its fullness can be presented to these people in the first instance, there is little likelihood of their relapsing into other forms of Christianity. The simplicity of the Catholic religion is its commendation.

So we teach in the familiar way the old truths, for since there is only one true God, there can be only one true religion. God is our loving Father. Prayer is converse with him. Sin interrupts this. Repentance removes the barrier caused by sin. Worship is giving God the honour which is His due. Grace is the power that comes from Christ's atoning death. The sacraments assure us of God's grace through Jesus Christ in His Church through the operation of the Holy Spirit. The preaching of the love of God is the most moving power in the world, for thus only is the consciousness of sin awakened. The preaching of forgiveness is of no effect until the consciousness of sin arouses the consciences of men. If this is omitted little need of a Saviour will be found. But when this duty of arousing the conscience is faithfully performed, the filial piety which the African of old showed when seeking to propitiate spirits in fear will now lead him to seek forgiveness and grace from the God of love.

In many places the slow movement towards conversion in days gone by is now giving place to mass movements towards Christianity among these peoples of less advanced culture. It is therefore necessary to form classes in preparation for Baptism after the first shyness is removed and a point of contact made. For our object must be to make Christians, and Baptism is the only gate of entrance into the Christian Church. But the way must not be too easy. The time spent as a catechumen by the would-be convert is a time of training ; we must ensure that it is a time of testing as well. Hence it must not be too short. The individual must be given encouragement as he goes along, for which the formal admission to the catechumenate gives an opportunity, when, after examination, the neophyte is signed with the cross and admitted to a special status on the fringe, so to speak, of the Church. Here he has a position higher than that of the " hearer," yet below that of the baptised. He is now encouraged to look forward to the grace that will be given him through sacramental means, when in the font he comes to receive spiritual regeneration and later kneels at the altar ; though it must be remembered that a necessary reserve should be observed when speaking to catechumens of the inner mysteries of the Faith.

It is in these classes that the value of native agents becomes apparent. A pioneer missionary may be able to preach either alone or with the aid of an interpreter, but he will find after a time that he is totally unable to deal with the numbers who come seeking for instruction. A selection from the small group of early converts will provide the nucleus of a body of catechists and teachers when the time arrives to require their services. The earnestness and zeal of these men will make up for many deficiencies in their training and preparation, but that does not exempt us from the responsibility of equipping them for their duties as well as we possibly can. In many cases they will start centres of teaching on their own initiative, and come in to ask for recognition and authorisation when the work is already started and in some degree established. It is thus (in Africa at any rate) that a great number of the small schools are started, and these humble beginnings often after a few years develop into centres of influential spiritual life. No one knows better than the European missionary the points of weakness in such schools, but, knowing also the possibilities of progress inherent in them, he is able to ignore the fatuous criticisms of superficial observers.

The " out-stations " begun in this way are the chief centres where the work of instructing the classes of hearers and catechumens is carried on. The type of catechist steadily and gradually improves, but all, even the best, need guidance both in the method and the matter of instruction. Experience shows that the best way of providing this is by means of a catechism ; and in spite of prejudice among many modern educationists against such compilations, a great deal may be urged in their behalf, which will probably be borne out by all who have to do with the religious instruction of the less civilised races. A catechism, if wisely arranged, provides a syllabus of systematic religious teaching, graded according to the requirements of those for whom it is compiled. In the circumstances we are considering provision should be made for a year's course for hearers in preparation for the catechumenate, and a two years' further course in preparation for Baptism, Confirmation, and First Communion. The answers should be as terse and concise as possible, providing a summary, easy to be remembered, of the instructions given, which should be made vivid and living by stories and illustrations.   Since the object of all religious instruction is to bring souls to the knowledge of God and of His self-revelation, it is difficult to imagine how anyone can dream that mere verbal knowledge of the text will be held to suffice, yet such is apparently the case among some who in these days criticise the use of a catechism.

Stories from the sacred Scriptures can be used to enforce and support our teaching, not beginning with the Book of Genesis or indeed with any part of the Old Testament, but with the Gospel of Jesus Christ, the Son of God. The Gospel according to St. Mark gives a plan that can well be followed, while later, when the hearers begin to grasp the facts, further questions as to His birth and parentage and the continuation of His work can be answered from the writings of St. Matthew and St. Luke.   Stories of the life and work of our Lord must, of course, come in the first place, but others such as those of the heroes of the Old Testament may well be used in sermons and instructions to illustrate and bring home special points of teaching as required.

Some missionaries of experience have gone so far as to question the desirability of using the Old Testament at all, but it seems difficult to take such a line as this when we think of our Lord increasing in wisdom and listening to the doctors during the years when He would be receiving instruction in the traditions and stories of God's chosen people. We can picture Him being told of the divine promises of old, of Noah and the patriarchs, of Moses and the prophets, and of all God's plan that led up to the Incarnation. And as we grow familiar with the folk-lore of the African peoples we can use their stories as well to illustrate the lessons of the Old Testament, showing how God's people of old were in darkness much like that of Africa to-day, and how God led them out of the gloom into the fuller light of that truth which is now brought to them through the Church of Christ. A speaker at the Le Zoute Conference in 1926 suggested the possibility of arranging a system of teaching from African folk-lore that might be used as a preparation for the Gospel. Whether that is either possible or desirable may be questioned, but it is at least true that acquaintance with such stories is of inestimable value in presenting divine truth to people of lower types of culture, and no missionary can regard his equipment as complete without some knowledge of this kind.

In these days, also, literature in the vernacular is necessary as part of the equipment of schools and missions. In most cases catechumens are taught to read during their time of preparation. The effort required for this helps, among other things, as a means of judging their moral earnestness. As a result they are able to study their catechisms, to follow the services intelligently in their Prayer Books, and to read the Holy Scriptures.[1]

Catholic belief in the value of sacramental grace will influence the dealings of the missionary with catechumens. He will be prepared to admit them to Baptism at an earlier stage than many other religious bodies, who, in failing to apprehend the fullness of the Christian revelation, are thus hampered in their dealings with their converts. This fact is recognised by a recent French writer, M. Raoul Allier, in his valuable study *La Psychologie de la Conversion chez les peuples non-civilisées*, where he notes : " Protestant and Catholic missions, while pursuing the same end, which is to make Christians, are inspired by principles which are at times dissimilar, and as a result put in practice divergent methods." Without entering into details, he refers to the difference of outlook resulting in different ideas of the

---

[1] Reference may be made here, in passing, to the tremendous help given to English Church Missions by the S.P.C.K., whose magnificent work in providing literature of this kind is too little known and appreciated by the rank and file of churchpeople.

character of the Church, involving also different conceptions of the sacraments, this last point being made plain at a very early stage by the difference of attitude in regard to infant Baptism.

The catechist carries on the round of daily instruction in the village schools which grow up in the way described above, but this makes it necessary for the supervising missionary to go round regularly inspecting the work that is going on. The Catholic system makes it essential that the supervisor shall be a priest, for once the stage has been reached when the first converts are admitted to Baptism, it will be his duty to see that they are regularly fed and nourished with sacramental grace. Candidates for Baptism and the catechumenate will have to be examined, children will need Baptism, confessions must be heard, Holy Communion must be given, the faithful need encouragement, discipline must be administered, the lapsed must be sought out, and the dying consoled.

The catechumens at the end of their probationary period will be called in to the central station for final preparation, which should last for about three weeks. During this time their course of instruction will be reviewed, questions as to possible heathen entanglements investigated, and final instruction imparted on details of Christian life and duty. The greater number will no doubt be well prepared, but some, for various reasons, will have to be held back till a future time.

It is thus that the way is opened for real pastoral dealing with souls, and one is thankful to notice the moral effort made to break, not only with the individual past, but with the social traditions of heathenism and all that they involve. Everywhere the old tribal restraints are breaking down, and the individual has more and more to stand by himself. As he is helped in this by the power of grace, he is also doing his part in raising the general level of public opinion around him, and thus working for the moral uplift of his own race and generation. Side by side with this there is often noticeable a real development of spiritual perception. Steps which in earlier days were not dreamt of as possibilities in the path of holiness are discovered and surmounted, as those who formerly stumbled in the darkness of ignorance come nearer to the Light that guides their feet into the way of peace.

Secondary Means of Evangelisation.—1. The very elementary type of school which had its origin in the necessity
of forming classes in preparation for Baptism is increasingly used for the purpose of imparting the rudiments
of " secular " instruction as well. At the present time,
in Bantu Africa at any rate, almost all the schools for
providing elementary education are under the care of the
various missionary bodies. At the Edinburgh Missionary
Conference in 1910 education was recognised as the most
prominent secondary method (after preaching, establishment of the Church and translation of the Scriptures) in
the propagation of the Gospel, and at Le Zoute in 1926 it
was agreed by all there that " the formulation and general
direction of educational policy, the general administration
of the educational system, and the supervision of all
educational institutions, are among the proper functions
of government." This is self-evident to anyone who considers the problems of modern domestic policy in any
country, but we must never admit that the State *alone*
can direct or adequately present the ideals of *Christian*
education. We must beware of allowing ourselves to
become so far involved with the State in our educational
activities that we lose control of our own schools ; and
missionary hearted people must be prepared—at any rate
for a time, till the local churches become firmly established
—to do more in the future in support of this important
branch of missionary activity. For the school is destined
to play a growing part in the later phases of the evangelisation of the less civilised, and our policy must be to take the
lead in this essential work. Missions cannot rest content
with merely conforming to the demands of Governments,
but must show them the ideal methods by which such work
is to be carried on.

2. Nor can industrial training be passed by without a
word of reference, since it is of far more importance in this
sphere of work than mere literary efficiency. The whole
man must be raised to a higher level, and if we seek merely
to save the soul or to raise the intellect, we shall often find
that we lose the man himself. By teaching organised
industry we are using a tremendous force in bringing
discipline to bear on the formation of character ; while by
widening the field of our converts' interests and activities
we do much to counteract those temptations to vice of

many kinds which beset persons living under conditions that often involve hours of idleness.

3. Medical work under the aegis of the Church has also its function as an important secondary method of evangelisation. To "heal the sick" was one of the commands given by our Lord to His disciples, and in obeying Him in this direction not only are prejudice and suspicion broken down, but the strongholds of evil are uprooted as gross and degrading superstitions are effaced and the influences of witchcraft are overcome.

4. No doubt the stimulating influence of contact with more civilised races is a factor that has to be reckoned with in presenting the Gospel under such conditions as we are now considering. In most cases the more civilised are Europeans, who in great number are at any rate nominal Christians. The natives recognise this, and being religious people, attribute the advantages the white man enjoys to the fact that he is blessed by God. They desire to enjoy these blessings too, and so seek to learn the white man's religion. That is perhaps a crude statement, but it contains an element of truth which makes it easier for the missionary in helping to open a way for the presentation of the Gospel.

The Building of the Native Church.—In conclusion, a few observations may be offered on the work which follows evangelisation.

1. For the preaching and teaching of the Christian faith, and the ministry of the sacraments, there is the necessity for developing a native ministry. The European missionary can but begin the work, and a great deal of his energy must be expended on training teachers, catechists, deacons, and priests to do as efficiently as possible what he can only attempt in a lame and halting manner, hampered as he is by the hindrances mentioned above. Such a ministry, adequately trained and equipped, is one of the first essentials to effective evangelisation. With this, training in the devotional life must go hand in hand. Meditation must have its place. Study of the Scriptures must be encouraged and the frequent use of the Sacraments plainly taught.

2. The efficient exercise of discipline is obviously essential. Baptism must not be too easily administered, training and testing must be provided for, and if by

grievous sin any should forfeit their privileges as Christians, signs of penitence must be shown before readmission to the fold.   No healthy church can be built up on a firm foundation unless a definite system of discipline is formulated and exercised.

3. Liturgical worship must also be presented with due dignity ; primarily because it is part of the divine plan, but also because decency and order in accordance with Christian tradition are appreciated.   Ceremonial has its meaning, and one has but to take part in the solemnities of the sacred seasons to realise the hold they have on simple folk.   The Crib at Christmas, the ashes at the beginning of Lent, the Procession of palms, the various ceremonies of Holy Week culminating in the joys of Easter—all these are no mere outward forms, but full of meaning in presenting the Gospel message.   And, above all, the drama of the Mass set forth day by day is soon understood as a mystic showing of the Passion ; while the feast on the Sacrifice and the fact of offering it on behalf of the departed is understood as the full unfolding of that truth of communion with the unseen, after which the elders groped in the gloom of heathenism.   The saints with Mary as their queen take their places with the angels round the throne of the Most High, and communion with them at the Christian altar is realised in a way dimly foreshadowed by the heathen rites, though never dreamt of by those who took part in them.

Music also has its place : the music of the Church is the music of the people.   If St. Jerome could write from his cave at Bethlehem that psalms and alleluias were the burden of the songs of ploughmen and reapers, labourers and vine dressers, shepherds and herdmen, it may equally be said that in many parts of the world to-day the influence of the Church can be traced and known by the music in the fields and on the footpaths.   Psalms and hymns are sung in place of the heathen ditties, though much scope still remains for those who will turn their talents to provide simple music for use in worship, suited to the needs and not remote from the genius of the backward races.

4. A characteristic that strikes the missionary on first contact with such folk as these is their active participation in church work.   All take their part, and to all it is a joy. Fellowship in worship is in a real sense fellowship in service ; and unless the sense of responsibility inherent in

this desire for service is encouraged and cultivated, there will be no growth into a healthy indigenous church life. The germs of this life are there, and the missionary from overseas will only be doing his rightful part as he seeks more and more to efface himself, while leading his flock forward in an ever-growing degree to shoulder responsibility, both in regard to finance and organisation. The tendency to do otherwise exists—perhaps more among us English folk than among other nations. " On all sides this is the complaint against England raised by her subjects of other races. ' You are just,' they say to us, ' you give us good laws and a large amount of liberty, but you despise us. As long as that is so, we can never love you.' If only missionaries can make their conduct an exception to that rule, they may do almost what they will with the ' inferior ' people that surround them."

Herein is the conclusion of the whole matter. It is love that supremely matters. If the Catholic religion is to win souls, it must above all things be presented as the religion of love ; a faith, indeed, to be held and taught, a system to be presented in its fullness, a worship to be offered in the beauty of holiness, but above all things a life to be lived as a witness to the transforming power of Jesus Christ. For we can only hand on to others that which we ourselves receive, as in union with our Lord we are transfused with His power and inspired with His Spirit—" I am come that they might have life, and that they might have it more abundantly." " This is life eternal, to know Thee, the only true God, and Jesus Christ whom Thou hast sent."

IV

THE PRESENTATION OF THE GOSPEL IN NON-CHRISTIAN SOCIETY

BY H. A. JONES

SYNOPSIS

It is inherent in the Christian faith to have a message to society.

I. FUNDAMENTAL PRINCIPLES OF THE GOSPEL BEARING ON THIS MESSAGE.

The nature of God as active in history.
The nature of man as a subject in the kingdom of God.
The teaching of our Lord.
New Testament emphasis on the interplay of the individual and the social.

It is evidently the task of the Church to build up a Christian social order as well as to change the lives of individuals.

It is impossible to live the Christian life in its fullness in a society which is not itself Christian.

We cannot escape our responsibilities by identifying the Church with the kingdom.

II. HOW ARE WE TO PRESENT THIS GOSPEL IN A NON-CHRISTIAN SOCIETY ?

The Church is clearly not intended to identify itself with any political or economic party.

But it must

(1) arouse a social conscience, especially in relation to avarice, responsibility, simplicity.
    The need of education in Christian sociology.
(2) judge the conditions and tendencies of the time in the light of the Christian standard. In doing this we must remember :
    (a) that our condemnation of the evils in society should be founded definitely on the fact that such evils are based on a wrong valuation of human life.
    (b) that the Church should Christianise rather than destroy as much of the traditional life and spirit of a country as possible.

Only in the Catholic Church can the various groups of men find a common life.

THE PRESENTATION OF THE GOSPEL IN NON-CHRISTIAN SOCIETY

THE growth of psychology and the tendency to analyse every aspect of human life from the psychological point of view have made us a self-conscious generation, not only as individuals, but as groups. The Church, the Nation, the Trade Union, the Social Class, or some other community, small or large, occupies the thoughts of the average man as much as, in some cases more than, his own individual life. Under such conditions it is impossible to avoid discussion as to the relationship of the Gospel to society. Even if the missionary wished to do so, the Chinese or Indian nationalist, the Moslem who sees the widely different social orders produced by the New Testament and the Koran, and the Communist arguing for the materialistic interpretation of history, would not allow him to do so. But there is more to be said than that. This essay is written in the belief that it is inherent in the Christian Faith to have a message to society as such, and that the difficulties of thinking out that message and of outlining a Christian social order under modern world conditions are no excuse for shirking what is perhaps the most vital of present-day tasks. We may believe that in recent years such an order has been identified too easily with some particular political or economic doctrine, but that again is no excuse for treating politics and economics as aspects of life outside the scope of Christian thought. It seems necessary, therefore, to outline some fundamental principles of the Gospel bearing on this matter before we can discuss profitably the presentation of the Gospel in a non-Christian society.

I

We begin with the Christian revelation of the nature of God. To us God is essentially " the living God " of the prophets, One who takes an active part in the course of

human history, not merely the logical glue which binds the
universe together. Philosophically and practically we
build on the truth. " There is no escape from pantheism,
and from a creed which, if not pessimistic, is without hope
for the future and without consolation in the present," says
the Dean of St. Paul's, " unless we abandon the doctrine
of equivalence between God and the world, and return to
the theory of creation by a God who is, in His own being,
independent of the world and above it." [1]   And Dr. Rawlin-
son has built up his Christological argument on the same
foundation. " What is really at stake in these discussions,"
he says, " is something which goes deeper than Christology.
It is the fundamental faith of the Jew in the living God.
It is the validity, as against what has been, upon the whole,
the pantheistic tradition of much European philosophy, of
that whole monotheistic apprehension and affirmation of
God as the Living One, operative in history, concretely real
and personal, which mankind owes to the Jew." [2]   That
faith of the Jew involved his recognition that God had a
purpose both for his nation and for the world.   That
purpose had very definite ethical consequences for society,
and the writing prophets were quite sure that their message
involved a reordering of the corporate life of the community.   That was natural in the earlier days, when the
individual was considered to have no relationship to God
apart from his membership of the nation.   But even when
Jeremiah and Ezekiel had passed beyond the purely social
conception of religion and had taught that the individual
is judged by his own relationship to God, they do not cease
to teach that the community as a community must express
the will of God.   From their day until apostolic times,
although the phrase " the Kingdom of God " might vary
its meaning, there was no change in the belief that the
world is God's world and that human life must be an
expression of His nature.   St. Paul's teaching was that
our Lord worked redemption on the cosmic scale and the
whole of the Johannine writings are inexplicable unless
this is true.   The Christian God is One who demands the
redemption of society through the redemption of the
individual, not the redemption of the individual through
society, but He does demand the redemption of society.

[1] *Outspoken Essays*, Second Series, p. 11.
[2] Bampton Lectures, 1926, pp. 18, 19.

When we pass on to consider the Christian doctrine of the nature of man, we are driven to the same conclusion. There is no indication whatever that our Lord looked upon His disciples as a collection of individuals. To Him they were " the remnant," " the true Israel," in accordance with the old prophetic teaching, and not only the parables but the Sermon on the Mount involve a reference to a community. This truth has been masked in the discussions of recent years because those discussions have centred round the question as to the *gradual growth* of the kingdom. We can grant that the kingdom begins by an inner acceptance of God's reign over the individual, and it requires little knowledge of the spiritual life to know that that acceptance can be made and yet the full results be a long time coming. This does not alter the fact that such an acceptance has a community reference and is (in the New Testament) inevitably followed by baptism. The phrase " the kingdom of God " means more than the reign of God over the individual life. It includes in its meaning the community over whom He reigns. So in the parables people are " cast out " of the kingdom, and in the Sermon on the Mount the disciples form " the city " set on a hill. This phrase " the city " became the typical one for the kingdom when the Church entered the Gentile world, and it is difficult to believe that such a fundamental misrepresentation of our Lord's teaching could have occurred. But this is not to say that Jesus was the equivalent of the modern social reformer, any more than He was the equivalent of a Greek philosopher exhorting His disciples to seek the absolute values of truth, beauty, and goodness. He was too " religious " in His outlook for either rôle. Rather does His attitude seem to have been somewhat as follows. He undoubtedly faced the evils of mankind in their corporate as well as in their individual aspects. No understanding of the Temptation narrative is possible without seeing this. But in analysing those evils it is possible to take up one of three positions. We may deal with them on the political plane, as did the Zealots and as does the typical party politician of modern times. Or we may go deeper and believe that our troubles are due to a bad economic system, and it is surely a matter for congratulation rather than for despair that in our own day we are concentrating on this rather than on politics in the narrower sense. Or we may go deeper still and find our solution on the spiritual plane, seeing men's chief difficulties as the result of men's sin, their refusal to seek and to hold fast to God's will. If the third alternative is the correct one, it is idle to suppose that political and economic salvation can come without spiritual salvation. The kingdom of God grows from within outwards, or it never grows at all, but in solving the spiritual problem (or, better, redeeming the spiritual life) we are in the way of solving the political and economic problems. They will require much thought and probably many experiments, but their solution does become possible. It is not the whole truth to say, with Professor Peabody of Harvard : " The kingdom of God, in the business world as elsewhere, is not an external growth but a spiritual revolution, to be created not by better machinery but by better men." For better men will create better machinery, or they will not be better men. Nor can they be stopped (nor should be) from the attempt to create better machinery until the majority of men are better.[1]

The New Testament writers are shielded from the danger of looking on men as merely a part of a social organism by their insistence on the fact that each one has an individual relationship to God. The nemesis which awaits all over-emphasis of the communal side of life is the destruction of individual initiative and therefore, in the end, the stagnation of the whole society. A healthy community is precisely one in which the individual has some kind of security of status which enables him to resist the aggression of the mass.[2] That interplay of the individual and corporate sides of life from which personality is achieved is rendered impossible by any form of " servile state." A community is distinct on the one hand from a herd, and on the other from a regiment. And that distinctiveness is obtained for the Christian from the sense of his personal relationship to God. This relationship is not independent of his membership in the Church, but an integral part of that membership. The Christian life reaches its fullness from the union between individualistic mysticism and devotion to the " beloved community." The balance between the corporate and the individual aspects of society may be difficult to reach, but it is one

---

[1] *The Church of the Spirit*, quoted by W. R. Inge, *England*, p. 220.
[2] *Cf.* Professor MacIver's *Community*.

which the New Testament writers never forgot, and which, in their view persists after death. For, although it is the individual who is immortal, he finds himself, even in eternity, a member of the Communion of Saints.

It seems clear from this consideration of the very fundamentals of the Christian message that it is the task of the Church to build up a Christian social order as well as to change the lives of individuals. There is another consideration emphasising the same truth, and that is the impossibility of living the Christian life in all its fullness in a society which is not itself Christian. That impossibility is hidden from us in the West partly because our civilisation is nominally Christian, and has large Christian elements in it, but chiefly because we both adopt a low standard for our ideal and also never think out the implications of much of our life. It is not enough to pay a fair (even an excessive) price for the food we eat, the clothing we wear, the coal we burn, if we never consider the conditions under which these things are produced. We have a real part in poverty, and cannot absolve ourselves from the duty of baptising the conditions of industry into the Christian spirit. In spite of the heroic spiritual lives of many individuals, any industrial parish witnesses to the impossibility of a high general level of Christian life under modern Western conditions. That material environment which should act as the great discipline of the human spirit has become so overpowering as to be almost its prison. But the effect of a non-Christian environment on the individual Christian life is most clearly seen outside Europe, in Africa, Asia, and the Pacific Islands. As the Report on *The Call from our own People Overseas* says, quoting an administrator of experience in the tropics : " I am, I confess, often astonished that our young men turn out as well as they do when all the conventions of life to which they have grown accustomed are suddenly withdrawn, and with eyes wide opened to life's possibilities they are jerked out into the midst of utterly strange conditions, where the best may seem not unlike the worst." [1] And if this be so with our own people, the case is still harder for the native convert. Internally he has a nature moulded by centuries of a non-Christian tradition, externally there is the opposition of his own countrymen, and the two are often combined at

[1] P. 21.

the present time, particularly in Asia, by the urgings of a patriotism which sees in Christianity only a form of Western Imperialism. There, at all events, the almost unconscious changing of society by the acceptance of Christian values is impossible. Not only the Faith but its corporate implications will only be accepted with full knowledge of all that it means in the ordering of the national life. Unless we can dissociate the Catholic Faith from its Western non-Christian accretions, and at the same time show its real significance for national and international life in the East, there seems little chance of winning the peoples of Asia for our Lord. " The Christ of the Indian Road " must be seen as the Christ of the Chinese (and Japanese) road as well. And it is worth while noting that the popularity of Mr. Stanley Jones's book in England is certainly due, in part, to our desire to find the Christ of the *English* road.

Before we pass to the consequences of this view of the Gospel as it affects its presentation, there is a question of a somewhat different character with which we must deal briefly. There are those who admit that the Faith has a corporate significance, but hold that that significance is fulfilled in the existence of the Church itself. That is to say, they identify the Church with the kingdom of God. They would read St. Matthew xxviii. 19 as if it were " make disciples *out of* all nations," being content if from the nations of the earth were gathered groups who as parts of the one Church would live the life of prayer and sacrament and worship and love of the brethren, but not attempting to influence directly the social order. Now it is true that in places our Lord distinguishes a Christian's attitude towards those within the Church from his attitude towards those without ; [1] that it took several centuries for the social consciousness of the Church to develop at all fully ; and that it is especially incumbent upon Christians to exhibit the spirit and life of the kingdom within the Church. But it is equally clear that in the New Testament the Church exists, not for itself, but for the kingdom ; that although it cannot be separated from the kingdom, but is integrated into the very structure of it,[2] yet its mission is to bring all life into captivity to Christ ; and that the

---

[1] *Cf.* J. R. Seeley, *Ecce Homo*, chap. xxiii.
[2] I owe the phrase to the Rev. P. T. Widdrington, Anglo-Catholic Social Series, No. 1, p. 18.

true interpretation of the phrase in St. Matthew is to be found in the Apocalypse of St. John xxi. 24, 26 : " The nations shall walk by the light thereof : and the kings of the earth do bring their glory into it. . . . And they shall bring the glory and the honour of the nations into it." For good or for evil the Church is committed in our generation to making the life of the nations of this earth an expression in all its aspects of the will of God as manifested in our Lord, to making actual everything that the God of life means to the whole man, and it is our belief that that is the vital message which God has for our time.

II

How, then, shall we present this Gospel in a non-Christian society ? To what does it commit the Church and the individual missionary (or parish priest at home) ? To dispose of a negative first, it does not involve the identification of the Church with any particular political or economic party, nor the adoption by the Church of the purely political or economic analysis of human ills. Nor is there any real tendency to do so at the present time. The habit of certain writers and speakers of saying that there is, betrays a lamentable ignorance of the trend of thought in circles devoted to the furtherance of a Christian social order. The members of those circles have steadily been moving away from such a position for years, and while still standing unfalteringly for a Christian social order, base that order on a spiritual basis and a spiritual change. It is true that in the opinion of the members of the League of the Kingdom of God, for example, such an order will involve corresponding changes in our economic and financial life, but that is because they are Catholic sacramentalists, and see that a religious life which has no social manifestation (or simply takes the present social order for granted) might receive the blessing of Plotinus, but not of the writers of the New Testament. The real truth has been put adequately in the Report on *The Call from the Moslem World* :

" Bound up with any Church policy for Moslem lands is the application of Christ's teaching to all our great international problems to-day. The Christianizing of our social, industrial, and political life in the West, the complete dissociation of political policies abroad from the true expression of the Christian message and the revival of new spiritual life in the Eastern Churches, freed from Western intrigue, are essential factors in the situation. . . . Missionary work in Moslem lands must make a permanent contribution to the present race problem. It must develop the social implications of the Gospel in lands where crying evils await solution. The range of this is unlimited. . . . Above all, missionary work must be centred, not only in the universality of Christ, but also in His absolute supremacy over all life. It must be the full interpretation of Him, as sufficient for all human needs to the whole Moslem world."[1]

When we turn to the positive side, the first consequence is the obvious necessity that the Church throughout the world should set itself to the arousal of " a social conscience." But this does not mean the perpetual denunciation of those in power after the style of the street-corner orator. It does mean the careful teaching of Catholic ethical principles not only on the general question, but particularly as they bear upon three things, which may be called roughly avarice, responsibility, and simplicity.

The fact that avarice is a deadly sin, fatal ultimately both to the individual and to society, has been masked by an economic and social order in which men believe that individual material advancement was bound to end in corporate happiness. It can safely be said that the majority of men have believed that doctrine only while there was any hope of their own advancement, and its hollowness has long been exposed. But it still survives as the typical rationalisation of selfishness, and there are few congregations who do not need to think more about avarice. Partly this can come as the result of sermons, lectures, and group discussions[2]; partly, also, through better direction and self-examination. The typical set of " self-examination questions " needs radical revision in this connexion. Most of them take up far too much time in tithing mint and anise and cummin.

The same is true with regard to responsibility. There has always been Christian teaching concerning the stewardship of wealth, but it has rarely gone deeply enough, and certainly at the present time does not take into account

---

[1] Pp. 66, 68.
[2] On the whole question of adult missionary and social education see Miss H. T. Jacka's excellent book, *A Mind for the Kingdom*, published by S.P.G.

the real forces which are moulding the world's life. For example, the industrialisation of India and the Far East would be impossible but for international credit and the " export of wealth " from the West. How many Christians with money invested in a way which may involve their being implicated in that industrialisation ever make any attempt to understand the consequences in Bombay and Shanghai ? In a world which is a unit from the economic and financial standpoint, it is not enough that we should be kind and generous to our more immediate unfortunate brethren. The world itself is now only a neighbourhood. That fact cuts very deeply into our ordinary English way of looking at such matters.

It is the same oneness of the world's life which is giving the question of simplicity a new orientation in our day. The racial problem is largely a problem of different standards of living. As matters are at present, economic equality is impossible between East and West because the peoples of the East have much lower standards of bodily needs. Racial conflict will be avoided only by the equalisation of standards of living. If we put on one side such a re-organisation of our credit system as that advocated by Major Douglas,[1] it seems clear that the white man is faced with the necessity of living on a simpler scale. That seems a hard gospel for our industrial parishes, but it is true concerning the community as a whole. Now the Catholic has no more reason than the Quaker to be afraid of simplicity. The story of the saints is full of examples of heroic poverty. We need a reconsideration of their teaching in the light of our modern conditions, where the danger is that men and women, in becoming poor, shall also become parasites on the rest of the community. In any case, a quiet, systematic teaching and discussion of these questions would do more to create a real social conscience than any amount of oratory.

But, it will be said, who is to do the teaching in such a complex world, and where will the parish priest and missionary find the help he needs to be sure that he is giving sound instruction ? The answer seems to be " Ichabod." It was one of the glories of the mediaeval Church that its thinkers did grapple successfully with the application of Christian ethical principles to their particular situation. It

[1] *Cf.* his books and *The New Age, passim.*

has required the publication of Mr. Tawney's Holland Memorial Lectures on *Religion and the Rise of Capitalism* (1926) to make us realise how Christians of all shades of belief slowly gave up the task of applying their principles to the different and more difficult conditions of later days. No book bears out better Mr. Chesterton's dictum that so far from Christianity having been tried and found wanting, it has been found difficult and not tried. Certainly no Catholic can read the book without shame—and, let us hope, without penitence, for that will lead to the revival of a Catholic sociology adequate for our own day and capable of application in each part of the globe. For that task we need the best Catholic intellects we can have, not only theologians but anthropologists, bankers, statesmen, and business men. It will not be completed in one year, or ten years, but the Anglo-Catholic Summer School of Sociology is a beginning, and should be looked upon as one of the most promising missionary movements of our time. Certainly the work which it is attempting to do should become an integral part of the training of candidates for the priesthood and for lay work.

There remains the difficult task, which would be difficult even if we had an adequate Christian sociology, of judging the conditions and tendencies of our time in the light of the Christian standard. The main work of a priest, at home and abroad, is to lead his people in the life of prayer, worship, and penitence. But, as has been said already, each of these has a corporate significance, and involves the condemnation of corporate as well as of individual sin. Two main principles seem to emerge. The first is that our condemnation of the evils in society should be founded definitely on the fact that such evils are based on a wrong valuation of human life. Slavery, child labour (whether in the England of the time of Shaftesbury or the China of to-day), industrial conditions which deny any real freedom to the producer, are all contrary to the Gospel because they deny God's value for men. And the more the upholders of the present system in any country say that those things are inevitable in the working of that system, the more do they convince us that the system itself is unchristian. It may not be. But if not, there is much to do to weed out the unchristian elements. Nor must the Church reject its prophetic office by keeping silence about such things. The application of our Lord's teaching to all life is an essential part of the salvation He has won for the world.

The second principle is that the Church should Christianise, rather than destroy, as much of the traditional life and spirit of a country as possible. Other essays deal with this question, but this much may be said. The Church is the fulfilment of the religion and life of Africa and the East as it was the fulfilment of the religion and life of the Jews. Our Lord came to fulfil, not to destroy, and Catholicism has always been much nearer to Him in this than has Protestantism. One of the anomalies of present-day theological controversy is that many Protestant Modernists urge the retention of as much as possible of the traditional life and customs of the East, and blame the Church of the fourth century for doing that very thing. They have yet to learn that only Catholicism can act on that principle with safety, for only Catholicism has a strong enough grasp of all the implications of the Incarnation.

It is the purpose of this essay to emphasise the fact that the Christian Gospel has a corporate aspect which is nothing less than the building of an international Christian social order. This is much more than mere social reform, not only because God means far more for men than only social righteousness, but also because, in result though not in method, it implies revolution rather than reform. All of which serves to bring into prominence the importance of the one society in this world which is based on God and on God's revelation of man. That is the Catholic Church. As the years go by it is becoming clear that the world can never be saved by individuals or by voluntary groups of individuals, however wise and saintly. It cannot be saved without them, perhaps, but they must be part of a corporate body which can extend over and affect all the closely interlocked and interrelated aspects of man's life. They must exhibit to the world a society which has solved in principle the problems of society. And a Church which gave the truly Catholic witness would do that. It is only in the common worship of God that men's differences can be reconciled, and the real meeting-place for men is not primarily in parliaments or assemblies, but at the altar. " It is the Mass that matters." That worship, too, would leave no doubt as to the way which would bring redemption for the nations. It is the Way of the Cross, which the Mass shows forth until the kingdom comes. And we have a long way to go before nations as nations accept that Way. In the meantime we surely have the right to claim that only in the Church can the various groups of men find a common life. This does not imply the domination of political or economic or intellectual life by the ecclesiastical authorities ; the world will never return to the conditions of the fourteenth century. The Church must learn the truth of one of our Lord's sayings whose wisdom has never been palatable to her : " The kings of the Gentiles rule over them, and their authorities take the name of ' Benefactor ' : not so with you. He who is greatest among you must be like the youngest, and he who is chief like a servant. Which is the greatest, guest or servant ? Is it not the guest ? But I am among you as a servant." [1] Then, and not till then, will men bring the whole of life to be baptised by her, and the kingdom of this world will become the kingdom of God and of His Christ.

[1] Luke xxii. 25 ff., Moffatt's version.

V

CHRISTIANITY AND NATIONALISM

BY E. L. STRONG, O.M.C.

SYNOPSIS

A. NATIONALISM.

By Nationalism is meant the tendency of the human race to form nations which manifest the common characteristics of human nature in different ways.

It is difficult to discover whether national differences are permanent or accidental.

Illustrations of this difficulty drawn from India. It seems to be part of God's purpose that nations should differ in their capacity for receiving and reflecting Christ's life, and so make their distinctive contribution to the Holy Catholic Church.

The unredeemed spirit of nationalism is a hindrance to the Church in its work for the fulfilment of the purpose of nationalism.

This unredeemed spirit of nationalism still exists in the British race and appears as the spirit of dominion even in the Church.

B. CHRISTIANITY AND NATIONALISM.

The Catholic Church is, by redeeming the spirit of nationalism, to produce a communion of nations in Christ.

The glory of the Church can only be partially manifested until the rest of the nations become part of it.

The gifts of the Indian races to the Church are likely to be :

1. An innate capacity for religious life.
2. The manifestation of the meekness and gentleness of Christ.
3. The self-effacing service of Indian womanhood.
4. The grace of courtesy.

C. THE SHARE OF THE ANGLICAN CHURCH IN THIS WORK.

The Anglican Church is fitted for this work in virtue of the fact that, in contrast to ultramontanism on the one hand and separatism on the other, it believes both in the one Catholic Church and in national Churches.

It is hampered in this work by the pride and self-assertion of the British race.

Criticism of the missionary methods of the past and suggestions for a new policy.

CHRISTIANITY AND NATIONALISM

I PROPOSE to consider first the part we can suppose Nationalism is meant to play in the working out of God's general purpose for mankind, and its natural spirit as greatly hindering the fulfilment of this purpose. Next, to consider the relation of Christianity to it : the task and power of the Church of Christ to transform its spirit—the chief temptation which besets the Church in its struggle to do this—the distinctive share in this work which we can believe to be assigned to the Anglican Church—and the main difficulty which has to be overcome if that Church is to fulfil its vocation.

A. Nationalism. — *The meaning of Nationalism.* — Nationalism denotes the fact that the human race on earth always tends to divide itself into groups, families, tribes, or clans which combine later on to form nations ; and that the common characteristics of human nature are manifested diversely by different nations. It seems probable that this will always be so as long as man is able to live on this planet. The gregarious instinct seems a permanent part of man's natural endowment ; divers large groups of men will have to live in the different climates of the earth, and will have divers energies evoked by their struggle to adapt themselves to their environments ; marked differences in national characteristics will no doubt remain. We have good ground for supposing that this is a part of God's purpose for man during his time of trial on earth.

But when we consider these differences as they appear to-day, we at once find ourselves on slippery ground. For it is no easy matter to determine which of them can be considered as permanent, and which are due, wholly or in part, to accidents of environment which can and ought to be modified or altogether removed. This difficulty, of discerning permanent from accidental national characteristics, is readily perceived by those who have lived for long periods in a climate and environment which are very different from their own. And it is no doubt because, owing to facilities of travel, anthropologists are able to live in the midst of races of men other than their own that, as Marett says, " in these days geography, in the form known as anthropo-geography, is putting forth claims to be the leading branch of anthropology." It may be of use, therefore, to give some illustrations of the difficulty as it presents itself to us of the English race who have lived for many years in a tropical climate.

There are several traits in the character of the Indian races of the plains which are very distasteful to most Englishmen, and appear as permanent national characteristics, but which are seen by us to be due, if not wholly yet to a very large extent, to concomitants of the climate that can be and are being removed—disadvantages which produce similar effects in our own countrymen who have been settled for two or three generations in the Indian plains. It is almost impossible for those who have lived always in healthy surroundings to imagine the enervating effects on the minds and characters of people who are not only subject through most of the year to great heat, but also to frequently recurring attacks of fever, especially malaria, and kala azar, or to hookworm, or dysentery, or cholera, which for the time prostrate them and take from them all desire to make any effort, even to get well. It is harder still for us to imagine the result to them of the fact that their ancestors through hundreds of years were subject to the same disabling attacks of illness.

We are also in a position to see what remarkable changes can be effected in national characteristics which seemed permanent by the establishment of a new religion in a country. The history of Christianity has shown this in most parts of the world ; but no changes have been more remarkable than those which have been and are now being wrought before our eyes in multitudes of the " Untouchables " whom Hinduism casts out as worthless.

We in East Bengal are face to face with a change caused by a new religion of quite another kind. The majority of the Bengalis in these parts were forcibly converted to Islam in the time of the Moghul Emperors. The result is that most of them appear now as people of a different race. Their mental outlook, their chief characteristics, even their

faces, are so different from those of the rest of their race
that one who did not know the cause would suppose that
it could only be a large admixture of foreign blood.

Similar instances are cited by witnesses in many other
parts of the world. They are sufficient to show how
difficult a task it is to discern permanent from accidental
national characteristics, and how dangerous and wrong
it is to judge of nations other than our own until that
task has been carefully and sympathetically attempted.
Probably most of the prejudices that separate nations
from one another would cease, if this were remembered.

But even if all were done that is possible to equalise
man's environment by removing remediable evils, and
when the Gospel has been preached and Christ revealed to
all the nations, permanent differences inherent in the
characters of the different nations will no doubt remain.
And it is the duty of the Church to try to discern them
even now, as far as possible to see them as God sees them.
Discerned in and by His light they are, we can be sure, the
differing capacities of nations for receiving and reflecting
Christ's life : for Christ is the end, as He is the beginning,
of mankind.   If, then, we inquire what is the meaning—the
purpose—of Nationalism, we are to find the answer in the
doctrine of the Holy Catholic Church.

The Church is the Body of Christ, which grows gradually
and, as it grows, manifests with ever-increasing perfection
the strength and beauty of Christ. He has become a
second Adam to the whole race, so that as in Adam all die
so also in Him shall all be made alive [1]—made, that is, a new
creation, alive with the life that He lives in His glorified
humanity in God. Of His fullness the whole race is to
receive, till it is filled with Him. Thus Nationalism is
already and is increasingly to become a manifestation of
what von Hügel called " the stupendous richness of God."

A parable from Nature may be of service to us here.

The beauty of the earth, which declares the glory of
God in kingdoms lower than man's, is produced by an
immense variety of living things, among which appears no
uniformity except such as can be discerned in processes of
life that we call laws of nature. But these multitudes are
also grouped together in large masses, such as mountain
ranges, forests, rivers, flat or undulating plains, each mass

[1] Cor. xv. 22 ; Rom. v. 12–21.

having a distinct character and beauty of its own, which it contributes to a vast living harmony of beauty. The beauty thus produced is, however, not inherent in the things themselves; they have only capacities for receiving and reflecting, each in its own way, the rays of the sun, which is the source of their beauty. So is it with the rational creation. While each individual differs from all the rest, multitudes are grouped together to form masses called nations, each with a distinct character and capacity for supernatural life and beauty, that is, for receiving and manifesting the Sun of Righteousness who is Himself the light and life of all men, and thus of producing a vast harmony of spiritual life which manifests the riches and the glory of God Incarnate. He sends His Church into the world that mankind may be fulfilled and that the vast harmony of human life may be produced, which is " the measure of the stature of the fulness of Christ."

The spirit of Nationalism.—This spirit, so long as it remains in its " natural " condition—that is, until it has been transformed by the Spirit of Christ—is the main hindrance to the Church in its work for the fulfilment of the purpose of nationalism. For its spirit is always at first the spirit of " the old man." [1] It is with nations as with individuals. As soon as a human person realises that he is a person he begins to assert his rights and to claim service from others. To describe a newly arrived child as " the home ruler " is to state accurately the position he soon begins to assume. But though this spirit has often such enchanting manifestations in young children that we cannot resist it, we know it is a dangerous one, and that if it is allowed to develop the child as he grows older will be spoiled. The same thing happens in each nation. As soon as a nation comes to realise that it is a nation it begins to assert its rights. If it finds itself a weak, downtrodden nation its citizens become " patriots " and strive for its freedom. If it becomes powerful, as compared with other nations, it asserts its right to dominion over them. A national spirit is always, till it has been transformed, an anti-other-nations spirit. It cannot brook foreign interference. It desires independence—liberty to go its own way and to assert its own individuality. It seeks intercourse with other nations only so far as its own safety or

[1] Eph. iv. 22 ; Col. iii. 9.

profit may accrue to it therefrom. We are all watching now the awakening of a national spirit in different parts of the world, particularly in India and China. And, in spite of many disquieting manifestations of it, we are conscious that we ought to be glad to welcome it, and in the case of India thankful that our rule has largely contributed to bring it into existence. We of the British race, who so greatly value liberty and who have, as we proudly say, striven desperately through so many centuries to achieve it, feel that it would be most ungenerous of us if we did not admire and hold out a helping hand to " patriotism," as soon as it begins to appear in any nation which is still in the making. That is why the British Government is trying to bring it about that the nations of India which are now being born (or the one big federation of nations which may perhaps be formed) shall be free to manage their own affairs as soon as they become capable of doing so.

But admiration of and sympathy with such a national spirit must not be allowed to blind us to the truth that this spirit in its " natural " condition is an anti-Christian rather than a Christian one, and is no more admirable than is the selfish spirit in men. We can be glad of its appearance in any new nation, but only on account of the fact that its present condition is an inevitable prelude to that which it is destined to become. As St. Paul says, " that is not first which is spiritual, but that which is natural; then that which is spiritual." Just as a person has first to become conscious of himself as such before he can become what God means him to be, so a nation has first to awake into consciousness that it is one before it can fulfil its destiny in and for the brotherhood of nations that is to be.

The national spirit, or patriotism, needs redemption and transformation, just as does the human spirit in each one of us. But though we are aware that our own selfishness has been the one great hindrance to the forming of Christ within us, we are apt to lose sight of the fact that the national spirit—the pride of race, the desire for dominion—has been and is the main obstacle to the fulfilment of God's purpose to form all the nations of the earth into the One Holy Catholic Church of Christ.

For in the first place, nationalism tends to produce and has hitherto produced all over the world not co-operation but antagonisms between nations ; and one main cause of

G

this has been the intolerance, arrogance, distrust, and even persecution, which have sprung from pride of race. Our own race has been guilty of it more than most, and it has blinded us to a great extent to the excellences of other nations and disabled us from imagining how greatly our national character might be improved, if we were to learn from the distinctive virtues of other nations. To say of a man, for instance an Indian, that but for his complexion he might be British would be considered by most Englishmen to be paying him as high a compliment as could be paid ; and this attitude of mind has been manifested only too clearly in our outward behaviour towards people of other races. To speak only of its effect in India, it is not too much to say that the deplorable antagonism which has been created between the British and the educated classes of India has been almost entirely due to the overbearing behaviour towards them of those who are wont to lay stress on the fact that they belong to the ruling race. No one who has lived sufficiently long among Indians in India to realise their point of view can be surprised that what they often call " the official manner," which might also be styled " the British manner," has produced in them such dislike and even hatred as to make them oblivious to the sincere desire the British people have and the great efforts they have made for the good of India. Though this attitude of mind is changing for the better very rapidly now, it remains as a forcible illustration of the deadly nature and effect of racial pride ; and it is better that the illustration should be taken from our own shortcomings than from those of other nations.

In the second place, this same spirit has taken root in the Church itself, the divinely appointed instrument for its transformation. At the first the Jewish pride of race was so strong as to threaten the very existence of the Catholic Church. It was almost impossible for Jewish Christians not to believe that Christ's Church must be a Jewish kingdom having dominion over other nations : they could not conceive that other nations could be equal partners with them in the new kingdom of Christ, until God had intervened with direct communications from heaven. A few centuries later the Church had to encounter a similar danger, which has not been overcome yet. The Roman imperial spirit with its passion for dominion over other nations was by no means killed or transformed at the " conversion " of the Roman Empire.   It entered the Church and assumed the Christian name.   The result was that the Roman Church gradually became more and more self-assertive, until it claimed dominion over the whole of Christendom as a right.   And just as the Jewish spirit led to the belief that all Christians were to be Jewish Christians, so the same spirit in the Roman Church leads still to the belief that all Christians are to become Roman Catholics. And it is this spirit which has been the main cause of the divisions of Christendom.   The lamentable separation of the Eastern and Western Churches was a direct result of it. It was not caused by diversity of doctrine—there had been greater diversities before which had no such result—but only by the fact that the Roman Church claimed dominion over the East, which the East would not consent to submit to. It was a similar claim by the Pope to dominion over England which was the main cause of the final rupture between the Churches of England and Rome in the reign of Elizabeth.

This spirit, which is the spirit of nationalism in its natural condition, was described and condemned as the opposite of His own by our Lord : " Jesus called them unto him and said, Ye know that the rulers of the Gentiles lord it over them, and their great ones exercise authority over them.   Not so shall it be among you : but whosoever would become great among you shall be your minister ; and whosoever would be first among you shall be your servant : even as the Son of man came not to be ministered unto, but to minister, and to give his life a ransom for many." [1]   The spirit of dominion and the spirit of service are contrasted as the spirit of " the old man " and " the new."   The latter manifests Christ ; the former hides Him.

Here we reach the root of the matter.   Therefore the Church will only fulfil its vocation of transforming the one spirit into the other in so far as it itself is purged from the spirit of " the old man."

It is dangerous to think of the faults of others rather than of our own.   Yet for our own warning it may be well to point out how this spirit of dominion obscures the true glory of the Roman Church from the rest of Christendom. The spirit of devoted service of God and man has been

[1] Matt. xx. 25–28.

wonderfully manifested in the Roman Church through a great multitude of saints and of holy missionaries in all parts of the world. Yet the claim of that Church to world dominion hides for the most part from the rest of Christendom the glory of Christ which is manifested so abundantly by its members. It appears to those outside it as the one despotism which still remains. If its supremacy was that of service—if the Popes had been in truth what their title proclaims them, " servants of the servants of God," instead of despotic rulers over them—most of the difficulty of accepting the supremacy of the Bishop of Rome would disappear from the mind of Christendom.

It is for us to take warning and consider the danger to ourselves of this same spirit. We belong to a race which loves to have dominion, an imperialistic race which has built up a vast Empire ; and there is no lack of men amongst us who easily become masters of almost any situation they find themselves placed in, who are conscious of possessing the capacity for ruling over others and enjoy its exercise. And this spirit does not necessarily die in those who go out as missionaries to spread the kingdom of Christ in non-Christian lands : they are still in constant danger from it. It is said, indeed, that there are very few of them who are content or at their best till they are " running their own show." Because of this we are singularly ill-adapted by national temperament for manifesting Christ to Eastern nations. We are apt to manifest just those qualities which hide Him from them, and to be deficient in those qualities apart from which Christ is not seen by them. In our case, also, the spirit of service, which is so abundantly exercised in India, is obscured by this evil spirit of dominion, so that those who would otherwise be ready to acknowledge the benefits that the British have brought them have their hearts hardened by the resentment produced by the domineering spirit of those from whom the benefits come.

B. **Christianity and Nationalism.**—*The work of the Church for the nations.*—The Catholic Church is sent to all the nations of the earth to transform the antagonisms caused by racial pride and selfishness into fellowship, and thus to produce a communion of nations in Christ. And the Church has the power to do this because it is the Body of Christ ; for possessing the life of His glorified Manhood it can manifest to the people of all nations the ideal life of man, and can communicate the power of Christ's life to all who desire to possess it.   It can in fact do, and is sent to do, in all parts of the earth precisely what was done with such success in the Apostolic age.   Christ's Church then witnessed to Him by manifesting His life to many different races, and communicating it to all in whom faith in Him was awakened through the beauty of His life which they beheld.   Thus were created Churches of various races, the different characteristics of which, informed by the life of Christ, were combined into one Church, so that even in its infancy it became manifest that Christ's Church was in essence Catholic.   The history of the infant Church in the New Testament has many lessons to teach us, which we are slow to learn.   Among them is this important one.   The Church of Christ, though from the first Catholic in essence, was then as it is still only beginning to be so in fact.   It is true that two thousand years have passed since then ; but two thousand years compared with the age of man upon the earth is not equal to two days of a man's lifetime. The Church is in its childhood still, and we can form very little idea what it will become when all the nations of the world have entered it and are filled with its life.

If we desire metaphors to describe the Church's present condition, we must employ a combination of such as the following.   It is like a vine, most of whose branches are at present dead or dying but can all be quickened into new life from the stem ; so that the beauty and fruitfulness of the vine that is to be can scarcely be imagined at present. Or, it is like a human body, most of whose limbs are at present paralysed, the whole of which however can be made alive and put into action by the new life which has already been infused into the body ; so that the strength and beauty of the body that will be cannot be gauged by its present condition : as its dead limbs receive the new life the whole body will have fresh activity, and its capacity for life in all its organs will be increased.   Or, once more, it is like the body of a child whose organs are intact, though, as yet, for the most part undeveloped.

The glory of Christ's Church can only be partially manifested by the Church on earth at present and is liable to be obscured till the rest of the nations become part of it. " The riches of the glory of his inheritance in the saints, and the exceeding greatness of his power to us-ward who believe " cannot be understood now as it will be when the Church has embraced the as yet non-Christian nations.

The point that needs special emphasis for our present purpose is that each new nation as it becomes part of the Church adds to the power and the beauty of all the other parts, and enables them more completely to fulfil their proper functions, just as its own proper function can only be fulfilled in combination with them.

Here it will be encouraging to consider what further manifestations of Christ's fullness can be expected when the Church has embraced the great nations of the East. Those of us who have worked for many years in the East have necessarily obtained some prevision of this. Let me try to describe by way of illustration what we believe about the Indian races.

1. Speaking generally, their capacity for religious life appears much greater than that of the Western nations. They can more readily appreciate our Lord's saying, " A man's life consisteth not in the abundance of the things which he possesseth." They have a truer insight than we into the relative value of things material and spiritual. Their life is saturated by religion. This is none the less true of them, although one effect of the presence of Christian Missions among them has generally been to excite their cupidity. There are obvious causes of this deplorable fact which we are all trying hard to eliminate; and even while we only partly succeed in this, we have abundant reasons for believing that as Christ becomes more plainly manifested to them the Churches of the East will put to shame, and it is to be hoped provoke to godly jealousy, those of the West, by their devotion to Him and willingness to sacrifice themselves and their worldly goods in His service. The capacity of the Indian races for religion is largely discredited among us on account of the fact that their moral consciousness has not been developed, so that they can be extremely religious and wicked at the same time. But this is to confuse two distinct matters—their capacity for religion and the actual religions on which it has been fed. Their religions do not tend to develop the moral consciousness, but have for the most part an opposite effect. We are to think of their aptitude for religion as it will be when it is fulfilled by the religion of Christ and they have

learnt to abide in Him who is invisible, and at the same
time to keep the two commandments of the Christian law.

2. (NOTE.—The following applies only in exceptional
cases to the Indian peoples who are under the dominion
of Islam.) The Indian races appreciate and their hearts
are readily touched by those virtues of Christ which the
majority of Western *men* scarcely acknowledge to be virtues,
namely, His humility, gentleness, meekness, longsuffering,
patient endurance of insult and outrage, and readiness to
forgive all who injure Him. This is none the less true
though most of them give way frequently to bad outbursts
of temper. The communal disturbances and hatred in the
midst of which we are now living, the anti-British feeling,
as well as the quarrels of individuals and families which
are seen and heard on all sides, seem to give the lie to what
we have said. It is nevertheless true. When their natural
weaknesses are overcome by the power of Christ, these are
the virtues which will develop in them, so that the future
Church of the East will enable the whole Church to manifest
to the world the beauty and strength of Christ's character
as it has indeed already been manifested by a great
multitude of individual saints, though not by the masterful
Churches of the West as a whole. Let us note that the new
manifestation will be of the *strength* as well as the beauty
of Christ's character. The longer one lives in India the
more one learns to realise the strength of humility, meekness, and patience, and to see in the overbearing masterful-
ness of the so-called strong men of the West deplorable
weakness that cannot bear injury or insult or racial
characteristics which they dislike, and tends to destroy
men's power of sympathy, and so to render them unfit for
the work of the kingdom of God.

3. Indian womanhood is, we believe, destined to enable
the future Church of India to show with a power that no
other national Church can emulate what it is to have the
mind of Christ, who took " the form of a servant, and
humbled Himself, becoming obedient unto death, yea, the
death of the cross." Indian women have been despised
and enslaved for ages ; and deplorable results have
followed. But they have undoubtedly developed a genius
for humble, self-effacing service, which, when their minds
are trained and developed by Christian education and their
spirits are fulfilled by Christ's life, will enable them so to

understand and love Him that they will become in the Church of the future wonderfully effective instruments for the winning of His kingdom on earth.

4. It can be said also of the Indian races generally that they have a natural capacity for courtesy, grace, and good manners which is destined, we cannot doubt, to add considerably to the attractive beauty of Christ's Church.

The races of India only afford one example, though a large and important one, of the distinctive capacities for receiving and reflecting Christ which are to be discerned in the new nations that are coming into being. It is indeed almost impossible for us to imagine what a power of attraction the Church on earth will have when these capacities are fulfilled and combined with those of the older Christian races.

But the capacity of each nation for reflecting the glory of Christ can only be fulfilled through the vision of Christ which that nation sees. The Church therefore has to manifest Christ as He is, not the kind of Christ that the Indians, or any other races, may desire or suppose Him to be, but Himself whose glory each of them has a special faculty for beholding and reflecting.

The share of the Anglican Church in this work.—We ought to believe that our Church has some distinct share allotted to it by God in the work of bringing the nations into one great brotherhood in Christ ; and it is worth while to consider in what respects it is fitted for this work and in what respects it is hampered for it.

It appears to be fitted for it on account of its traditional beliefs about the Catholic Church ; that is, while holding firmly to the belief that the Church of Christ is one, and meant to include all the nations of the earth, it sees in the difference of national characteristics an indication of God's purpose that there should be national Churches, each having a distinct contribution to make to the life of the whole. The implications of this belief are most readily understood when it is considered in contrast with the two extreme theories about the Church, between which it holds an intermediate position. On the one hand is the extreme ultramontane theory held in the Roman Church. This is that there is no place for national Churches within the Catholic unity, that the oneness of the Church implies uniformity rather than the harmony which we hold to be the Catholic ideal.   The recognition of Uniat Churches by the Roman Church, in so far as the national rites, ceremonies, and customs of such Churches are loyally respected, is a genuine concession to a Catholic ideal which is supranational rather than hyper-standardised and anti-national, but it remains true from the Roman Catholic point of view that the endeavour of the Church must be to induce people of all the nations of the earth to become Roman Catholics. The extreme opinion on the other side is the Protestant one, that all distinct bodies of Christians are intended to be separate Churches, and that the union of all of them in one great body is not desirable.[1]   This opinion is now, however, being abandoned in many quarters where it was formerly strongly held ; it does not evoke enthusiasm, and there is not much reason to suppose it will long survive.

The most recent manifestation of the beliefs of the Anglican Church is the Indian Church Measure, which is a careful attempt to set free the Indian Church of the future to manage its own affairs and become a national Church, or a federation of Churches, within the unity of the one Catholic Church.   This action of our Church is but the latest instance of the policy we have consistently adopted for translating our belief into practice.

But though by our beliefs about the Catholic Church we are fitted for our task, we are at the same time handicapped for it by our national characteristics.   So much is this the case that it might at first appear to be the irony of fate rather than the providence of God which has sent us to manifest Christ in India.

Our difficulty is of an opposite kind from that of the Roman Church.   That Church in its official capacity is remarkable for self-assertion and aims at world dominion, while its members in all parts of the world are manifesting Christ's spirit of humble, loving service.   Our Church officially desires to act as a humble instrument in Christ's service, though its representatives in all parts of the world incline so strongly to self-assertion and to lord it over God's heritage that they all too often hide Christ from those to whom they desire to manifest Him.

Moreover, the plan on which most of our " missionary work " is done has the effect of evoking and accentuating this most undesirable national characteristic.   It is time

---

[1] See, *e.g.*, Dale, *Ephesians*, chap. xv.

for us to face the situation afresh and consider our special temptation in the light of our Lord's experience, and so to alter our methods of work that they help rather than hinder us in following His example. This is a favourable time for making a new beginning, for there is at the present time undoubtedly a fresh outpouring of the Spirit of God on Churches and nations. There are abundant signs of the transformation of the spirit of lordly self-assertion into the spirit of humble service. It is being recognized, even in very unlikely quarters, that meekness is not weakness but strength. Christ's principles are beginning to be seen to be the only practical ones for the welfare of mankind. The old spirit of nationalism is beginning to be transformed into the spirit of national brotherhood, and the Churches are longing for unity, dwelling on one another's virtues rather than faults and realising that they need one another. One of the latest and most remarkable signs of this is the action of the present Pope, in requesting the Benedictines to devote one of their abbeys entirely to the work of the union of the Churches and their response to his appeal. The letter he wrote and the publications of the " Moines de l'Union " since they began their work manifest an attitude towards the rest of Christendom which is almost the exact opposite of the usual attitude of the Roman Church.[1]

Let us then consider that temptation in our Lord's life which corresponds to that which so persistently besets our race, and then conclude with a suggestion for a change of method in our work in non-Christian lands, taking India as our example.

Before He began His work our Lord was tempted to use His power to become the royal, conquering Messiah whom the Jews expected. The same temptation beset Him till His death, the chief written accounts of which are : when He had fed the multitudes and the people desired to make Him their king ; when He was asked for a sign, that the people might believe in Him ; when the crowds welcomed Him as a king on Palm Sunday ; and when, at the last, He was tempted to come down from the Cross and justify the title which was written over Him. This was the temptation which evoked the response, " Get thee hence, Satan," with which we should compare the stern rebuke to Peter in

[1] Those who have not yet done so should take in *Irenikon* and procure its back numbers. Apply to Prieuré d'Amay, s/Meuse, Belgique.

St. Matthew xvi. 23. Our Lord could only obey His Father's will by choosing to win His kingdom by whole-hearted self-sacrifice and humble service.

This temptation, to win His kingdom by lording it over people instead of by meekness and humility, is the most dangerous of all those which beset Christ's representatives in our Church ; and it is one which, on account of our national capacity for ruling over others, is so plausible as not to appear to be a temptation at all.

Moreover, the methods by which we have worked hitherto are such as greatly to accentuate the force of this temptation. The usual plan of the missionary societies has been to send men and women in small parties to many places to do pioneer work. They have for the most part lived isolated lives. They have attempted far more work than they could do, and have frequently become over-strained. This has accentuated the worst of our national characteristics. Without meaning to do so, they have become domineering, impatient of the slowness of their Indian workers, anxious that the work should progress faster, and so have dictated to the Indians how it was to be done, lording it over both their minds and consciences. And the results have at last in many, probably in most, districts been such as to cause dismay to those who have brought them about. The Indian workers have lost heart ; they show no initiative or enthusiasm, and have settled down, very often with anger and bitterness in their hearts, into being what they were usually called—" Mission agents." The mistake is seen now and recognised as probably the principle reason why there are still so few signs in India of even the beginning of an Indian Church. It is felt on all sides that we must retrieve this mistake, and the following suggestion is made with a view to this.

A time seems to have come when in India, at any rate, we foreign missionaries should undertake no more pioneer work ; should cease to open up and " run " new Mission districts, and as soon as possible should cease to superintend the old ones, leaving them to become parishes of the different dioceses worked by Indian priests directly under the bishops, so that there should be no more people either called or thought of as S.P.G. or C.M.S., or any other Society's priests or workers or Christians.

Secondly, that our main energies should be concentrated

on forming centres in various parts of India, where the Christian life can be generated at high power—spiritual oases in the non-Christian desert, where Indians and we can live together in a condition in which Christ can abide in us and we in Him, so that through Him we become one family in love. Such centres are the only effectual training places for Indian workers—priests, deacons, readers, catechists, teachers, Sisters or other women workers. The training that these all need for the difficult pioneer or parish work they will have to do in a non-Christian atmosphere cannot be given them through mere teaching by word of mouth or by books. Christ Himself must be made manifest to them. They must learn by experience what the Christian life is, that it is a life of fellowship, in which His disciples abide in close union with Him and one another. Such centres must be places in which there is abundant time for prayer, where habits of prayer can be taught and formed, and where there can be created an atmosphere of mutual trust and affection. And also the situation of these centres should be carefully thought out, so that they can be abiding, not temporary ones ; for they are to be spiritual homes to which those who go out from them to work can return from time to time for rest, quiet, and more teaching : and also Christian shrines, to which tired workers or pilgrims can come from many parts of India to rest awhile with our Lord.

Such centres can no doubt be formed most readily by Religious Communities, but they can be and are formed already by other Communities not under vows. Their power for manifesting Christ and for drawing Indians to Him cannot be overestimated. It would be well if the great missionary societies were to withdraw isolated workers, especially women, from many places, in order that they might be formed into such families and their work done from central homes.

In such an atmosphere of Christian life the lordly, domineering spirit dies and a passion for serving Indians and India takes its place. When we thus abide with one another in Christ, who we know loves and believes in us in spite of our sins, we are at our best and we think the best of others, so that they feel at their best with us. Thus is created the necessary atmosphere or spirit, in which Indian Christians gladly come to receive from the West the fruits of its long experience and go out into the dark places of

India to make use of it, feeling sure that they are loved and trusted by those through whom their training has come.

As such situations develop in India or other Eastern countries, it will become increasingly possible, as it is altogether desirable, for the older Churches of the West to live and work in harmony and loving concord with the Eastern national Churches that are coming into being, East and West learning from each other and contributing to each other what each is fitted to give, and so helping and inspiring one another to bring nearer the great consumma- tion whon " tho kingdom of the world is become the kingdom of our Lord and of His Christ," who reigns not as the rulers of this world, but from the Tree.

VI

CHRISTIANITY AND EDUCATION
BY H. H. KELLY, S.S.M.

SYNOPSIS

Education is concerned with a wealth which consists in all that man has learnt : and may be considered as the science of the processes by which the mind is trained to appropriate this wealth.

The purpose of this essay is to consider (1) what this training of the mind implies, the difficulties in which it is involved, and the confusion in which it must end ; and (2) the nature and meaning of Christianity, and how it meets these difficulties and redeems this confusion.

I. ALL EDUCATION IS CONCERNED WITH THE FACTS OF EXPERIENCE AND THE ATTEMPT TO UNIVERSALISE AND UNIFY THIS EXPERIENCE.

As experience widens, our effort to understand reaches out and progresses towards the centre of being.

Three distinct lines in this progress :

(1) In the realm of material science.
(2) In the realm of human ideas.
(3) In the realm of philosophy.

The progress of civilisation is a progress by which men, in formulating ideas, pass from the present to the future, and from the future to the eternal.

Every idea has value in so far as it embodies

(1) the unity of things, or of truth.
(2) the unity of persons, or of righteousness.

But (3) there can be no unity of truth or righteousness without faith in God, in whom alone truth and righteousness are one.

Faith in God is thus the inspiration and life of all progress.

II. CHRISTIANITY IS FAITH IN GOD, AND A GOSPEL OF HOW THAT FAITH BECAME POSSIBLE THROUGH CHRIST.

The Gospel is actualised in the Church, which cannot exist effectively without a mechanism. But the mechanism and the society are not to be merely identified. Catholicity can be predicated only of God and His Gospel.

God and His kingdom come down to men, bringing the assurance of faith in the reality of progress.

All modern attainment has been gained in the atmosphere and under the inspiration of the Gospel. Ultimately, therefore, it springs from the work of those " religious " people who have preached the Gospel and have *held to* its faith. Actually, however, the best progress has been the work rather of those who have been *held by* that faith—not always very consciously. The " visible " Church—in the sense of its authorities and of professedly religious people—has often seemed to hamper progress through the instinct of conservatism, at least in regard to the unity of truth. Nevertheless the Church has always been an educative power, often the only one, not necessarily by the insight of ecclesiastics, but by the instinct or necessity of its witness to the universality of God.

CHRISTIANITY AND EDUCATION

ECONOMICS is the science, knowledge, study of the processes by which material wealth is acquired, and we assume the meaning of wealth to be simply the accumulation of what makes human life secure and comfortable. So far, it is hardly a matter with which Christianity is more concerned than it is with the science of billiards or of navigation. If, however, for comfort one reads happiness, if one asks why mankind should seek material wealth, we are launched on an inquiry which is in the first place psychological, and in the end theological. Here Christianity may have a great deal to say. Always the " why " dominates the " how " ; the end, our conception of an end, determines the processes we use to gain it.

By education properly we mean the science of the processes—some would take it as the art—of training the mind ; but here education differs from economics at the very start. Material wealth, like all material ideas, is easy enough to define ; consequently, it is possible to consider the processes without any further analysis. The training of the mind is a very complex idea. Education is the process by which all that men have learnt is handed on in order that it may become a permanent possession of mankind. It is primarily traditional. All that men conceive life to be is part of what is handed on. The end determines the methods throughout, and the end itself is singularly indeterminable. The conception which men have of the end is constantly varying.

I propose, therefore, first to consider what the training of minds does imply to men, taken simply by itself, then to show the difficulties in which it is involved and the confusion in which, as it seems to me, it must end. Secondly, to consider the nature and meaning of what we call Christianity, in what way it meets those difficulties, how by it the resultant confusion of human life is redeemed.

H

In each case we will consider the abstract or *a priori* principles first, and then see in what fashion they appear in the facts of the actual history of mankind.

I

All human life, therefore all education, is concerned with two things, which we may call, distinctively, the facts of experience and the theories of reflection, using " theory " in its Greek sense of a bird's-eye view of many facts, a group of facts, seen in their connexion. All education is based upon instruction ; that is, upon some attempt to put the student in touch with an experience wider than his own observation can give him, but its real substance consists in teaching the habit of generalising or universalising experience in order to find in it what is of permanent value. When the savage shows the boy a snare, and how it lies on the beast's track, it is not that snare, that beast, or that track with which either is concerned. The boy is learning how to study the habits of animals for himself, and to turn his knowledge to advantage in years to come. The savage is working from instances to rules and principles, and he may serve as an instance to us ; for we all, from the mechanic with his apprentice to the philosopher with his inferences, are doing just the same thing.

We can draw a picture of life as a whole diagrammatically, if a little confusedly. Mankind lives all round the outer circumference of things, that is, of experience. The individual mind moves or orbits through some very limited, and very disjointed, parts of experience. The experiences of the doctor, lawyer, soldier, and tradesman belong, as it were, to different sectors. But the lawyer gets ill, and the doctor goes to law. Both play golf, buy at the grocer's, and have wives and children, so that there is a good deal of overlapping ; sometimes we impinge as we move into one another's sectors. Yet there is in us all an instinctive craving for unity, wholeness, comprehension. We want to understand, and every effort to understand consists in just that universalising of the discordance of the mere facts under common laws. How far are we going to take this unifying process ? As individuals, mostly, we do not trouble ourselves to go much beyond our own immediate concerns. Medical work is very exacting. If the doctor can keep up with the best practice of the day, and understand enough of golf to play a decent game, enough of politics to give a sensible vote, the mystery of life does not touch him much, though his family affairs may worry him.

The mystery of life, however, is not so easily disposed of. The doctor knows that his own science is the result of a very long development, and has much ground yet to cover. Can one make an education based purely on sectors ? Life is in fact a whole, and all these lines of development cross one another. As experience widens we take in more ground, our effort to understand reaches out, as if it were hopeful at last of reaching the very centre of being. Life is essentially a progress ; to what else, except that final centre, can it be progressing ? I call that a hope. What we experience is of sight ; the existence of the unreached is of faith, and what progress can there be without faith as to something which can be reached ?

There are three very distinct lines of this progress :

(1) The common mind is most impressed by the progress of material science, which in its own respect, in its own sector, is the most universal, or Catholic, we have. The Western doctor, electrician, chemist, or engineer is equally effective on any continent. A Japanese, Chinese, or Indian can take up the work of them equally well, provided he has studied in the same way ; for the solidity of the material facts alters for no one. Scientific history, psychology, economics, and politics—so far as these also rest on facts and the handling of material evidence—are also common in method. In all this scientific work it is peculiarly obvious that the greatest advances have been made by the co-ordination, or unifying of different lines of inquiry—as in the new atomic theories. Nevertheless, all these material facts make up one side of life only ; they cannot possibly reach to an interpretation of life as a whole. They may cover the doctor's work ; they can be stretched to cover the lawyer's work. They do not explain the doctor's family ; they may make wealth, but they have little enough to say to his happiness.

(2) When we come to deal with human thoughts, motives, happiness, we are concerned, not merely with the facts, but with the values, of life ; we are involved in quite another atmosphere. In the first, we find at once how far we have got away from that common unity of method

which forms the catholicity of material science. The difficulty of language is symbolic ; for it lies, not in mere difference of sounds, but in difference of ideas, in a different grouping of experience, so that no one word in one language corresponds to any one word in another. The Greek " Logos " does not correspond to the English " Word." In cognate languages there may be close approximations ; in remote languages the differences are baffling. The further our thought develops the more the lines diverge. That is what I meant by " impinging." Even amongst ourselves, when the doctor goes to law, or the lawyer falls ill, each enters the other's sector, but the expert who lives in that sector of things, and the layman who only enters it for a special reason, think of it so differently that it is not easy for them to understand one another.

(3) Philosophy is an attempt to reach universal ideas by the aid of pure thought, leaving the differences and confusions of mere experience behind. In the realm of pure thought one does reach unities far beyond what one can render in experience, but the ideas we so reach in thought are very abstract. At the end of all, that centre from which we believed all being or reality radiates only presents itself to us as what philosophers call the Absolute, where all thought ceases.

We have then three lines of progress, which I might call subjects of inquiry, dealing with material facts, with human ideas, and with philosophy or pure thought. The first is represented by material science. In its higher forms the facts are so numerous, often so novel and difficult to remember, that we get rather lost, yet the conclusions are in such close touch with the facts of experiment that with time and patience we feel no inherent difficulty over them. When we come, secondly, to deal with human ideas, the difficulties are not due to any want of time or brains. We know well enough that those who have most studied the subjects still go on differing. The facts of life seem so clear, so certain and positive. They are different facts, but we are, or may be, in unity over them. The interpretations, ideals, values men have are so speculative that no unity seems possible. There seems to be a unity in philosophy, that is, in our ways of thinking, but to most people philosophy has no meaning at all. In any lending library you may find a small vegetable garden of technical books, useful and interesting to those concerned.   There is an herbaceous border of history and biography.   If you look for the meaning of it all, instead of a philosophy, there is only the open moor of fiction, where writers group any story of common life round any theory or interest which may occur to them or excite the reader.

So far I have been considering the idea of progress as the basis of education.   I have pointed out that all education is the same, based on the same principles.   The savage teaches his boy, and is himself learning, being educated in, the known ways of doing practical things and the common ways of thinking, which enable him to live and work with his fellows.   This is nothing other than we are doing.   The attempt to state its general principles, as it were the philosophy of education, makes it look a little abstract, though I hope that my analogy of the lending library may serve to show how practical it is, to show also what are the difficulties of education.

One thing, however, I want to make plain.   There is a notion that intelligence, sometimes called reason—though reason properly speaking is rather the process of intelligence—is opposed to faith.   On the contrary, intelligence is wholly concerned with faith.   The progress of civilisation is a progress by which men pass from the things seen, which are of the moment, to the things unseen, which are first of the future, but which, as future reaches to future, must be ultimately of the eternal.   Present, future, eternal —these are the same three factors.

Vegetables, and perhaps the lower animals, live because they use things, but have no intelligence in so far as they anticipate nothing.   Men, however, seek an end.   No doubt in the first place they anticipate and seek only what is immediately and personally obvious, as the tradesman seeks his profit and the fighting man strives to win, but that carries us no further than the methods and motives of the card-sharper, or the savage with a club.   No real attainment, whether in peace or war, is possible that way.

Secondly, therefore, it is both the aim and result of that mental life on which civilisation stands—which education is to maintain and hand on—to lead men away from the immediate and personal to the understanding of those common causes and common ideas by which ideals can be built up and followed.   And ideals, all ideals, are in some

sense of faith. But then, again, men's powers of anticipation are very small. Ideals are only consciously
visualised so far as they are capable of being stated as a
programme and explained as a policy. They must be
something more than personal, but they will very rarely be
universal. They are the ideals of those who entertain them,
that is, of some group as large as a nation, or as small as
a trade company or a party. In regard to time, men's
imagination seldom goes beyond what may be attainable
within their own life. Neither the middle Roman Republic,
nor the East India Company, nor "perfidious Albion," had
any definite vision of the empires they were creating.
Where men such as Charlemagne, Hildebrand, or the
French Revolutionists, perhaps St. Francis, Cromwell, or
Napoleon—should we say President Wilson ?—tried to
formulate the ideals of a long future, the results were very
different from what had been planned.

The programme-ideals, therefore, which men are capable
of formulating and following, are limited to what can be
seen. By themselves they end in disillusion, yet there is
no progress without faith ; for there can be no achievement by an age which has ceased to believe that there is
anything worth achieving. In spite of all their failures and
disillusion men are drawn forward, thirdly, by ideals of
quite another kind, by a vision of certain principles to
which men constantly appeal, which are yet too general
and too dimly seen to constitute a policy. Yet every
policy, every idea men do shape in their minds, has value,
becomes a step in the progress of mankind, just so far as
these principles have been realised and embodied in it.
The two primary principles I would call (1) the unity of
things, and (2) the unity of men.

(1) The unity of things I might otherwise call the unity
of science or, better still, the unity of truth. In material
science it is very plain how far progress lies in the co-
ordination of different branches. It is the same in all the
practical affairs of life. Agriculture needs a great deal
more than ploughing and sowing and reaping. It is
dependent on markets, transport, stable money, chemical
research, and much else. Business is more than manufac-
ture and sales. It has to adjust itself to, and is affected by,
every change in fashions of living, even of thought.
Religion may think itself aloof from the world, but in fact

nothing provides so complete an expression of man's inner thinking. Faith certainly looks beyond the world, but the Gospel is nothing less than the answer God has given to the difficulties men find in the world.

(2) This unity of things, which is a unity of truth, implies a unity of men, which is a unity of righteousness. At one end of the long line we fancy to ourselves the isolated self, as it were a stray fragment of matter, but neither the one nor the other exists. Every particle of matter moves in its place in the whole network of material force. So even the card-sharper, perhaps the most selfish and useless being the world holds, is the member of a little community with which he discusses, drinks, boasts, and he works in the centre of a circle of dupes, of whose foolish mentality he is a product. It is only that his world is held together by bonds so frail and mean. The progress of the world consists in a growing realisation that everything a man does belongs somehow to the universal humanity. Only death is his own, and " those things " which he would have stored for his own use—they include all he has gained and done—are left to mankind, by whom, in fact, they were garnered. Thus it is that in history the village passes into the tribe, and the tribe gives way to the city or territory. The nation—whether it be the United States or Denmark —is the largest area which can shape itself upon the recognition of common ideals. Yet even the nation only stifles itself—as in the discredited economic theory called Mercantilism—if it tries to prosper in isolation, if it cannot recognise its place in the fellowship of peoples, if it cannot recognise its dependence and its duty in respect to others.

Here, therefore, mankind moves, somewhere between the impossible fancy of an isolated individualism at one end and the unattainable hope of life-unity at the other, while the whole road is littered with broken ideals which once seemed to mean so much, which in fact meant a great deal, but which did not reach, nor could reach, the unattainable. No wonder man is disillusioned. Is anything worth pursuing ? Are we doing more than chasing rainbows ? If there is a unity, where is it ? Are not the unity of truth and the unity of righteousness themselves disunited ? The one solid truth we have is the unity of assured fact. Righteousness belongs to ideals, and the ideals we can frame are neither solid nor assured. The facts do not bear them out. I do not think that is disputable, and it is the basis of unbelief.

(3) There is in the depth of the human soul a third principle without which the other two cannot exist permanently, for they lead to nothing. There is no progress without faith. There can be no real faith in the truth we have, for it is a mere fragment ; nor in the ideals we frame, for they are half dreams. Faith is the ground of hope, but it is not the same as hope. Hope is an expectation of something the self desires ; faith is a looking to something beyond the self which is a source of good. Real faith can only be a faith in God in whom alone Truth and Righteousness, Being and Good or Value, achievement and purpose, material fact and human ideal, are one. By God we mean that centre of being which we have seen to be implied in all human thought. When St. Anselm, Descartes, Leibnitz, tried to prove that the existence of God was involved in the very nature of the thought itself, the argument seems extraordinarily difficult to follow. Nevertheless, all thought and meaning, all anticipation and aspiration, involve an ultimate meaning and an eternal value. If the fool said " to-morrow shall be as to-day," the saying was absurd ; when he added " and much more abundant," he denied that there could be any progress except in quantities. The arguments for the existence of God, when stated, look very complex. The whole world about you rocks under the effort to state the reasons which justify posting a letter or boiling a kettle. Explanations always look complex, yet, in fact, one's mind moves so simply.

Nevertheless, while the posting of a letter is done with confidence, belief in God, though to the simple soul equally simple, is the most difficult thing in all life to keep to, just because it is so central and universal. By God we do mean the centre of all things, the one Reality of all ; that is the basis of religion. But our thought of God is of an ideal, no doubt the highest and most inclusive ideal, none the less an ideal, framed by man's mind like any other ideal. That is the essential principle of idolatry ; for an idol is just that which the imagination shapes for itself. Whether we carve it in wood, or let it rest in the mind, or explain it on paper under the titles of " My religion," sometimes even " My Faith " is a mere accident of local habit. Folk do it one way in Africa and another way in

England or America. If the idol is not all God is, it is for us all there is of Him ; it is all we have to worship. Yet what else can we do ?

This image, or ideal, of God is not a unity. It is one of many ideals the mind holds. It provides neither for a unity of things, nor for a unity of men. On the contrary, just because it expresses so much, it reflects and expresses all our confusions and differences. The limitation, variety, uncertainty of our conceptions, and the difference of ideas between us and other people is the ground of polytheism. As to the unity of all thought, that goes no further than the Absolute ; it involves the impossible emptiness of Pantheism. Heathenism in its proper sense denotes the religion men come to by natural process of reflection and inference—and religion is primarily a heathen word. The antithesis of its two conclusions—popular polytheism and philosophic pantheism—is the cause of that religious despair which had come over men's minds about the time of the Christian era. There was only a choice between a polytheism which no reasonable person could believe, and a philosophical phraseology rather fascinating to intellectual people, but in whose vague abstractions neither they nor anyone could find solid meaning, comfort, or use.

I have maintained that faith in God, faith in the reality of what is ultimate, eternal, infinite, is the inspiration and life of all our present and very limited idealism, therefore also of progress. The failure of one was certainly coincident with the failure of the other. The long ages we call pre-historic show a continuous growth of material civilisation from eoliths to the age of iron. No doubt there must have been a concurrent growth of intelligence, but, as in childhood, it did not suffice to constitute a history ; for it had not advanced far enough to be capable of self-conscious expression. There was, however, a very real intellectual progress, therefore there is a true history, of Greece and Rome. These two people were not merely progressing ; they knew they were making progress, meant to make it—the one distinctively in the unity of truth, in the things of the mind, representatively in philosophy ; the other, in the unity of righteousness, representatively in law. It was not till the seventeenth century that, partly from the impulse of geographical and scientific discovery, mankind got definitely beyond the attainment of what we still call the classical ages. In the first century A.D., by the unity of the Empire, the diffusion of Greek culture, classicism seems to be within reach of a success of which in its earlier stages it could not have dreamt. Surely this will be an age of hope. Nothing is more plain than that the age has lost hope. Its highest moral attainment is the Stoicism of Seneca, who tries hard to bring the philosophy of truth and righteousness together ; but they will not meet. The most he can offer is the ideal of the self-perfected soul, and, if that can answer to righteousness of life, it does not correspond to the truth of life. The first century is the beginning of decadence, although the old ideals died slowly. Philosophy said its last word with Plotinus in the third century. Classic law was a little later in reaching its final formulation under Justinian. Politically, however, the second century of the Empire, Gibbon's " Golden Age," ushered in chaos. Diocletian reconstituted a mechanism, but a mechanical government meant death. It no longer has faith. Diocletian was a fierce persecutor, because on behalf of mechanism he was at war with faith.

At this point there is another beginning. Trajan was a greater, probably a better, man than Constantine, but Constantine was an infinitely greater man by vision, because he had won hope. In the full tide of the Diocletian recovery, of which he was the heir and executant, he saw where hopefulness could be found, and that life had passed over from the Empire to the Church. He thought the Church would regenerate the Empire, and in fact it did enable the Eastern, the most Christianised, part to hold together for long centuries, but nothing could really Christianise an institution so fundamentally heathen ; nothing make living and spiritual what was so fundamentally mechanical.

II

I have been emphasising above the very primary distinction between the true principles, ideas, or aims, and the forms in which men are capable of visualising them. Now that we turn to the Christian side, that distinction, and the confusing of that distinction, beset us in every word we use.

Christianity, as set out in the Creeds, is first of all faith in God ; secondly, it is a Gospel of how that faith became possible, in that God made Himself known to us, and reconciled us to Himself, in Christ. Yet we often use the word Christian to denote the moral, or even cultural, system which springs from that faith.

By *Faith* in God we mean a looking for something which God can do for us, but the word is quite often taken as equivalent to belief, that is, the holding of certain doctrines as stated to the mind.

Religion, on the other hand, denotes the response men make to God, or what they take as God. It is always an activity of our own. There is a response to what we believe God has done for us, but belief in religion must not be confused with belief in God. Again, in the narrower sense religion is most commonly used only of those activities, such as prayer, which are addressed to God directly, but anything may be part of our religion if considered and intended as God's service.

The Gospel is realised, actualised, in the Church, which is the unity, society, family, of the redeemed, called together by God out of the world, to whom the Gospel is given that it may be God's witness in the world. On the one hand, then, a Society is not a merely collective name for a number of similar individuals. It cannot exist effectively without a mechanism whose acts shall be determinable as its acts. On the other hand, the mechanism and the society cannot be simply identified. The government is no more the whole substance of society, or the only means of its expression, than what a man says is the whole of his mind, or necessarily explains what he is doing. All through history, the doctrines and policies of ecclesiastical authorities are attempts, at times very crude attempts, to express, or to realise, what at the time is understood of the inner faith of the Church. They do not and could not give us the whole of that faith, nor the whole of its influence upon men's lives. Often enough, the acts of authority express only the ideas, or even interests, of the officialty.

Speaking intellectually, and of education, we use the Latin words generalise or universalise to denote the line or direction on which thought and understanding move. By common instinct we use the word Catholicise for its religious equivalent, though the meaning is the same. In the proper whole sense of the word, Catholicity can be applied only to God Himself. So far as we apply it to created things, it covers the whole sweep of the divine purpose. Therein, the unity of truth and the unity of righteousness—science and philosophy, business and politics, religion and morality—are all included. If we break them up into departments, "sectors," as, tentatively and uneasily, we cannot help doing, so far they cease to be catholic. Our notions and ideals of these things, even of God, are only ours. They differ with all the differences in human minds. None of them can be catholic, for no man's mind and no group-mind can be universal.

Catholicity does, however, belong to the Gospel. From that centre of being which man could never reach no mere Absolute of intellectual abstraction but the living God has reached to man, made Himself known in that He took manhood to Himself. The Gospel is catholic with a fullness nothing else on earth can equal. It is not philosophy or a fashion of thinking, a teaching or a doctrine. It has that catholicity of a material fact which is the same, unaltered for all, whether in Europe, China, India, or Africa. Yet it has nothing of the limitation of the merely material. Here the material and spiritual are brought together, combined and reconciled. That which we saw and our hands handled concerning the Logos of life was God Himself.

We are, however, dealing with the very practical subject of education, which is concerned with the agelong, and for individuals the lifelong, labour of mental progress. What does this Gospel effect ? Plainly, as for the boy starting on laboratory chemistry, or Greek literature, studies in the Creeds or in the Bible will do his work for him no more than they will for the statesman trying to see his way through the tangle of European politics. Furthermore, there are scores of instances—fundamentalism is the latest—that only mischief can result from the notion that our questions can be settled that way. Surely, if we understood the Gospel, we ought to have seen that God never meant it that way. The mediaevalists were rather fond of picturing a ladder up which the saints climbed safely, while sinners fell off on the one side or the other. Once we are told of a ladder ; but the patriarch was not invited to go up it. Only the angels of God went both up and down. We have step-ladders only, and they do not reach to heaven. The Gospel does not speak of men climbing up to God, but of God coming down to men.

It is, therefore, true that the Gospel does not answer any one of our immediate questions ; but, when the reality of God broke through the emptiness that besets all mere speculation, it brought with it the assurance of faith in the reality of progress. It answered at least this question, always pressing on the mind, whether anything is worth doing. Are faith and hope ever things which go with us for more than a few steps, weakening with every effort ? Are they not always something which meets us on the way, needing to be renewed from the other end ?

There is one other thing shown as coming down from heaven, and that is the kingdom of God, the city of the New Jerusalem. Neither do men go up to reach or find this, but they enter into it, bringing into it all they have achieved of glory and honour, that it may be part of the common joy and possession. I pointed out that in the first century A.D. the classic world was palpably dying. It had lost hope. In this very century history is born anew ; and it is born of a new faith. There is at least *prima facie* justification for saying that the history of the Church, which holds the witness and promise of the Gospel, is the centre and motif of all that follows. That at, least, shall serve as a thesis.

Here there is a distinction of great importance. On the one hand, it can hardly be denied that all modern attainment, whether in politics, science, or economics, has been gained in the atmosphere which the Gospel has created. On the other hand, those to whom the advance has been due are not necessarily men of deep religious conviction. The faith seems to hold them, yet many have lost or renounced the faith. If we take the kings of England as typical and well known, of those to whom England owes most—Alfred, William I, and Edward I were deeply God-fearing men, but Henry II was notably worldly, and Elizabeth disputable. (For my part, I think I see in her an essential sincerity.) But there is no denying that those notably and primarily religious, with some claim to saintship—Edward the Confessor, Henry VI, Mary,

Charles I—were all singularly incapable, and their reigns disastrous.

It can be contended that what I gave as a *prima facie* thesis is contrary to the facts of history. I offered above two great principles which human life is struggling to realise. The first was the unity of truth, the sanctity of all the activities of life. There are times when churchmen seem to assert it strenuously, and times when they seem practically to deny it. When we consider the narrow outlook of monasticism and its modern forms of puritanism and pietism, the condemnation of Galileo and Copernicus and the anti-Darwinian controversy, the Bible Commissions and the futilities of fundamentalism, has the Church led, has she not hampered progress ?

Secondly, in regard to the unity of men, which I called the unity of righteousness, has not the Church, like all religions, been a conservative force ? Churchmen have indeed maintained the equality of all men before God. In practice they have made excuses in early days for slavery, in the Middle Ages for serfdom, in later times for autocracy, for oligarchy, for capitalism. As Mr. Carlyle has pointed out Seneca and the Stoics condemned slavery far more whole-heartedly than St. Augustine, or even St. Paul.

One thing is, I suppose, not plain, since so many people miss it, yet it ought to be plain. If we believe in God, history must be understood as the story of God's doings. To evade, to refuse to face, to tamper with, the facts of history, will be to misrepresent God's doings, and to substitute for them some meaning or theory of our own. The facts of history are pressing upon us this lesson—not very welcome to our self-satisfaction—that the faith, power, catholicity, of the Church is in a faith in the Gospel—in God, not in men. Churchmen, Church leaders and authorities, are set to maintain that faith, but they are no wiser than other men in following out its development. Even the very fact of their absorption over the Gospel may make them indifferent to business, to " billiards and navigation"—though it ought not to. It must somewhat distract their minds from those studies which God has given to other people that they also may have something wherein to glorify Him.

Can we say then that the Church—the actual and visible Church—has been the leader or educator of civilisation, of progress, intellectual, political, and material ? There have been times when she has. When, however, the Church believed that that leadership and guidance were hers by right, so that her authorities were competent to lay down what direction progress should or should not take, the Church falsified her own witness. Then it hampered progress. I doubt if, in fact, it hampered it very seriously ; since the Spirit of God is not easily bound, and, stirring in men, found His own fulfilment.

But there is another question. Has the Church provided the hope and inspiration of human practice ? I think we must answer—Always. The relation between these two questions shows itself in every age.

(1) Is religion a department of life, or the whole of it ? We met that question at the beginning. Certainly, it is matter of faith that we should say it covers the whole. On the other hand, the human mind is very limited. The laws of billiards may be of God, but to say that a billiard champion is *ipso facto* a religious man, is only to confuse the issues of life. These departments do exist, and we have to recognise them.

The early patristic age of the Church was essentially evangelical. It meant to preach a Gospel. It was concerned only with the Gospel; for " the Catholic Faith is this that we worship one God—one God in Trinity." But thereto it is also necessary that we understand, think rightly concerning, the Incarnation. None of the fathers, except St. Augustine, troubled their heads over political and social questions. The apparent stability of the Empire and the jealousy of its rulers did not encourage such questions.

(2) In Western mediaevalism it was very different. In the chaos of German tribalism and its warrior caste, reaching up to the eleventh century, the Church had not merely to inspire men with the conception of unity, she had to teach them the bare elements of the methods of orderly government, and even to find men with the necessary education to carry it on. It was not ambition on the Church's part. There was no one else to do the work. And it is important to note that the inspiration came mainly from the monasteries, because no where else was a reasonably peaceful life possible.

In this earlier part there was hardly anything worth

calling an intellectual life at all, but the scholasticism of
the twelfth and thirteenth centuries reached a very definite
conception of the unity of truth in which all sciences were
subordinated to theology, just as it conceived of all
political institutions being subordinated to the papacy.

There we have a very human ideal of Catholicity, but
it was very far indeed from being a Catholic ideal in any
single respect. "The mankind " of mediaevalism was a very
small unity indeed. France, Italy, Germany, England,
comprised the known world. Its ideals were common only
to a very small international group, educated in one
way ; but there were no other ideals to set against them.
Science is represented by the mediaeval " bestiary "—tales
of animals ; history by the legends of Constantine, or the
hagiologists. When knowledge of this sort was being
made up and interpreted at will, there was no difficulty
in systematising it.

Then the scholastic ideal broke up, first of itself, when
Occam denied the unity of truth, affirmed two truths of
religion and of philosophy ; concurrently, when the
lawyers and politicians asserted the independence of their
own sphere, claimed therein to be answerable to God alone.
It cannot be denied that they did their own work far
more effectively than the Church, as an instance will show.
The curse of the Middle Ages was the independence and
private wars of the feudal lords. The Church established
a Truce of God. Lent and week-ends were " close times "
for brigandage ; but there was no Truce of God in
England. William I and his successors allowed no private
wars at all; nor did any king who knew and could do
his business.

Scholasticism was a system of strictly deductive inference from a narrow range of ideas. The Renaissance of
the fifteenth century launched out joyously on voyages of
discovery in the vast ocean of experience. First, it discovered Plato and Greek literature, where it had to meet
that wide view of life which had only puzzled it in Virgil
and St. Augustine. Then it discovered the new worlds,
where life was not ruled by syllogisms. It went on to the
inductive science of Galileo.

Thus it was, from the century before Protestantism to
this day, that life broke up into sectors, of which religion
was one, concerned with certain psychological states or

experiences of the soul. Luther made an honest attempt to break through, claimed that he had vindicated the sanctity of married life and politics, but, even in his own life, he had reverted from faith in God to faith in a state called Assurance. His truest result was *Pietismus*. Religionists of all sorts maintained the separation. It is as obvious in Wesley and the Evangelicals as in Liguori. One of the most eminent of Anglo-Catholic bishops was quite satisfied that Protestant countries were more civilised and prosperous than Catholic countries, but Catholicism made more saintliness, as if the two had nothing to do with one another. The Counter-Reformation expended itself in a devotionalism, "stirring to piety." In our Christian Socialism there is at least a tendency, in mediaeval fashion, to regard secular business as sacred rather in its moral restraint than in its effectiveness.

Is the Church Catholic ? By the Church we mean a Society among men. If we mean the Society of our own day, how can any day be universal ? We are only just ourselves, struggling with our own ideas, as limited and imperfect as those of any other day. It must include all that men have ever learnt, by failure and error, not less than by achievement. It must include the generations yet unborn ; for of the past it is true that they without us, and of the future it is true that we without them, shall not be made perfect. But the Catholicity of the Church lies in the Gospel, in the universality of God. So far as it is realised among men, it is realised in reverence for God ; it is abandoned wherever we seek, believe we have attained, or can attain, the pride of human achievement. The claim to Catholicity as a thing possessed is the rejection of its very principle ; for it is the principle of denominationalism. The patience that seeks, the humility that receives, the penitence which confesses, the faith which looks upward and works onward, these things are the gift of God and they are bases of all education.

Thus it is that the *prima facie* view of the Church's influence is as true as the historical view of the limitation of churchmen. St. Paul's view that all men are one in God was more fatal to slavery than anything Seneca could say. The first chapter of Genesis is a far more secure basis of evolutionism than the poem of Lucretius. The Catholic Creeds affirm a unity of all life.

I

VII

THE CHRISTIAN APPROACH TO
NON-CHRISTIAN CUSTOMS

BY W. V. LUCAS, BISHOP OF MASASI

SYNOPSIS

I. STATEMENT OF THE PROBLEM.

Preservation of the individuality of nations at Pentecost.
The importance to-day of a right attitude to non-Christian customs.
The difficulty is moral : the conscience of the young Church needs guidance in the realm of conduct.
This guidance depends on the foreign missionary, a stranger to native life.
This guidance is specially needed in equatorial regions.
Avoid too ready acceptance of pagan standards, equally with too great timidity resulting in detribalisation.

II. THE ATTITUDE OF THE CHURCH IN THE PAST.

Acts of the Apostles and Corinthians.
Three principles :
(1) The law of charity.
(2) The law of liberty.
(3) The claims of perfect holiness.
Pope Gregory's Letter to Mellitus, seventh century.
Council of Ratisbon, eighth century.
Bishop Grimkill, tenth century.
Otto in Germany, twelfth century.

III. THE ATTITUDE OF MISSIONARIES IN RECENT TIMES.

At first ignorantly indulgent.
Pastoral care brings knowledge of evil.
Such knowledge should be gained without questioning.
First discovery produces the reaction of wholesale condemnation, but such zeal is not according to knowledge.
The Church admits mistakes, which might have been graver.
Damage is greatest when a party of revolt arises amongst converts.
Conversions hindered by such a party.

IV. THE ATTITUDE OF THE CHURCH TO-DAY.

Strange customs are not necessarily bad.
Conservation to be aimed at, consistently with Christian holiness.
Substitute good for the evil removed.
The assistance of anthropology.
Interdependence of different elements of culture necessitates toleration of less than ideal conditions lest whole social fabric be endangered.
Organic unity of religious systems and evidence of preparation for Christianity.
Assistance of native converts essential.
Enactments must appeal to general Christian conscience—this requires real care in preparation for Baptism.
Conclusion.

V. THE PRINCIPLES APPLIED.

Clothing. Dancing. Divination. Funeral Rites (see also Sacrifice).
Hospitality. Housing. Hygiene. Initiatory Rites. Marriage. Music.
Names for converts. Religion, i.e. Sacrifices to departed spirits.
Sickness. Vows. Witchcraft.

THE CHRISTIAN APPROACH TO NON-CHRISTIAN CUSTOMS

I

WHEN the Holy Spirit of God descended upon the Apostles on the day of Pentecost, Parthians and Medes and Elamites, with all those other different races which were represented amongst the dwellers at Jerusalem at that time, heard the Christian message of the wonderful works of God, every man in his own tongue wherein he was born. The form of the approach respected the individuality of every man, and its appeal was adapted to be perfectly intelligible to each separate nation. On that day there were added to the Apostles' fellowship about three thousand souls, and their unity in the Catholic Church in no way destroyed their characteristics as individuals belonging in the providence of God to varying tribes, but the Divine inspiration made possible the full development of the individual nature and gifts of each. Our Lord came to destroy nationalism in churches, and henceforward all were called to live in the one family of God ; but nations with their racial characteristics, equally with the individual personalities of which nations are composed, are not thereby stereotyped into one monotonous uniform pattern, but enabled to grow up, each and all, into the measure of the stature of the fullness of Christ. There were Cretans present on the day of Pentecost, and within a few years there was a church in Crete under Bishop Titus ; but, as Canon Scott Holland inimitably said, " the Cretans who became Christians would remain Cretans none the less, though (we hope) no longer liars and evil beasts, and with bellies less slow."

This essay represents an attempt to consider what the Christian approach to-day should be to non-Christian customs, lest in our missionary work the Church, while seeking to win souls to Christ, denationalise them. The

wrong answer to our question would result in Christianisa-
tion coming to mean Europeanisation. The right answer
will mean that the characteristics of all are preserved.
The Indian Christian comes into the Church bringing all
those special gifts which in the providence of God India
alone can contribute to His kingdom ; and in the Church,
enabled by God's grace, the Indian Christian should
become the best of India's sons. The Zulu who becomes
a Christian in no way ceases to be a Zulu, but his life is
raised to a higher and supernatural plane as a Zulu
Christian.

But the arrival at this end in practice reveals problems
and complications demanding for their solution real
wisdom and statemanship exercised in dependence on the
Spirit of God. The problem will begin to make its pressure
felt in the realm of morals. The new Christian rises from
the waters of the font and goes back to his home in the
village with his fellow tribesmen, men of his own nation
and race : what is to be the practical relation between
the new life and the old ? As a catechumen he has tried
to face it, but now, white from the laver of regeneration,
it comes home to him with a new urgency, how shall he
walk worthy of the vocation wherewith he is called ?   In
grace he has come into a new society, his life has been
raised to a new plane. But though no longer of the world,
he is still in the world : he has to live out his faith in
everyday life. Again and again situations will arise in
which he may easily imperil his soul's new health. Custom
will demand his participation with his relatives and
kindred in much of which he may feel a real distrust, and
yet, if he refuses to be associated with his fellow tribesmen
in what are regarded as essential acts of citizenship and
duties to the community, he begins to be in danger of
cutting himself off completely, and at the end becoming
an outcast. If his own tribe into which he was born no
longer recognises him, it is impossible for him to become
a real member of any other tribe or people. He can indeed
do his best to imitate the ways of another race, and another
race may do their best to offer him comradeship and make
him their associate to the utmost extent to which this is
possible ; but more than an associate he cannot become.
Having lost his own tribe, he is tribeless ; and, except in
the rarest cases, his whole life will have suffered a loss

which cannot be remedied. It happens that here and
there faithfulness will necessitate that the right hand be
cut off and the right eye plucked out if the soul's health
is to be saved, but this loss and maiming are none the less
lamentable because in rare cases they are inevitable. In
practice, therefore, he will in his perplexity tend to do one
of two things : either he will come to the missionary and
ask for guidance, what he may do and what he may not
do ; or, if his conscience is only barely awakened or his
faith has not led to a true conversion of heart, he will
acquiesce too easily in the ways of the old life and lapse
from religion, behaving at times as barely more than a
baptised heathen, losing his sonship in slavery to the old
life.

It is true that ideally he should be able to find the
answer to his doubts through religion, faith should issue
in life, Christian belief should result in Christian conduct ;
and theory would suggest that he, who was born in the
old life, has grown up with it and lived in it, and knows
and understands all its ways and demands and reasons,
should be able, better than any stranger, to determine for
himself in each instance a line of conduct which will
express the purity of his creed. Perhaps this is the case
with those dwelling in northern and temperate zones,
where the Church's supreme difficulty is to rouse men to a
real belief in the importance of faith in God ; and therefore
each coming to the Faith tends to be preceded by so great
and real difficulty that the realisation of the paramount
importance of a consistent life follows almost naturally,
and care lest the hard-won treasure of faith be imperilled
will lead to a high standard of morals, persevered in in
spite of taunt and opposition. Nevertheless some instruction in morals will be needed even in temperate zones,
and the conscience must be trained before it can be relied
on to guide rightly. Otherwise there will be failure
through over-confidence on the one hand, or timidity—
fearing where no fear is—on the other.

But near the equator the emphasis falls quite differently : the stage of the decisive contest is changed from
the region of faith to that of morals. To all equatorial
people a vivid belief in spiritual powers all around, helping or harming at every turn, comes naturally and calls
for no argument or proofs : and, wheresoever tribes are

encountered as pagans, they press into God's Church with a ready eagerness that hardly waits to be called ; but the translation of faith into conduct is a real difficulty: religion seems able to co-exist in the case of many with lamentably frequent moral lapses. Here the training of the conscience, the relation of the neophyte to native custom, the attitude of the infant Church to the life of the village and tribe, is of paramount importance ; for it is in the realm of conduct that the real battle has to be fought.

But we return to the difficulty mentioned above. Those in whose hands the care of the Church lies, to whom the instruction of the earliest converts is entirely due, are in every case men of another race, their habits of life and social customs different, perhaps utterly remote, from those of the people amongst whom they are working. To teach the Faith has had its difficulties, difficulties of language and expression, but in almost every instance they will appear small compared with the far greater difficulty of guiding the early native Church to a right line of conduct in everyday life. For it is fatally easy to jeopardise per-fection of morals, on the one hand by a too hardy presump-tion that ignorantly accepts pagan standards and customs, not realising the danger that lurks within, or on the other hand by a too great timidity that insists on such a degree of prohibition as cuts off the native Christian from any further effective membership in his tribe or race. The difficulty of the problem is very great but not insoluble, for the Church born on the day of Pentecost is for ever indwelt by the Spirit of God, guiding into all truth of faith and morals.

II

At this point, inasmuch as it is plain that it is no new problem as to what the attitude of the Church should be to those non-Christian customs with which all unconverted life is so closely bound up, but a problem which began from the very birthday of the Church, we should do well to examine such evidence as has been handed down to us as to the guiding principles which have determined the answers given.

In the Acts of the Apostles the question is debated as to what Jewish customs are binding on Gentile converts, and in St. Paul's Epistle to the Corinthians what Gentile customs must be given up in the interests of the love of man and the love of God. The first question was of so great importance that, though it had arisen locally, no decision of a merely local council satisfied, and the matter had to be referred to Jerusalem itself and the Apostolic conference. It was, no doubt, not merely the magnitude of the question which caused its reference to Jerusalem, but, inasmuch as Jerusalem was the centre of Judaism, the question raised primarily by Jews needed to be settled where the Jewish point of view could be completely presented.

St. Paul, as the Apostle to the Gentiles, gives his own counsel to the Corinthian converts as to their attitude to meat which may, perchance, have been offered to idols before it is served up as part of a friendly feast. A right relation to heathen sacrifices, the duty of a married Christian who lives with an unconverted partner, divorce, the reference of disputes between Christians to heathen courts of justice, all these several problems of conduct are solved by the application of the following principles : the law of charity, demanding special consideration for the weaker brethren; the law of liberty in Christ Jesus, delivering men from an oppressive yoke of legal prohibitions which had proved a burden crushing to the human spirit; and the recognition of the majesty of God to whom is due the service of perfect holiness at whatever cost to human carnal desires. St. Paul therefore directs that the Church is to impose no unnecessary burden; her members are to avoid scrupulous questioning, but to dare quite definitely on occasion to " eat not "; there must be no fellowship with devils; Christians must not lose sight of the ideal of devotion to God in the unmarried life; Christian marriage, moreover, is indissoluble.

An exhaustive study of early Christian literature would certainly reveal again and again the Church's efforts to guide her children in doubtful cases of conscience. The following references must be taken as a mere indication of decisions made from time to time.

The letter of Pope Gregory to Mellitus at the beginning of the seventh century, which may be found in Bede's Ecclesiastical History (i. 30), cannot but have special interest to English Catholics.

" When Almighty God shall bring you to the most reverend Bishop Augustine, our brother, tell him what I have, upon mature deliberation on the affair of the English, determined upon, viz., that the temples of the idols in that nation ought not to be destroyed ; let holy water be made and sprinkled in the said temples, let altars be erected, and relics placed. For if those temples are well built, it is requisite that they be converted from the worship of devils to the service of the true God ; that the nation, seeing that their temples are not destroyed, may remove error from their hearts, and knowing and adoring the true God, may the more familiarly resort to the places to which they have been accustomed. And because they have been used to slaughter many oxen in the sacrifices to devils, some solemnity must be exchanged for them on this account, as that on the day of the dedication, or the nativities of the holy martyrs, whose relics are there deposited, they may build themselves huts of the boughs of trees, about those churches which have been turned to that use from temples, and celebrate the solemnity with religious feasting, and no more offer beasts to the devil, but kill cattle to the praise of God in their eating, and return thanks to the Giver of all things for their sustenance ; to the end that, whilst some gratifications are outwardly permitted them, they may the more easily consent to the inward consolations of the grace of God. For there is no doubt that it is impossible to efface everything at once from their obdurate minds ; because he who endeavours to ascend to the highest place, rises by degrees or steps, and not by leaps. Thus the Lord made Himself known to the people of Israel in Egypt ; and yet He allowed them to use the sacrifices which they were wont to offer to the devil, in His own worship ; so as to command them in His sacrifice to kill beasts, to the end that, changing their hearts, they might lay aside one part of the sacrifice, whilst they retained another ; that whilst they offered the same beasts which they were wont to offer, they should offer them to God and not to idols ; and thus they would no longer be the same sacrifices. Thus it behoves your affection to communicate to our aforesaid brother, that he, being there present, may consider how he is to order all things. God preserve you in safety, most beloved son."

The fifth Canon of the Council of Ratisbon, in 742, states as follows :

" We have decreed also that each Bishop so order his diocese that God's people do nought that is pagan, but rather cast from them and utterly eschew all the contaminating filth of heathenism ; whether it be the heathen sacrifices in connexion with the dead ; or resorting to divination and unlawful prying into knowledge hidden from us ; or participation in sacrificial offerings, which foolish men offer in the very church's precincts but in the pagan manner, daring to name in their offerings holy martyrs and confessors ; these and all other such rites of paganism are to be unremittingly forbidden." [1]

In the tenth century, when Olaf Haraldson became king of Norway, and

" succeeded in establishing Christianity as the national religion, he summoned an assembly at which a code of laws was drawn up known as Olaf's Kristentet which was apparently the joint work of Olaf and Bishop Grimkill. The law which related to the observance of heathen customs is of special interest from a missionary standpoint. It made no attempt to suppress the social customs connected with heathenism, but endeavoured to associate them with the observance of Christian customs. It directed that wherever three families could meet together and have a common feast the custom of drinking beer was to be observed, the beer having first been blessed 'in honour of Christ and the Blessed Virgin for good years and peace.' Fines were imposed in case of a breach of this law. A step towards the abolition of slavery was made by the law which provided that, instead of offering a slave as a sacrifice at the meeting of ' the assembly of the people,' one slave should be set free, and that one should be liberated every Christmas." [2]

In the twelfth century

" Otto in Germany made a clean sweep of temples and idols. He proposed to the assembled people that, inasmuch as the worship of the true God could not be combined with that of idols, they should proceed to destroy the temples of the false gods. When they hung back, moved by superstitious fears, Otto and his assistants, armed with hatchets and pickaxes, and having obtained their reluctant consent, proceeded to carry out the work of destruction. The first temple to be attacked was that of the Slavic god Triglar, *i.e.*, the three-headed, which contained an image of the god and was decorated

[1] " Decrevimus quoque ut . . . unusquisque episcopus . . . gerat . . . ut populus Dei paganias non faciat, sed omnes spurcitias gentilitatis abiciat et respuat, sive profana sacrificia mortuorum, sive sortilegos, vel divinos . . . sive hostias immolatitias, quas stulti homines iuxta ecclesias ritu pagano faciunt, sub nomine sanctorum martyrum vel confessorum . . . sive omnes quaecumque sunt paganorum observationes diligenter prohibeant " (Council of Ratisbon, 742, Canon V. Quoted by Robinson, *Conversion of Europe*, p. 29).
[2] Robinson, p. 466.

with sculptures and paintings. As it had been the custom to dedicate to this god a tenth portion of all the spoils taken in war, its temple contained much treasure. The Bishop having sprinkled the spoils with holy water and having made the sign of the Cross distributed [them amongst the people. The heads of Triglar he afterwards sent to Rome. A sacred oak, which was valued for its shade, the Bishop allowed to remain, but he insisted that a horse which was used for purposes of divination should be sent out of the country and sold." [1]

In all these instances we may trace the working of the same principles laid down in apostolic times which we have summarised as the law of charity, the law of liberty, and the recognition of the holiness due to God. Pope Gregory directs that care be taken to avoid any grave dislocation of the people's customs ; they are to be modified and redirected and enriched, but idols were to be destroyed. The Council of Ratisbon suggests that things had gone too far in the direction of toleration, and offerings to the dead and divination come under special condemnation. Bishop Grimkill treads closely in the steps of Pope Gregory. Otto's actions suggest that paganism had again become a danger, and the horse also used in divination had to go ; but the distribution of the blessed spoils and the preservation of the sacred oak show the same spirit careful not to bind on man burdens too grievous to be borne.

III

Of the history of this problem in more recent times it is dangerous to generalise. What has tended to happen is as follows : missionaries have gone to a new country to work among people of an entirely different race and have at first naturally been so engaged in trying to establish contact with those for whose conversion they were working that, so far from entertaining a critical spirit as regards the manners and customs of the people, they have smiled indulgently on all men and such of their ways as have come to their notice. It could hardly be otherwise. There is the primal difficulty of language : one cannot hope to begin to understand a people until a considerable advance has been made in learning their language. Then also the

---

[1] Robinson, p. 466.

most intimate rites and customs of the people are never paraded before the gaze of strangers, and in many cases all knowledge of them is jealously guarded from those who have not been initiated. A missionary is, in fact, a foreigner in the country in which he is working. However much he may desire to enter whole-heartedly into the lives and deepest interests of the people amongst whom he has come to live, they seldom can be expected to feel a like urgency moving them to admit the stranger to more than an external friendliness. In many cases his coming may have given rise to a measure of uneasiness ; he will be suspect, perhaps for a long time. He may proclaim his disinterested desire for their truest good, but ulterior motives will be imagined and can hardly fail to gain belief ; for the Christian message is unknown to them and the true motive for missionary work is therefore unintelligible.

Time passes on, contact with individuals is established, instruction is accepted, catechumens are made, Baptism comes, and then to the directly missionary work pastoral care of the new converts begins to be added. The new converts cannot be fully warned of the danger of some tribal customs and the direct evil of others, for the missionaries themselves have not yet come to understand more than a fringe of all that village and tribal life involves. A glimpse is granted them from time to time as the country-side is moved, it may be, to joy over the growing of the boys into manhood or to anxious sorrow over the failure of the rains.

So for a longer or a shorter time work goes on until a day comes when with something of the shock of a rude awakening they stumble, as it were, upon some evil which seems the more terrible inasmuch as all the circumstances of it sound so strange and sinister. This knowledge may come, as we have thought, through the movings of conscience of a convert sincerely desiring to live not after the flesh but after the spirit, who turns for counsel to those who have taught him all. To some knowledge will come because the course of circumstances has made the Mission responsible for the bringing up of orphans, the care of whom from childhood to marriage will inevitably reveal many of the demands of tribal custom. Or, again, the care of some derelict strangers, unable to return to their own country owing to difficulties of distance and travel, and handed over, perhaps by the action of Government, to live in the difficult conditions of an artificially created mission village, will disclose hitherto unknown elements of native life. Or it may be children vanish from the schools for a period, having been taken away to a rite of tribal initiation. The duty also of striving to reconcile those who have quarrelled will bring to knowledge new points of tribal custom.

But it is necessary to remember that, in whatsoever way knowledge comes, it will be the more reliable in so far as it is not the result of any direct questioning. Direct questions, seeking for information about the agelong customs of intimate tribal life, may seem to those questioned like ill-mannered prying, and the answers will, in that case, be chiefly valuable as examples of courteous prevarication. Moreover, many simple pagan people have a very marked sense of modesty, and dislike the discussion, apart from their environment, of rites and ceremonies which they perform quite naturally in their own due season.

In whatever way knowledge comes, we have reached the point in our consideration when the missionary discovers for the first time that there are aspects of village life which strike him as terribly evil. The reaction from his former attitude of trustful confidence will be great. Is not the new convert himself, growing now in grace, repelled by what " heathen " practice allows to go on ? These children in mission hands and care, are they to be exposed to the contamination of such unheard-of wrong ? Can the people of the mission village be allowed to organise rites which are unknown in the Christian home life of the old country ? If dancing and drumming are used in orgies, can the Church countenance any dancing at all for her converts ? Is not bride-price plainly a thinly veiled form of selling women into slavery ? Questions acutely affecting morals must be dealt with with as little delay as possible ; the anxious avoiding of all appearance of evil will tend to seem the only safe course. Are Christian ideals of purity and perfection possible if such customs are to be permitted ? And so the missionary in his isolation is moved to denounce, blindly and indiscriminately, much which he had at first ignorantly blessed.

It is easy to condemn this attitude, and it is increasingly being understood that such zeal is not according to knowledge. But many missionary decisions had to be made before the immense assistance of anthropology became as accessible as it is to-day. That mistakes have been made the Church increasingly realises. For some of them she must admit the responsibility ; others are the evil result of contact with European civilisation ; but the far-reaching results which have followed too sweeping a condemnation of tribal customs cannot be denied : artificial sins have been created ; tribal life has been dislocated ; in seeking to root out the tares, so much of the wheat has been destroyed that the old social life has in some cases starved and died.

That the result of our mistakes has not been more grave is due to various causes. In lands where Christianity has proceeded steadily but without the rush of a mass movement, enough paganism has remained to keep the old customs alive and give the Church time to revise hasty legislation in the light of fuller knowledge. In certain other cases the missionary's prohibitions have been promulgated, but shortage of staff and pressure of work have made it impossible to enforce them, and the old customs have survived except in the minutes of the missionary's log-book.

But the damage will be greatest when, as happens here and there, there are found converts who welcome an attitude of revolt. Missionaries from Great Britain can hardly fail to carry with them a prestige and status which are impressive to the people to whom they have come ; their manner of life, their belongings, however simple, speak almost everywhere where missionary work is done of a power and knowledge which cannot but exert an influence on the minds of a simple people. Moreover, the lives of love and devotion and sacrifice which many missionaries have lived add further weight to their counsels, and it is not to be wondered at if in these circumstances judgments which are, in fact, ill-considered, and will be recognised as such later on, are nevertheless accepted without question out of reverence for the source from which they come. And so a party may arise which in great measure will despise the old life and the village chiefs and elders and many of the customs and rites of the past, and seek to model themselves on their conception of the European pattern.

As an example of this, it is a cause of real anxiety to see the way in which tribal life in some parts of Africa tends to an increasing disintegration, natural respect for native authority disappears, and many Africans seem to desire nothing so much as to abandon what is essentially African and adopt what, in their judgment, appears to be European. So much is this true that efforts at conserving and enriching all that is best in African life, arising from a real reverence for its essential genius, are regarded by some Africans as nothing more than a plot to keep them back because we are jealous of admitting them into the fuller life that is ours. That the whole world will suffer loss if the African forsakes the contribution which he alone can make through striving to confine himself in moulds that are not his is an undoubted and deplorable fact. And where older and responsible non-Christians continue to hold aloof from Christianity, distrusting its influence and misliking what they imagine to be its message, it is, in a number of cases, because the evils of detribalisation have filled them with a right alarm, and those who have imitated our civilisation, contemning their own, are regarded as the inevitable product of the teaching of Christianity.

IV

What, then, should be the Christian approach to non-Christian customs as we come to know them ? First of all we must do our utmost to keep far from us the attitude of mind which considers customs, that seem to us perhaps uncouth, bizarre, far removed from European ways, to be therefore bad. Our first aim must be to conserve all that can possibly be conserved of essential native life. And only when consultation with the best local opinion clearly establishes the fact that the retaining of any particular custom is inimical to the attaining of Christian holiness should that custom be proscribed and abandoned. And at the same time it should be our serious endeavour, where it is necessary to condemn some particular point, to substitute in its place another custom which will not conflict with high moral ideals.

The position to-day is immensely clearer through the help that anthropologists bring, but, while availing ourselves thankfully of their aid, we must be on our guard against adopting an ultra-anthropological attitude which resents the slightest alteration in the rites and customs of a people. If we could justly regard the rites and customs of a people as an antiquary regards the uncovered ruins of some ancient temple or buildings, the problem would be immeasurably simpler. It would seem sacrilege to move a single stone, even though one substituted a more beautiful stone in its place, or to make any addition to supply what is lacking in the remains as they stand. But a living people cannot be treated as a dead ruin : they are dynamic, not statio. And though tho utmost oaro and skill is needed in remoulding any ancient rites and customs, our Lord, who came not to destroy but to fulfil, wills that it be done ; for nothing can rightly be allowed which would make perfect holiness unattainable. For a long time it may be necessary to tolerate less than ideal conditions of hygiene and bodily health out of respect for the interdependence of the different elements of culture among primitive peoples. For it is frequently the case that the destruction of one custom may damage and endanger the whole social fabric far more than was realised to be possible. Indeed, it cannot be too strongly emphasised that the ceremonies and beliefs of peoples of lowly culture are so closely bound up with economic and social factors of various kinds that the ill-considered destruction of its ritual and beliefs may involve vital wounds to the whole social structure. The evil of institutions " often lies on the surface while the good only becomes apparent as the result of prolonged and painstaking investigation " : but " the more a missionary knows his people, the more he finds to admire " and marvel at even in the lowliest forms of religion. It is impossible to regard the religious systems of savage and barbarous peoples as merely the work of the devil. That they do invariably contain elements which are directly opposed to Christianity, and must therefore be destroyed, cannot be denied ; but the more they come to be understood, the more they show that the light that lighteneth every man that cometh into the world has not been without its witness in the darkest parts of the earth : and in the providence of God a substructure has been prepared to which the firm building of Christianity will wisely be related.[1]

[1] For passages in the above I am indebted to an article, " Anthropology and the Missionary," by Dr. Rivers, *Church Missionary Review*, Sept. 1920.

K

No real remodelling of non-Christian customs can safely be undertaken without the assistance of native converts of sufficient age and standing and maturity in religion to be competent to give the guidance required. Moreover, with whatever care necessary adjustments in non-Christian customs are made by the Church, with the aid of all the expert advice and help that can be obtained, the enactments will be in danger of remaining for the most part a dead letter, unless their wisdom and fitness find an answering note in the conscience of the Christian community concerned. This can hardly be looked for unless real individual care is exercised in the preparation of all candidates for Baptism. Every effort must be made to obtain real conversion of heart in those who come to the font. It may well be that the Church in Europe is still suffering to-day from the wholesale admission to Baptism of those to whom Christianity is but a thin veneer, covering a heart in which the enemies of the soul hold barely disputed sway. To avoid the reproduction of this danger in missionary work to-day, it behoves us to do our utmost to keep our standards high, and in the preparation of all whom we baptise to lay great stress upon the demand of Christianity for real holiness of life.

I will close this section of my essay with a recollection of a speech made by a lady on the first day of the International Conference at Le Zoute, September 1926. A point in her speech she illustrated by the difference between the European and the African method of beckoning with the hand. The European holds his hand with the fingers uppermost ; the African holds his hand, when he beckons, with the fingers pointing down ; our European beckoning seems to him to be so unseemly as to be almost unthinkable. The Christian Church goes forth to its missionary work in many lands, seeking to call God's children scattered abroad into the true knowledge and love and fellowship with Him for which they were created. But must we not admit that the greatest message with which man could be entrusted, the most tender calling ever made to the human soul, have failed to win the response that is their due ? If this is so, is it not in part because in our eagerness and zeal we have not given that respect and care to the language and customs of those to whom we have gone ? We have beckoned with the beckoning of the white man, and the wonder is that

God has so overruled our mistakes as to make the response as great as, in fact, it has been. But new knowledge brings new responsibility, and though we have taken many outposts, strong walled cities remain unshaken, unimpressed. If, then, our love and longing for the souls of those as yet unwon is to overflow the region of the emotions and be translated into effective act, we must needs learn the beckoning which will be understanded of the people, and show that we have come not to destroy, not to breed disrespect for age in custom or in man, but to interpret, ennoble, and enrich all the best that their own life has prepared for the coming of Him in whom all things are fulfilled. A new chapter may then begin in our missionary work, as all the prayers that have gone before come to their answer and the seed that has been sown matures to the harvest.

V

We pass now from general considerations to an attempt to apply our principles to some of the problems which meet the missionary in his desire to make a sympathetic approach to non-Christian customs. It is inevitable that a writer cannot speak at first hand except of those conditions with which his own life as a missionary has been surrounded : and therefore it is right to say in preface that almost all that follows is concerned with missionary work in Africa amongst pagan people matriarchally organised, the tribes in question being Yaos and Makuas.

Clothing.—The preaching of the Gospel should not involve any change of customary native dress in those who become converts. The New Testament does indeed plead for a simplicity of raiment as worn by Christians, and there may well be a need in certain parts of the world to-day to make a similar appeal that no undue expense be incurred on unnecessarily costly clothing. In educational institutions there may be reasons for adopting clothes of a uniform type, cut on the general lines of the local native dress, as is the custom of the majority of public schools in England. Where radical changes in attire have been encouraged or required of converts, it has happened in some places that serious results have followed in reduced stamina and liability to diseases of the chest. European civilisation, alas, presses its way so rapidly these days into the coast hinterland that the adoption of European clothes goes on apace : but this is another subject which cannot be dealt with in this essay.

It merely remains to consider whether the European missionary is well advised to try himself to wear the normal native dress. Cardinal Lavigerie, the founder of the Congregation of White Fathers, ordained for them a habit which is an almost exact replica of the Arab burnoose as worn round about Algiers, where their work originally began : the place of the Mohammedan rosary being taken by the Christian rosary. But when the White Fathers extended their work into equatorial Africa, they made no change in their habit ; and it is difficult to believe that Europeans could adopt the clothing of the Central Africans consistently with health and seemliness.

Dancing.—Dancing is a universal recreation in Central Africa. It is hard to picture normal African life without drums and dancing. Certain dances in connexion with special ceremonial occasions are suggestive and obscene : with the help of local African Christians of standing a list of these can be, and should be, compiled and sent to responsible leaders of society, and the Christian conscience will not be slow to acquiesce willingly in their being given up. Certain conditions of the ordinary dances of joy make what is innocent in itself a proximate occasion of sin, such as continuance of the dance too late into the night, and the gathering together of young men and maidens from other villages who at the conclusion of the dance must return to their homes by dark forest paths, or sleep where no adequate provision for them exists. For this reason a dance that goes on all night until the dawn is in some ways less dangerous than a dance terminating at midnight or at 1 or 2 A.M. But many an ordinary dance does not go on after nine, for Africans go early to bed, as most of them have to be early abroad in their fields. A regulation that 10 or perhaps 11 P.M. should be regarded as the limit of the dance is soon accepted ; but the education of the Christian conscience is worth far more than rigid rulings, for, unless the African conscience assents, rigid rulings will be of no avail except within earshot of the European mission station. Many missionaries find it strange that the African dance has such an appeal, for it often appears to us to be a very dull affair ; but those who are tempted to find it shocking will be those who find European dances no less blameworthy. And the dancing of men and women together, as in European countries, seems to all but the most sophisticated coast African shocking beyond belief.

Divination (Swahili : *Kupiga bao, kupiga ramli* ; Yao : *Chisango*).—The very widespread habit of resorting to a diviner, or witch-doctor, in order to discover the cause of your relation's disease, or of the rain shortage, or of any other grave and perplexing trouble, leads to such lamentable enmity, hatred, and malice, the breaking up of homes, and cruel torturing of the aged, that the Church to-day will stand by the fifth canon of the Council of Ratisbon and condemn as mortal sin any participation in the resorting to divination. Those who have been under instruction as hearers should promise on admission to the catechumenate that they will have nothing more to do with this practice.

Funeral Rites.—The up-country African Moslems, who rarely know anything about the tenets of Islam, in districts where they live in any numbers urge on their co-religionists who may be tempted to seek instruction as Christians two considerations : (i) that a Moslem who forsakes his religion and becomes a Christian develops leprosy ; and (ii) that the Christians cast away the bodies of their dead with no reverent burial. It is as difficult to trace the authority for this second statement as for the first. But attendance at a Christian funeral disproves at once their allegation. At a funeral last year of the Christian wife of a Government clerk in the Mohammedan country round Tunduru, the African priest who buried told me that as many as three hundred Moslems came to the funeral to see how Christians do bury their dead, and all their misgivings were banished. Following the custom of the country, the friends and relations of the deceased dig the grave, and in the bottom of the grave they make a further excavation somewhat in the shape of a coffin. The body is laid out and wrapped in cloth : and when the service in church is over and the graveside is reached, a near relation or, in the case of an adult, two go down into the grave and receive the body into their arms and lay it to rest in the hollowed-out earth coffin, placing rough-hewn small logs of wood to form, as it were, the lid, and then covering all with a mat. The pagan custom is to lay the body on its side, and

sometimes the cavity is hollowed out in the wall of the
grave instead of in the floor, and before leaving the body a
hole in the cloth is cut close to the ear, presumably in order
that the deceased may hear petitions addressed to him :
this custom is not allowed.

Some little difficulty is experienced at times on account
of the strongly held belief that bereavement, with its consequent necessary contact with the dead body, and the
holding of the head and shoulders in the burying in the
grave entail a ceremonial pollution (Yao : *Ndaka*) which,
unless it is removed according to custom, exposes the con-
taminated person to grave danger of illness and death.
The removing of the pollution is partly by a ceremonial
lustration in water which has been treated with certain
herbs and partly by an act of immoral intercourse with a
near relation. For a time a form of " churching " of the
bereaved was attempted in order to dispel the fear of the
results of contact ; but this has now been abandoned, as it
tended to prolong the erroneous belief that the performance
of one of the corporal works of mercy could bring with it
defilement. Where there is hesitation in taking the head
and shoulders in the burial of a stranger, and thereby contracting defilement for the sake of one who has no claim of
kinship, a good object lesson has been afforded by the
missionary himself going down into the grave to lay the
stranger's body to rest. Nothing but persevering instruction will remove this wrong, but not unnatural, fear of
contact with death. It may be that the ceremonial
lustration with herbs will be long continued, and scientists
may establish later that the herbs in the water have the
effect of a disinfectant, but it is obvious that there
can be nothing but condemnation for seeking to remove
a supposed bodily defilement by an immoral act.

In the pagan practice, when the grave has been filled in,
a thatched roof on poles, sheltering the whole grave, is
built over it, at any rate in the case of the more important
people of the clan. There seems no reason to object to this,
though the offerings of tobacco and cloth are not allowed.
The pagans take great care of their graves, keeping them
swept and clear of vegetation. It is unseemly if our
churchyards are less carefully tended. And the desire to
serve, benefit and appease the departed finds its outlet in
the arranging of Requiem Masses. Persevering instruction

will make this Christian act on behalf of the departed so satisfy their desires to serve their dead as to make the old offerings seem puerile, a mere shadow compared with the substance. Offerings, though perhaps better not the actual old offerings in kind, can be given as alms at the Mass of Requiem. Great care should be exercised to keep an accurate list of the faithful departed, so that at each Sunday Mass the names of those whose year's mind falls in that week may be read out.

The sacrifices offered to the departed are referred to under " Sacrifice."

Hospitality.—The greatest care and courtesy are shown in the customs of real African hospitality. When a guest of importance is expected special care is taken that the house to which he will come, with the ground round it, is swept clean. Firewood, water, flour, and other foods are prepared, and when the guest arrives the whole house is handed over to him, adorned and made as beautiful as the owner's possessions can make it : the owner himself turns out and sleeps at a building near by. The analogy of these customs provides a simple and effective way of teaching Africans the preparation necessary in our souls if we are to receive rightly our Lord in Holy Communion.

Housing.—Just as wise missionary zeal will be most careful not to interfere with the customary clothing of the people, so the housing usual in the country will remain untouched. Nevertheless, as in the matter of clothing the ideal of cleanliness will inevitably find its place, so with the home the tendency will be in the direction of improved housing, more attention to space and ventilation ; but all this as a natural development initiated by the people themselves under no kind of compulsion. To substitute permanently built dwelling-houses for the customary dwellings lasting a limited number of years might have a disastrous effect on the health of the people until the general level of life, as regards cleanliness and sanitation, is ready for more permanent dwellings. And where the custom is to scatter houses sparsely over a wide area, each house with its farmlands around it, to compel an artificial alignment of houses after the manner of a street might mean that endemic diseases became epidemic with the gravest result to the health of the people.

If it is possible for the missionaries themselves to live in houses built in the native pattern, the gain in accessibility to the people will be really great : they should be able to come in and see the members of the Mission with the same ease with which they visit one another. And, incidentally, such improvements as will occur to the European missionary in his own house construction will exercise any influence that is needed towards the improvement of local housing in the interests of hygiene.

Hygiene.—In this matter of hygiene reforming zeal will need specially careful direction ; there are so many points in which twentieth-century European practice may be indisputably hygienically superior to the customs of the people amongst whom one is living. For example, it is the custom of the greater part of Central Africa for no one person to eat by himself, but always to share, two, three, or even more persons, the food from one plate. It is the custom where a leaf filled with tobacco is twisted up into a small cheroot for the smoker after a few puffs to pass his cheroot to his neighbour, the one cheroot being thus shared by all those present until it is finished. Amongst the Yaos and Makuas circumcision takes place round about the ages of thirteen or fourteen.

Health experts would condemn all these practices and many more, but to insist, or even to suggest strongly, that a man should eat by himself and smoke by himself would revolutionise the habits of the people and wound vitally that admirable belief in the solidarity of mankind which is the very basis of our African society ; and to alter any part of the initiatory rites, except in the interest of purity of morals, would endanger our whole influence in this most important matter, more of which we will consider in the following section. This intense belief in the solidarity of mankind, which can hardly be better expressed than in the Pauline phrase that we are verily and indeed members one of another, imposes moral restraints for which scientifically there can be little, if any, ground. One's first impulse is to say that whatever makes for moral restraint must be an unmixed good, but this is to forget that, when some untoward circumstance occurs, the averting of which is the express purpose of the moral restraints imposed, blame tends to fall unwarrantably on persons who may be innocent. But, although the failure in restraint cannot rightly be charged as the direct cause of the bewailed event, there may well have been a failure, and I do not call to mind any single case in which this unscientific belief has resulted in real hardship. It seems better, therefore, not to risk the licence and the undoubted harm which would follow from it by a premature destruction of strongly held beliefs. Where, let us say, a man has committed adultery, his wife being pregnant and drawing near the time of her delivery, local custom demands a ceremonial lustration with water herbally treated, and relies on this to remove the added peril which through this sin awaits the woman in her child-bearing. No Christian supposes for a moment that this bath can remove moral guilt : for this they must have recourse to the Sacrament of Penance ; but it seems safer not to forbid at present the ceremonial bath. The contamination removed by this ceremonial lustration may be paralleled by that contracted and similarly removed after contact with death.

One other point remains under this heading. The complete ignorance of the physiological causes of disease and infection almost certainly results in the unnecessary spreading of yaws and leprosy and other grave diseases. In the days before European occupation lepers whose condition had become a real trial to those with whom they were living were taken out into the forest and shut into a small house, with three days' food and water, to die. European Governments have put a stop to this summary treatment of the disease, and this may be partly responsible for the swing of the pendulum the other way to a fatalism which treats all care or caution as futile. Here some instruction in the ways of avoiding infection or contagion must be attempted. With the Yaos and Makuas probably the surest way of spreading this knowledge without wounding the African kindly susceptibilities will be to establish something on the lines of an initiatory rite, for sufferers at any rate from leprosy, wherein instruction may be imparted and right lines of conduct imposed. There are restrictions immemorially imposed, in an initiatory rite, on women expecting the birth of their first child : many of them coincide strikingly with what is desirable in the avoidance of contagion, and these would form the basis of the rite suggested above. The policy of compulsory segregation for life of known cases of leprosy in the past invariably led in this country to concealment of the disease, except in the case of those sufferers who had no relations to care for them. To-day medical treatment is extended freely to all those who will come for it, without any compulsory segregation, and quite early cases are being brought for treatment with good hopes of cure.

Simple rules of hygiene, stressing specially cleanliness and the necessary battling with flies and mosquitoes, form now part of the curriculum of our schools.

Initiatory Rites.—In the customs of the Yaos and Makuas no boy comes to marriage and manhood without circumcision, which takes place during the initiatory rite called the "lupanda." In the case of women and girls there are four rites of initiation : (i) " chiputu," in which a certain physical act is taught to young girls ; (ii) the rite which follows on puberty as soon as the fact that puberty has been reached is established beyond doubt ; (iii) the rite which takes place in about the sixth month of the first pregnancy ; (iv) the rite which follows the birth of the first child. In all these four rites invaluable instruction is given, mixed with varying amounts of futile old wives' fables and some teaching which is definitely opposed to the Christian ideals of holiness. The second and fourth of the women's rites contain hardly any instruction (perhaps in the fourth none) that is immoral ; the third gives most occasion for obscenity, and as the purpose of the physical deformation taught in the first seems to be directed to the increasing of the sexual appeal it must be regarded as morally dangerous. That a girl who had not been through the rites could survive child-bearing is not believed. All the five rites are accompanied by the singing of definitely obscene songs accompanied with undesirable dancing to the drums.

There is no doubt that in the case of the boys' rite it is a religious ceremony : tribal marks are given in it ; relation to the ancestors of the tribe is established through it, their aid is invoked, sacrifices are offered to them ; the " lupanda " tree with its lopped branches, which is brought and set up in a mound in the middle of the open space before the chief's house, may be designed to take back the memory to the hill, Yao, in Portuguese East Africa, which is said to have been surmounted by such a tree and near to which they first became conscious of themselves as a tribe, or it may, perhaps, more probably be a phallic emblem. Add to this connexion with pagan religion the undoubted elements of positive evil mingled with the rites, and the danger of it, religious and moral, seems so manifest that a campaign for the complete suppression of these customs is easily initiated. I say " easily initiated " advisedly, for where circumcision has become to be regarded as essential before marriage it will be by no means easily suppressed. Uninitiated boys are debarred from being present at any funerals even of a near relation, and certain other restrictions fall upon them ; for example, they are not allowed to cut hair, or to kill an animal for food, and they are voiceless in the village assemblies.

What shall the attitude of the Christian Church be to these non-Christian initiatory rites ? The first answer of almost all European missionaries would tend to be condemnatory. The Church may condemn the whole system from A to Z as incompatible with faithful Christianity. Where circumcision is not part of the boys' rite, after a long struggle, suppression may be accomplished for weal or for woe. Or the result of the edict of proscription, especially where circumcision takes place in the rite, may produce an open or a secret defiance ; and of the two, the secret defiance, the clandestine carrying out of the rite in concealment, and therefore with a bad conscience, seems the more damaging to the characters we are trying to build. So much for the men. But on the part of the women and girls the struggle will be even more prolonged, and it may result in the impossibility of baptising any women until the last of the tribal rites has been finished. So much for the alternative of suppression.

Can the Church, then, allow the rites to continue as they stand ? I imagine that there are no Christian missionaries who would maintain for one moment that the rites should be allowed to go on according to the old customs.

Is there no other way ? Is it impossible to preserve all the undoubted good, to tolerate for the present those elements which are not incompatible with Christianity, to eliminate the teaching which is contrary to morals, the obscene songs and dancing, substituting positive moral instruction and any other instruction which makes for manliness, citizenship, and general integrity of character ? Traditionally the rules of politeness, all that is comprised by " good manners," the way to receive and entertain guests, the way to wear one's clothes and to behave politely and modestly to members of the opposite sex, some traditional rules of a rare refinement equal to the most perfect courtesy known to us at home, are imparted to the young in these rites.   Is it impossible to turn the elements concerned with paganism to the ends of Christianity, as the light of day succeeds to the half-light before dawn, correcting or removing the misapprehensions the semi-darkness had conveyed ?   If we have admitted that detribalisation is in itself a grave evil whatever people it may befall, surely we shall desire to do all we can to preserve such a very important element in the present constitution of African tribal life as are these initiatory rites.   The difficulties are admittedly immense and the dangers equally so, but if it be possible to purge the rites of all that is dangerous to faith or morals, substituting positive good for all that we remove ; if it be possible with the willing consent of the Africans for the Church to be entrusted with effective control of all the rites involving Christian and catechumen initiates, and for the Africans themselves so to recognise the unity of the Christian rites with the former pagan rites as to continue to call the Christian rites by the old names ; and if, over and beyond this, pagan chiefs are able to be so satisfied with the Christian rites, carried out under the direct supervision of the European missionaries themselves, as to write and ask permission to send pagan boys to be admitted to the Christian initiation, would not the gain make the burden, however great, more than worth while ?

Some one will rightly ask, How do you know that the elements of pagan religion and immoral teaching do not remain unknown to the Europeans, or perhaps added when the rite outwardly ends on the return of the initiates to their village homes ?   That the latter may take place after the rite has ended is true : I think I know one instance in which it did happen.   But it is contrary to African custom that such instructions should be given outside the rite ; they lack all the solemn auspices of the rite itself : and one can no more defend people from bad advice and bad conversation in Africa than in England : what one can do is by positive teaching of good try to counteract the appeal of evil.   To believe that evil takes place in the rite under our very eyes is possible, but the unmistakable good that is effected and the evil that is avoided would seem to make a risk that some dregs may have filtered through an entirely insufficient ground for giving up so much that is positively good.

A detailed description of the rites as the Church has adapted them would be out of place in this essay as being of too local interest, but it may be of value to indicate briefly the main points of the adaptation.

The ceremony for the boys divides itself naturally into three main divisions: the opening day, the month or six weeks' seclusion in the forest camp, and the close. The ceremonial use of sacrificial flour offered to the spirits of the departed, the setting up of the tree with the lopped branches (the " lupanda "), the invocation of the spirits of the great ones of the past are too intimately and plainly pagan religious rites to be tolerated by the Christian Church. The whole ground, therefore, on which the rite will take place is blessed with litany and prayer and sprinkled with holy water, replacing the flour ; the Cross takes the place of the " lupanda " tree ; and the invocation of the Saints of Christendom replaces the appealing to the great ones of the tribal past. All this is done after dark on the vigil. The all-night dance is allowed, though the dances themselves must be chosen from an approved list, and in the morning all gather into the church for the Christian Sacrifice, the offering of the true Flour and the true Cup. The circumcision follows, done by an African who holds the licence of a European Government doctor that he is qualified for the purpose. The great dance of rejoicing when the rite is safely over follows, and then all the relations disperse, leaving the boys in seclusion in the forest camp. The customary provision of a sponsor guardian for each of the initiates seemed too great a risk, and the boys therefore are committed to the care of two carefully chosen Christian teachers, unless the number exceeds, say, forty, when a further teacher is added for each additional twenty, or fraction of twenty, boys. Food is cooked for them by a cook provided, and medical care is supplied by African dispensary assistants. Local chiefs come from time to time to give instruction in the manners and customs of the tribe, the Christian teachers being present (but no European) to check any tendency to teach unauthorised subjects. And this instruction by chiefs is supplemented by teaching given by a senior African teacher on the following seven points : truth, honour, purity, a right relation to drink and heathen customs, humility, the love of man, and to honour God above all. Hunting is taught ; discipline is strict ; and care is taken to ensure that morning and evening prayers and grace before and after food are the habit of all. As the period draws to its end special efforts are made to move each boy to a true repentance for all the sins and failures of the past, and on the day before the end each boy makes his confession, as he does also in the heathen rite. Heads are then shaved, new clothes brought, and early in the morning of the last day all that belongs to the old life is set fire to and burnt, and the boys come to the church for the solemn Mass of Thanksgiving with a real determination to lead a new life. In the heathen rite they would be given a new name, but their new name in Christianity belongs to their Baptism. At the Mass of Thanksgiving they are received into the chancel of the church and separately censed as potential bridegrooms, and at the end of the Mass receive a special blessing. And then the priest takes the boys to the west door of the church and, amid a scene of wonderful enthusiasm, restores them to their waiting mothers and other relations.

With the girls' Christian rite the period of seclusion lasts ten days. They also begin and end at the altar. The physical rite has been disallowed. But the same efforts as with the boys are made through the teaching of African women, under the direct supervision of European lady missionaries, to instruct the girls in the manners and courtesies of the home and village and establish them in the practices of the Christian life. And they too are moved to repentance for the past, confession of sin, and leaving behind all that belonged to the former life, and on the final day, clothed in the new garments their parents provide and anointed with the oil of gladness, they come to the church for the solemn Thanksgiving Mass.

Later on, when a generation has grown up knowing only the Christian rite, it will be possible again to provide each initiate with his or her own godparent, and the rite will go back from the quasi-quarantine in which it at present has to be to become a normal part of Christian village life. The opportunity which these intimate relations with all the Christian boys and girls of the parish give to their priests and teachers is of an importance which cannot be exaggerated ; and, rightly used, a relationship is established which remains for years.

The three remaining women's rites are semi-private in their character. The girl who has reached puberty is instructed by a trustworthy African Christian matron, her mother listening near-by : no singing or dancing or concourse of people is allowed. In the sixth month of the first pregnancy the husband sits also with the young wife listening to the teaching given ; but again there must be no singing or dancing or concourse of people : and equally after the birth of the first child.

A criticism made of this effort to Christianise tribal customs is that it is dangerous, inasmuch as it stresses too much the ancient sanctions. But the only alternative seems to be a cutting adrift from the old sanctions, and though it would be presumptuous to claim that no improvements or further precautions could be adopted, it is precisely because it does stress the old sanctions that what began as an experiment has seemed to some of us to be of real value.

Scholars could measure how far this effort to Christianise the mysteries can be compared with the Church's attitude in her earlier years to pagan festivals and the " mysteries " of the early Roman Empire. Confession, which in the old rite was extorted under pain of death if the truth was not told, and which takes place also as far as regards sins of unfaithfulness whenever a woman labours in childbirth, makes the Sacrament of Penance seem to our Africans a very normal provision for the soul. And the anointing with oil which marks the close of these rites of initiation (as it marks also the close of mourning), when the entry is made through the *rites de passage*, upon the new life makes natural the Church's use of consecrated oil in the sacraments. Moreover, the ashes with which rejoicing parents disguise themselves lest jealous Fates strike them in judgment give a special African meaning to the imposition of blessed ashes on Ash Wednesday, rejoicing in the mercy of God who has brought the soul safely to the beginning of another Lent, and realising that it is only by His mercy that divine judgments are still averted from us.[1]

Marriage.—So many troubles of the missionary are concerned with marriage, and so much time has to be given

---

[1] Some further notes on initiatory rites have been printed in the *International Review of Missions*, April 1927, p. 192 *et seq.*

to the endeavour to reconcile husbands to erring wives or wives to erring husbands and help on those who are tempted to tire of their marriage tie, that we cannot afford to neglect any help which native custom can render to the establishment of the holiness and indissolubility of Christian wedlock. Amongst the Yaos and Makuas there are no specific pagan marriage ceremonies : the marriage contract is arranged by the relations on both sides, with the consent of the bride and bridegroom. But the union is regarded as tentative and experimental, and can be terminated if it proves childless, or if the husband is lazy, or if grave unfaithfulness has occurred on either side. The contracting parties are frequently far too young, with the result that their consent is the consent of immaturity, submitting placidly to the arrangements of their elders. This consent of relations thus constitutes the main feature in non-Christian marriage ; and the Church rightly asks for the same formally expressed consent of relations on both sides, as well as of the bride and bridegroom, but to a union which they must understand is indissoluble. Care therefore has to be taken that the contracting parties have reached sufficient maturity to enable them to give a valid consent to the union. First cousins who are the children of two brothers or two sisters are regarded as within the forbidden degrees, and may not marry : this restriction the Church here maintains.

In countries where bride-price forms a necessary part of the marriage contract there is no reason against permitting the practice to continue, and there may be much danger in disallowing it. In one district missionaries forty years ago forbade bride-price in Christian marriage, but they had some few years later to allow the practice to be restored, for parents having no longer an incentive to guard their daughters' morals for fear lest her marriageable value should decrease, a considerably lower level of morality began to prevail, and the restoration of bride-price adjusted this once more.

Amongst the Hindus the sign of marriage is a wreath of flowers. It is plainly desirable that, although the ring be used in marriage, the wreath of flowers be given also its due place.

Music.—There are probably no parts of the world where a form of music indigenous to the country does not exist.

In the Africa of to-day there are those who correspond to the old English bards and compose songs by the way commemorating events grave and gay. In the rendering of them a fixed chorus is answered antiphonally to the varying story of the bard. A real genius for this form of song exists. It is a definite loss to religion and worship in particular if use is not made of native melodies sung to suitable words composed for singing antiphonally, or in whatever manner the local custom prescribes. Care, however, has to be taken that the melodies used are not familiar to the district in which the Church uses them, or there would be danger of the original words being sung through the mere force of association. But both in India and Africa, where an effort has been made to vary the singing of European hymn tunes set to vernacular words by introducing the melodies of the country sung in the traditional manner, the success of the experiment has been beyond question.

Names for Converts.—A somewhat parallel native gift which, adopted into Christian practice, would do much to preserve the character of an indigenous Church is the power of inventing personal names that express a suitable meaning. Instead of baptising all our converts with European names, let new names with Christian meaning be invented for some according to the custom of the country.

Religion, *i.e.,* **especially Sacrifices to Propitiate the Departed.**—In the Yao and Makua customs, when events appear sinister, one of the elders will dream that the spirit of a departed great one appeared and complained that suitable offerings were not being made to him, and only by a sacrifice of the customary flour and beer on a generous scale can deliverance be won from the troubles that oppress them. A day is chosen, specially white flour is prepared, and five days' brewing will provide the beer for the drinking that follows. Those concerned go to the place of sacrifice, usually an " msoro " tree, *i.e.* a particular kind of forest tree chosen, it is said, originally as suitable to shelter the offering because its leaves only fall at night. Here the head of the family makes the offering, interceding the while for deliverance from evil and the granting of their pressing needs, while the people in attendance express " Amen " by a slow rhythmical hand-clapping. As he makes each petition he takes a handful of flour and allows it to dribble

L

through his fingers into a little cone on the ground ; at the end, while all the remaining flour is poured out to unite the tiny separate cones into one big cone, the only invariable words of the Sacrifice are said, "We beseech Thee, O Lord God, have mercy upon us." (Yao: *Chonde Ambuje Mlungu mtukolele chanasa.*) This petition, thrice repeated, closes the rite. They are also the only words addressed to God and not to the spirits departed. No Christian can be allowed to take part in these sacrifices, but great good may be done by linking the points of the pagan sacrifice with the perfect Christian Sacrifice, to the offering of which they have now come. Many African peoples tend to regard Christianity as a beautiful European religion into which certain specially kind Europeans are prepared to enrol them as associates, and anything that will show that Christianity is the fulfilment for them of what had already been adumbrated in the immemorial customs of their past will do perhaps more than anything to help the Church to become really indigenous. An African of intelligence—when it was pointed out to him that the flour and cup of the pagan sacrifice were the way in which God prepared them for the offering of the true Flour and the true Cup, that the "msoro" tree corresponded to the tree of Calvary, and that although Africans offered flour as being the whitest, purest, cleanest, shiniest thing that they knew, there is that which is purer and whiter still, the Body of our Lord, while the thrice repeated petition to God is an address to the Holy Trinity—coming then for the first time to realise that Christianity is an African religion in a very real sense, and that God had been preparing his fathers until the time of the full revelation should come, was so moved that he could not speak until he had been first into church to pour out his thanksgiving to God. It is surely not merely a coincidence that, for quite other reasons, more than twenty years ago the site chosen for the building of the only stone church in this district, which has now become the cathedral church of the diocese of Masasi, is on the lower slopes of a conical hill named, as far back as man can remember, "Mtandi" —*i.e.* The Hill of the Personified Sacrificial Flour, or, in plain English, the Hill of the Living Bread. An equally striking "coincidence" is true of the cathedral in Korea.

Ancient Hindu literature reveals in the Bhagavadgita,

"The Divine Song" (dated, I believe, 400 B.C. to A.D. 400), a most striking scheme of religious devotion called Bhakti, that is to say, Love, Worship, Faith, and Devotion *to God Incarnate.* There are in Bhakti nine spiritual degrees :

(i) Devotion to the most Holy Name.
(ii) Devotion to the most Holy Feet.
(iii) Hearing (or reading) the Holy Scriptures.
(iv) Kirttan—Devotion by means of song.
(v) Worohip.
(vi) Devotion to the saints.
(vii) Work for God (as His slave).
(viii) Friendship with God.
(ix) Oblation of self—thought, word, and deed.

Here prepared in the providence of God lies ready a scheme of Retreat addresses, framed in the East for the East. God Incarnate is Jesus Christ. Christianly interpreted, the degrees are :

(i) Devotion to the Name of Jesus.
(ii) Devotion to the Sacred Feet on the Cross.
(iii) Meditation.
(v) The Mass.

The preaching of Retreats in the Hindu (Mahratta) country based thus on Bhakti has met with a very wonderful response, because it brings home to Hindu Indians the blessed truth that in Christianity is found the interpretation of the best in their own religious past, the fulfilment of what without it remained partial ; in a word, that Christianity is Eastern, the religion for them, and not merely, as they are tempted to fear, Western and European.

It is perhaps not beside the point to plead here for careful consideration of the use we are making of pictorial art. If our great aim is to present the Christian religion as God's call addressed directly to those for whom we work, His longing to bring to them that which alone can perfect and complete what without it will necessarily remain partial ; and if, as is the truth in many cases, the hesitation and fear of so many is that Christianity is in reality an exotic, then those pictures which represent our Lord and the saints as Europeans justify their worst fears. Art could do so much, but it must be an art that illustrates and aids our work, instead of keeping alive the very apprehension which is hardest to dispel. I have seen an African looking with tears of grateful joy at Byam Shaw's picture of our Lord in a Zulu hut; but such pictures are so very, very few.

Sickness.—The first thought of the African in medical cases is that some enemy has cast a spell on the sufferer, and, moreover, that although medicines may help considerably, no one can remove the spell with certainty except the person who was responsible for putting it there. It follows that a diviner will be sought to trace the identity of the enemy. Surgical cases, however, often have such an obvious explanation that the supernatural origin is not needed, though an accident in hunting is usually blamed to infidelity on the part of the wife at home, and certain other accidents are considered to be unlikely to be quite independent of human malignance. In extenuation it must be remembered that nothing is known of the physiological causes of disease.

But it follows that the mental state of the patient, tortured by fear of the supernatural, will gravely aggravate the physical condition of disease, and direct efforts will be needed to try to establish confidence and a measure of calm. African treatment, on the contrary, tends often to aggravate the fears of the sufferer, despairing relations and neighbours surround him, and the whole atmosphere is one of helpless impotence in the presence of supernatural evil, complicated by a heaviness born of the consciousness that any one of them may be charged as the enemy responsible. Mortality in medical cases is therefore high, far higher than would be the case with European patients suffering from the same diseases. That this is not due to any inherent bodily weakness is shown by the fact that in surgical cases Africans recover frequently where Europeans would almost certainly die.

The above facts explain the extreme gullibility of the African when charms claiming to protect the wearers against all malignant influence, and so preserve them in immunity from disease, find a ready sale. That a spell will best be counteracted by a stronger spell is the argument; and the value of the spell is shown by the number of people buying it, therefore it is as well to be on the safe side and buy.

Or, again, a witch doctor will arrive who will claim to be able to deliver the village from all who cast spells—that is to say, from witches and wizards alike—and thus maintain or restore the health of the inhabitants. He also will carry off large sums, for those who invited him to come will pay him; and those also whom he declares to be witches he can, if they pay him, deliver from their malign powers, which he will say in certain cases they may be exercising unconsciously—" carriers," as it were, of evil.

When herbal remedies are sought for sick persons, the almost universal rule is that divination must first be resorted to in order to discover who is the enemy before the suitable drugs can be selected. That some drugs are extremely efficacious cannot be doubted. A most interesting article on the scientific knowledge of savages occurred in *Blackwood's Magazine* of, I think, June 1927. And it would be a very interesting study to collect the herbal remedies, but it would be extremely difficult to do, because the knowledge of them is jealously guarded by those whose property and means of ready gain they are. As regards the Christian attitude to all this, divination cannot be tolerated, as has been recognised above : moreover, the possession of charms, which claim to give a quasi-divine protection from all dangers and disease (Swahili : *Hirizi*), must also be forbidden to Christians. But real herbal remedies should never be referred to contemptuously as " heathen medicine " ; probably no small part of the concealment of native remedies is due to the consciousness that some Europeans treat their drugs with derision and deny utterly that they could have any efficacy.

It is necessary to be patient also when European medical care does not immediately command the respect and confidence which is its due. Visible results are the test—does the dose of medicine break the spell and banish the disease ? For this reason treatment by injections is very popular, and the measure of the popularity is in direct ratio to the degree of visible result secured.

Some simple practical instruction in the laws of hygiene given in schools should do wonders after a time to reduce the aggregate of unnecessary fears which beset the primitive African.

Vows.—It is a normal African instinct to endeavour to win safety in danger or recovery in disease by vowing to make an offering if the relief sought is granted. In pagan life the offering usually takes the form of a feast of native beer. There seems no reason why this instinct should not have its place in the Christian religion. It is essential that the native mind should be directed to God as the sole Giver of all our good. Alms are gladly brought to the Church as a thankoffering to Almighty God, and the feast for friends and neighbours follows.

Witchcraft.—That everything which breaks the even tenor of life disagreeably has its source and cause is a natural belief. In Central Africa, whenever the source is not obvious, the explanation that follows most ordinarily assigns the untoward event to the powers of witchcraft. Missionaries hear the word frequently and with varying degrees of patience, but probably they only realise a fraction of the extent to which the fear of witchcraft casts its shadow over the lives of Africans. This is not the place to attempt any detailed study of this very perplexing subject, but something must be said of the attitude due to this non-Christian custom which looms so large in the lives and thoughts of primitive people at any rate in Africa.

Suggestion and auto-suggestion probably account for part of what is ascribed to witchcraft ; deliberate poisoning must not be excluded as a possible explanation of some deaths or debilities assigned to witchcraft in the native mind ; hypnotism, too, may play its part ; but he would be a rash man who refused to admit the possibility of the existence of some occult powers not yet classified in the lists of applied knowledge. The persecution and torturing of poor old men and women suspected of having stopped the rainfall arouses a righteous indignation, and every effort must be made to bring this impudent cruelty to an end.

The firm belief that by the use of " medicine " a man can turn himself into a lion or a leopard in order that he may be able to kill his enemies safely while remaining himself unknown is almost universal ; as is also the similar belief that a man may possess a lion or a leopard which will kill his enemies for him at his bidding. The complete abandonment in modern European countries on the part of all educated people of any fears of witchcraft and belief in werewolf stories suggests that after the lapse of long years the similar beliefs and fears will be laid aside by primitive African peoples also, and come to be regarded as mere nursery bogy stories cast away as the race passed from childhood to a status of greater maturity.

In the meantime the attitude of missionaries should be educative and not derisive. Their people should be shown all sympathy in their very natural longing to know the causes of events, and, wherever explanations covering the facts can be found, every effort should be made to gain credence for them and oust thereby the too ready resort, natural to primitive man, to the supernatural solution. We should try to lead people to require adequate evidence before condemning others for a witchcraft of which they may be entirely innocent.

Witchcraft itself must be categorically condemned, and every assurance given that where it is proven against anybody it will be regarded as an abhorrent crime. But mere mockery and derision of those who are "foolish enough to believe in such nonsense" will considerably reduce our hope of helping people to shake off unnecessary fears. They will not bring their fears to those who will only mock at them ; and mockery tends to be regarded as a mark of the ignorance, not unnatural on the part of strangers, of the true gravity of the situation.

The difficulty of dealing with witchcraft increases considerably when those on whom suspicion falls are said to have confessed and boasted of what they have done. It may well be that if the missionary finds himself confronted with a man or woman who maintains that he is responsible for the wrong done, the truth may be that it is a case of poisoning, or some misuse of a known natural gift, or an example of mere megalomania ; but, in any case, the person must be regarded as a danger to the public peace, and a period of detention, where Government takes cognisance of such conditions, will be no act of injustice.

VIII

MISSIONS AND GOVERNMENTS

BY E. R. MORGAN

SYNOPSIS

The mind of our Lord on the relations of the Church to the civil power suggests the need both of an aloofness from and of an intimate association with states, empires, governments.

There seem to have been two ways of approach to missionary enterprise in Post-Reformation Europe—the imperialistic and the individualistic.

But the imperialistic and individualistic approaches have tended to converge as the idea of toleration has gained acceptance, and there has been increasing mutual respect between Church and State for the freedom of each entity. Illustrations of this in connexion with missionary work.

Difficulties in considering present relation between missions and governments. There is undoubtedly much fruitful co-operation, but there is on the other hand evidence of uneasiness lest, by becoming too much identified with the humanitarian schemes of civil authorities, Christianity should lose its savour.

Certain features in the modern situation.

GOVERNMENTS AND THE COMITY OF MISSIONS.

Co-operation between missionary societies has naturally led to co-operation between the representatives of these societies and governments, with many excellent results.

But there is a subtle danger in the looseness with which we speak of "the churches and the Church" which has a bearing on this question.

THE PROTECTION OF MISSIONARIES.

The missionary must come close to the people among whom he works, and yet bring with him the best heritage of his own country. While he cannot repudiate the authority of his home government, he can under certain circumstances decline to accept government help. He must act with and in obedience to his bishop.

MISSIONS AND GOVERNMENTS IN MEDICAL WORK.

The primary purpose of medical work is to give Christ His chance to manifest Himself through the human ministry of healing. This aim must govern the relation of such work to government work of a similar character.

MISSIONS AND GOVERNMENTS IN EDUCATION.

The crucial problem to-day arises out of the increasing responsibility felt by governments for education. This is good, but the very enthusiasm of governments raises embarrassing questions for the missionary.

Warnings suggested by the story of educational development in India.

The desire of the Imperial Government to avoid the mistakes made in India in developing education in Africa.

It is vital that missionaries should agree as to the aim of Christian education.

Conclusion.

MISSIONS AND GOVERNMENTS

THE relation between missions and governments is but a part of the great epic of "The Church and the World in idea and history." The intricacies of the modern situation, resulting from the occupation of continents by explorers, traders, colonists, and missionaries can only be understood in the light of the mind of Christ and Christian history. Yet within the limits of a short essay it is possible only to make the briefest historical survey in order to introduce the discussion of present-day relations between missions and governments.

Two sayings of our Lord seem to give the key to His mind and intention in this matter :

"Render unto Caesar the things that are Caesar's, and unto God the things that are God's." [1]

"Before governors and kings shall ye stand for my sake, for a testimony unto them. . . . And when they lead you to judgment, and deliver you up, be not anxious beforehand what ye shall speak ; but whatsoever is given you in that hour, that speak ye : for it is not ye that speak, but the Holy Ghost." [2]

The divine message to the Church seems to be :

"The purposes and policies of human governments are inevitably inconsistent, shifting, and mixed, a prey to prejudice and circumstance. And yet through their laws and organisation they are striving to express the righteous stability of a higher Law which is of God. If you condemn them, beware lest the judgment recoil upon yourselves. Be not blind to the evil, but recognise also the good. Expend your energy, not in opposing governments, but in striving, through repentance and faith, after a consistent discipline and dependence on God, an uncompromising loyalty to Him, and an unfailing respect for every human being. You are the salt of the earth—a city set upon an hill. Be prepared to be loyal to these principles to the point of crucifixion, and you will be the means of new life

[1] Matt. xxii. 21.   [2] Mark xiii. 9, 11.

to the world, you will be the ministers and witnesses of repentance unto remission of sins, you will fulfil the Church's
Mission."

Such a task involves at once an aloofness from and an
intimate association with states, empires, governments ;
an independence of the existing standards of the state,
and a concern not merely with individual citizens of the
state, but with its home life, laws, commerce, public
health, education, and international relationships.

The break-up of the Middle Ages left open two avenues
of approach to missionary work in the modern world : the
one, chiefly characteristic of Catholic countries, may be
called the imperialistic approach ; the other, characteristic
of Protestantism, the individualistic approach. But the
imperialistic and individualistic approaches have tended
to converge as the idea of toleration has gained acceptance,
and this convergence was stimulated by the blow struck
at the autocratic idea of sovereignty by the Revolt of the
American colonies and the French Revolution. Throughout the nineteenth century the idea of constitutional and
federalistic sovereignty developed both in Church and
State, accompanied by an increasing mutual respect for
the freedom of each entity.

By the middle of the nineteenth century governments
were beginning to embody the idea of toleration in treaties
dealing with colonial possessions and relations with foreign
countries. The expression of this in a treaty between
Great Britain and Portugal (June 11, 1891) may be taken
as characteristic : " In all territories in East and Central
Africa belonging to or under the influence of either power,
missionaries of both countries shall have full protection.
Religious toleration and freedom for all forms of divine
worship and religious teaching are guaranteed."

In applying the principle of toleration in colonies and
dependencies where the inhabitants profess different faiths
the British and American governments maintain the strict
religious neutrality expressed in Queen Victoria's proclamation to India in 1858 : " Firmly relying ourselves on
the truth of Christianity and acknowledging with gratitude
the solace of religion, We disclaim alike the Right or the
Desire to impose our convictions on any of our subjects."
Of this policy the bishops of the Anglican Communion

reaffirmed in 1920 their approval, " having no desire to see any kind of political influence brought to bear on people to induce them to change their religion."

The Covenant of the League of Nations makes two declarations which bear on the relation between missions and governments. Article 22 in recognising that " the well-being and development of peoples not yet able to stand by themselves under the strenuous conditions of the modern world form a sacred trust of civilisation and that securities for the performance of this trust should be embodied in this Covenant " accepts responsibilities which bring the work of Mandatory Powers into closer partnership with missionary work. Article 438 in dealing with German missions implicitly accepts the principle of missionary freedom.[1]

The consideration of the relation between missions and governments at the present time involves the risk either of being lost in a maze of intricate detail, or of being lured into a slough of dangerous generalisation.

Some nations are in comparative stability, others are undergoing or living through the after-effects of social political and economic revolution. Stability itself may be the outcome either of a steady idealism or of a stagnant lethargy.

Governments are in their very nature and function changeable because they express and reflect the changing or developing policy of nations.

Moreover " government " is in itself an abstract term. What it means in any given area where missions are working is the ideas (or prejudices) of certain administrators, magistrates, consuls, medical officers, or educationalists on the spot, or the interpretation put by them upon the ideas (or prejudices) of certain other people for whom they act.

There is undoubtedly much happy and fruitful cooperation both within and outside the British Commonwealth. The League of Nations has been working with the Conference of British Missionary Societies on the opium question ; and there is the likelihood of common action

[1] For documents dealing with the relation between missions and governments see *Treaties, Acts, and Regulations relating to Missionary Freedom* (International Missionary Council, 1923.)

over the traffic in women and children and in the fight against tropical disease.

In the British Commonwealth many mission hospitals receive government and municipal grants. Grants are given to Leper Settlements started by missions. Missionary doctors are invited to take charge of government hospitals and sanatoria. Civil surgeons give voluntary service to mission hospitals. In the diocese of Dornakal, South India, the Church and the municipality have co-operated in the founding of a women's hospital. In another district in India the government asked the mission doctor to train all the midwives for the district.

A well-established co-operative scheme in social work is seen in the criminal tribes settlements in India which are shepherded by missions at the invitation and with the help of the government.

In Central Africa laws have been passed against witchcraft and excessive payment for wives.

The Church in Singapore and Ceylon has taken a noble lead in rousing public opinion to the dangers of sexual immorality.

In education, the Prince of Wales College, Achimota, stands as a symbol of the new experiment in co-operation whereby a government college is staffed by missionaries.

It is to be hoped that this co-operation will before long bring about the removal of certain disabilities at present attaching to service overseas in the teaching profession, and the adoption by the Imperial Government of the concession granted to missions by the German Government before the war, namely, the remission of duty on mission stores.

There is on the other hand evidence of uneasiness lest by becoming too much identified with the humanitarian schemes of civil authorities Christianity should be losing its savour. Here the relation of missions to governments is seen to be part of the whole problem of Christian witness in social life. In the Early Church this problem

" hardly existed as we know it. The Church and the world stood over against each other in such violent contradiction that on some points the only possible witness was the witness of complete non-co-operation, whilst on others the opportunity of formative influence had hardly arisen. In the Middle Ages, on the contrary, when some attempt had been made to mould the laws and customs of Christian countries according to Christian principles, the problem was non-existent for an opposite reason. What Christianity required of its members was conformity to the accepted social ideals of a society that could fairly be described as ' Christendom,' the domain of Christ.

" The problem is acute to-day for two opposite reasons. On the one hand it is acute because we stand at the end of a period when for some hundreds of years society has not reckoned to be carried on on Christian principles, owing mainly to the change from the mediaeval economy to the modern economy and the gradual abandonment of Christian idealism as impracticable.

" It is acute, on the other hand, because of the growing sensitiveness of the Christian conscience to all that is comprised in the Christian ideal, and the increasing interpenetration of religious and general thought, making it certain that Christian principles will either be increasingly embodied in social and political life or increasingly abandoned altogether." [1]

An observer in Africa writes :

" Missions are in a cleft stick, and it is not the hostility of the government that causes the difficulty, but its goodwill. Christian missions need to re-emphasise their Christian Mission. Theologically speaking a doctrine of grace needs to replace the present doctrine of nature. . . . The aim of Christianity is to rescue the world from sin, not misguidedness, or an untidy mind, or bad habits."

Another writes :

" The religion of a government can seldom be other than the common ground of agreement among its supporters, and though at the present time governments may be friendly, one must always remember the lesson of secularisation of the Church in the fourth century. . . . The fact is that governments can never afford to allow large corporations to exist in their midst with a complete field of independence, and with ideals which may possibly conflict with those of the State, and so they are prepared to get some measure of control under the guise of a friendly subsidy. The Church itself has at times in the past shown that there are few more effective ways of silencing a tiresome priest than by promoting him to be a dignitary ; it is not surprising if the State tries to follow the same plan in its dealings with the Church."

It is, therefore, with a full sense of the signs, both of hope and of danger, that we venture upon the indication of certain features in the modern situation.

[1] From a pamphlet on *Christian Action in Modern Social Life.*

Governments and the Comity of Missions.—It is obvious
that the increasing comity of missions tends to invite the
co-operation of governments with missionary work. As
long as the missions of various denominations were going
their own way, none of them, except those of the Roman
Church in some countries, were strong enough to be active
partners with governments in the working out of any
common policy. Governments were in so much the
stronger position that they could dictate the terms of the
relationship. They could refuse or grant toleration, decide
what constituted conformity to law and order, and make
grants in aid if it seemed in the interest of good government
to do so.

But since the Edinburgh Conference of 1910 gave expression and impetus to co-operation between the different
missionary bodies, the next step of co-operation between
representatives of those bodies and representatives of
governments became natural enough.

The Committee appointed in 1912 by the Conference
of British Missionary Societies to assist in matters arising
between missions and governments did notable work in
the years succeeding the war. It seemed likely that the
British Government would insist upon missionaries of alien
nationality obtaining a licence to carry on their work in
India, and thus impose upon missionaries a disability which
those engaged in civil occupations were not required to
accept. After friendly negotiations " the government submitted proposals under which the government undertook
to ' recognise ' all societies recommended by the Conference
of Missionary Societies and the corresponding body in
North America. The missions of British and allied
countries were accepted without further question ; neu-
trals were recognised on the recommendation of the
Conference of Missionary Societies ; and missions of enemy
countries were excluded for a term of years, afterwards
fixed at five years from the termination of the war." [1]

It is obvious that co-operation of this kind would not
be possible unless the missionary societies were themselves
prepared to work together. " Neither the government
departments nor the mission houses could stand the irri-

[1] See *Treaties, Acts and Regulations*, Memoranda A, B, C, pp. 10, 19,
and Kenneth Maclennan, *Twenty Years of Missionary Co-operation*
(Edinburgh House Press).

tating strain of an effort, on the one hand, to maintain separate relations with some forty different mission headquarters, nor, on the other hand, of the effort to secure attention to the problems of each when presented separately."

The twenty, or more, national missionary organisations and Christian councils which are allowed to send representatives to the International Missionary Council are no doubt of varying strength and importance, but many of them are bodies with which it is worth the while of governments to co-operate, especially if they have the backing of the International Missionary Council behind them. The way thus opened has already achieved much and is fraught with possibilities for the future.

But associated with this most fruitful advance there are drawbacks and dangers which it would be foolish to ignore.

There is a subtle danger in the looseness wherewith we are growing accustomed to speak of the " churches and the Church."

Dr. Headlam in his Bampton Lectures, after calling attention to the threefold use of the word *Ecclesia*, for the whole Church of God, for the local church, and for the actual assembly of Christians for worship, goes on to say :

" It has been suggested that the expression ' the churches ' might be used (in the literature of the early Church) in the same manner as has become customary in certain modern circles, for a number of different societies in each place separate from one another, just as there are what are called Anglican, Romanist, Wesleyan, Congregational churches in one city. It is difficult to conceive of anything more fundamentally alien to the whole spirit of the New Testament than this. As there could be only one Church of God in the world, so there could only be one Church of God in Corinth, although it might and probably did consist of many congregations. In fact, a considerable part of St. Paul's First Epistle to the Corinthians is devoted to preventing such a state of things arising as the modern world presents. . . . No justification can be found in the New Testament for our modern divisions."

No doubt the thoughtful among the leaders of all denominations are aware of the danger of treating organisations which express the comity of missions as though they were identical with synods of the Church. But Anglo-Catholics cannot fairly be accused of bigotry because

M

out of a sincere desire for organic unity they are shy of a federalism which does little to curb idiosyncrasy, and which is in danger of being content with something less than a unity compacted in Holy Order.

The habit of negotiation with governments through an organisation which, though composed of representatives of different missions and earnestly desiring to interpret their mind, yet tends inevitably to develop a corporate character and outlook of its own, means that this organisation may commit individual missionary bodies to a policy in relation to governments which they cannot conscientiously accept.

To the present writer these dangers are real and need to be constantly remembered ; but they do not in his opinion warrant an attitude of cold aloofness on the part of Anglo-Catholics from mighty movements in which the Holy Spirit is palpably at work. They are rather a challenge to humble and sincere and critical co-operation, and should spur us into more and more fervent and penitent prayer and work for unity in Faith and Order.

The Protection of Missionaries.—

" Christian missions involve the largest possible identi-fication of the missionary with the people of the country of his adoption."

" The missionary need never apologise for being a foreign evangelist. It was our Lord's plan, so that people of different nations might make friends in the process of learning the truth."

These two quotations express two necessary aspects in the attitude of the missionary to the people among whom he lives. He must come into the closest sympathy with them ; but he must remain himself, and a true son of his own spiritual and national heritage.

It is fashionable to imagine that it is more important for the Westerner to learn the mind of the East than to bring to the East the best heritage of the West. Both are necessary and both are possible.[1]

With the increase of self-consciousness in the native churches there has grown up among some missionaries a desire either to become citizens of the countries in which they are working or to vacate their own citizenship altogether and be without a country. There is in this

---

[1] *E.g.* Sir Stamford Raffles. See Professor Coupland's *Raffles* (Oxford University Press).

attitude the danger of bowing down to the very idol of nationalism which it is presumably the ambition of such missionaries to overthrow. It seems to be contrary to truly Catholic principle which never bows down to nationalism but in respecting and using national characteristics and differences transcends them.

But if it is right for a missionary to remain a citizen of his own country while he resides in a foreign country, he is thereby entitled to all the protection claimed by the traveller and the merchant. If he accepts it he is said to lay himself open to the charge of relying on armed force —though to rely, in times of danger, upon armed protection is not the same thing as the propagation of Christianity by force.

If, on the other hand, the missionary rejects the assistance of his government the position of the ambassador or consul who acts for his government may become very difficult. If a missionary can be robbed or maltreated without official protest, why not others ? If a missionary's property can be taken with impunity, why not the property of a merchant or other civilian of the same nationality ?[1]

The Catholic principle seems to be that missionaries owe obedience to their bishop, and bishops cannot repudiate the authority of their own government. They can, however, under certain circumstances decline to accept government help—as, for example, in compensation for the destruction of mission property—or deliberately decide to neglect government warnings at their own risk either for themselves or for the missionaries of their diocese. And ambassadors and consuls can in certain circumstances safely leave it to the discretion of the bishop or the individual missionary whether a worker should return to or be withdrawn from a dangerous area.

Missions and Governments in Medical Work.—The Commission of our Lord to His Church to heal the sick is clearly given that He may continually manifest through His mystical Body the same recreative power and compassion of God which He showed on earth.

Medical missions have too often been regarded as a means of preparing a way for the preaching of the gospel, or as essentially philanthropic in character. Obviously

[1] See J. L. Barton, "Missions and Governments : A Study of Principles," *International Review of Missions*, July 1924.

they are both, but only as a consequence of their primary purpose of giving Christ His chance to manifest Himself through the human ministry of healing.

Unless this is clearly recognised by the Church the salt of its witness through healing will lose its savour.

1. The best type of non-Christians will tend to regard medical missionary work as a disreputable attempt to exploit their suffering and poverty and bring their poorer brethren within the range of Christian propaganda.

2. The difficulty of getting workers will tempt the Church to accept men and women as medical missionaries who have a general sympathy with missionary work but no real missionary vocation.

3. There will be no standard by which to judge within what limits co-operation with governments in medical work is right in principle. Christian doctors and nurses may conceivably be able to bear their finest witness to the power of the Living Christ to heal in a government hospital, but nothing short of an impelling sense that God is calling them so to do, no vague idea that " it is all the same work " should tempt them to desert the distinctive life and witness of medical missionary work.

4. Missions will be too easily content to leave the training of Christian native doctors and nurses to government, again on the assumption that " it is all the same work." It is vital that missions should take the initiative in native Christian medical education.

Missions and Governments in Education.—The mission school has to adapt itself to a situation, broadly speaking, of one of two kinds—the situation created by the unfriendliness of a government to its work, and that created by the goodwill of a government. Countries like Turkey and Persia tend to make it difficult for the Christian mission school ; and it still remains to be seen what effect the registration of all schools in China will have upon missionary education.

Where the government attitude hampers the freedom of missionary education the bishop on the spot must ultimately decide how far compromise is possible, and at what point it may become necessary to withdraw from the particular country where restrictions are imposed.

The crucial problem for missionary thinkers at the present time arises out of the increasing sense of responsibility felt by governments for the education of peoples whom they have been content in the past either to exploit or merely to keep in order.

The British Government has for a hundred years recognised its responsibility for the education of at least some classes of the peoples of India, and since 1854 has worked in partnership with mission and other voluntary schools.

As the fruit of regular consultation with the missionary societies since 1923 it has formulated an educational policy for the natives under its protection in tropical Africa which encourages " all voluntary educational effort which conforms to the general policy," and recognises that in the education of the pagan peoples of Africa " the greatest importance must be attached to religious teaching and moral instruction " ; and that such teaching must " permeate the whole life of the school." The aim of education, it is said, " should be to render the individual more efficient in his or her condition of life, whatever it may be, and to promote the advancement of the community as a whole through the improvement of agriculture, the development of native industries, the improvement of health, the training of the people in the management of their own affairs, and the inculcation of true ideals of citizenship and service. It must include the raising up of capable, trustworthy, public-spirited leaders of the people, belonging to their own race." [1]

It is cause for rejoicing that the humanitarian obligations of Christian civilisation are being increasingly accepted by the State. And yet the attitude of sympathy to missionary work which accompanies such acceptance raises embarrassing questions. Are the aims of missions and of the British Government in India, for example, or in Africa, the same ? Are we pretending that they are when they are not ? What is the aim of education ? What is religious education ? What is the relation of educational missionary work to the aim of missions ? Such questions are being eagerly canvassed ; and inevitably the shortage of personnel and of funds in missionary work confuses the real issues and introduces subtle complications. The problem will certainly not be solved by mere insistence on the Scripture hour, nor by any plan which divorces the spiritual from the secular. If religion

[1] *Education Policy in British Tropical Africa*, White Paper, Cmd. 2374.

covers the whole of life, all education must be based on faith in God through Christ. We cannot be content with the policy of the Roman Church which leaves secular education to the government on condition that its missionaries shall be responsible for the religious instruction.

The story of educational development in India under British rule is a record of much admirable work both by government and by missions, but suggests two warnings :

1. India has been cursed by excessive bureaucratic control of education. The paraphernalia and machinery of educational administration have gravely hampered the life of the schools.

2. In 1835 those who favoured an Oriental education for India were overruled by the famous decision embodied in Macaulay's minute to concentrate on Western studies with a view to (1) training Indians to help in administration, (2) increasing material prosperity, and (3) breaking the power of idolatry, superstition and immorality by a "useful" education. From the beginning this aim was differently interpreted by the government officials on the one side, who hoped by means of education to serve God and Mammon, and by the missionaries and reformers on the other who welcomed it from altruistic motives. The result of this alliance against a common foe has led to much mischief, with the result that in the opinion of many thoughtful Indians missions have become hopelessly enmeshed in a godless system.

But even the aim of Westernisation as defined in Macaulay's minute was never whole-heartedly accepted, and the aim of supplanting Eastern by Western culture has become gradually transformed into an attempt to combine what is best in both, or to oust the influence of the West altogether.

The experience of educational development in India thus warns us clearly of the danger of muddle-headed thinking and vacillation as to the aim of education.[1]

Though the educational problems of the Indian Empire are widely different from those of the native territories under the control of the British Colonial Office, it will be well for all who have the education of the African at heart to remember, first, that the Colonial Office has defined its aim in African education; and, secondly, that the greatness

[1] See Arthur Mayhew, C.I.E., *The Education of India*, especially chaps. i., iii., and vi.

of a government's educational policy is to be judged by its generosity and power of self-effacement.[1]

Sir Gordon Guggisberg in a prophetic speech delivered at the Prince of Wales College in January 1927 said :

" It is my firm belief that Achimota will not attain complete success, will not become of the greatest value to ourselves and to Africa, if it does not become free to work under its own constitution, and on a certain known income.   In other words it should not be a department of the government.   If it remains a government department it must become in time merely *an administrative machine*, like all other government colleges are to a very great extent.   Thus it will work in an atmosphere of popular suspicion, largely cut off from the enthusiastic co-operation of the people, and from benefactions.   Educational institutions do not live well under a system of rules and regulations.   Imperial Rome, historians tell us, was first swaddled in and then strangled by red tape.   Schools are much more sensitive than empires, and red tape kills them quickly.   For the essence of a school is a family life.   The personality of the staff is more important to a school than the subjects taught ; and personality, in order to grow, must have free conditions."

It is above all vital that missionaries should continue to think out and try their very best to agree upon the aim of Christian education.   This is not quite as easy to do as might appear.   There would probably be very general agreement among Christians that the aim of Christian education is to " form Christian character and advance the kingdom of God in the minds of man,"[2] but the fact remains that Thomas Arnold of Rugby, Clutton Brock, and von Hügel would not define Christian character in quite the same way ; nor would the idea of the kingdom of God in the mind of Mr. G. K. Chesterton be the same as that in the mind of Dean Inge.   Character and conduct inevitably depend upon creed and philosophy, upon our answer to the question, What think ye of Christ ?   There is no subtler danger in the religious world to-day than that of a fantasy Christ, a Christ created in our own image. Without the correctives of the historic creeds, seasonal fasts and festivals, and the objectivity of sacraments as Catholicism has understood and used them it is extra-ordinarily easy to confuse Christ with our idea of Christ.

[1] See the important pages 76–82 in Mr. Mayhew's book.
[2] Dr. Garfield Williams, " Relations with Governments in Education," *International Review of Missions*, January 1925.

The *Jesus of History* is a most attractive book, but the Figure there presented is largely a fantasy Figure. If we need a compensation for our pugnacity, the Christ in our midst is fashioned in our minds as the Great Pacifist ; if, on the other hand, it is our natural timidity that needs compensating, Christ will be our Fighting Hero in the cause of social righteousness. The " Catholic " Christ easily becomes a " Sacred Heart " or a " Sweet Sacrament," and may be a mere projection of miserable self-pity, or sentimental affection.

Granted that we all to a greater or less extent fashion the Christ in our own image or in compensation for our own defects, we need every help to keep before us and over against our one-sided littleness the objective grandeur of the whole Christ.

In conclusion, both history and the present situation seem to remind us that the Church's Mission must be undertaken by people who have the boldness given to those who have been with Jesus, who are missionaries first and professionals second. There is real danger of a cult of efficiency in mission schools and hospitals. Efficiency is vitally necessary, but must be the fruit of loyalty to Christ and not of any lower motive.

Missions if they are faithful to their trust are bound to embarrass governments, simply because the Gospel is a fermenting influence, and Christians can never be content with the *status quo* which government officials are often too anxious to preserve. But missionaries must distinguish between the offence of the Cross and human cantankerousness. " Many people claim the blessing of being persecuted for righteousness' sake who nurse an imaginary grievance and only suffer through self-consciousness. Self-made martyrs are numerous, but they have no place in the ranks of that noble army which came out of great tribulation. When we analyse the amount of pain we suffer through our fellow-men, it is surprising to discover how much is due to a cantankerous disposition, and how little to any bold championship of our principles. There are those who court persecution by a tactlessness which brings religion into disrepute. They are hated of all men, not for the kingdom of heaven's sake, but because they are persons with whom it is impossible to live." [1]

[1] Minos Devine, *The Religion of the Beatitudes.*

On the other hand governments, the more enlightened they become, will be a constant temptation to missions. But this cannot be made an excuse either for compromise or intransigeance. The Church must always, in humble dependence upon God, be calling to repentance, and if the world rejects the call, must be ready to be crucified with Christ.

IX

CATHOLIC ORDER AND MISSIONARY DEVELOPMENT

BY GODFREY CALLAWAY, S.S.J.E.

SYNOPSIS

I. Fulfilment of the Primitive Order.

(*a*) " I came not to destroy but to fulfil." The moral values of the primitive order will find their fulfilment in the Order of the Catholic Church.

(*b*) The impact of European civilisation, while bringing much that is valuable, has also been destructive of moral values.

(*c*) Missionaries have not been altogether guiltless of sharing in that destruction.

(*d*) A new attitude of respect for primitive order, even apart from the awakened ideal of Catholic unity.

(*e*) The nature of the primitive order amongst the African peoples.

II. The Task of the Catholic Missionary.

It is the Catholic missionary who is best prepared to see :
(*a*) The moral values of the primitive order.
(*b*) The gravity of the destruction.
(*c*) The need of penitence.
(*d*) The direction in which to seek recovery.

III. Three Outstanding Qualities developed in the Primitive Order which are to find Fulfilment in the Order of the Catholic Church.

(*a*) Respect for authority.
(*b*) Reverence for :

(1) Fellowmen, resulting in manners.
(2) The spiritual world, resulting in worship.

(*c*) Fellowship resulting in communion.

Browning's " Saul " as an inspiration to the task before the Catholic Church.

CATHOLIC ORDER AND MISSIONARY DEVELOPMENT

I. Fulfilment of the Primitive Order.—" And other sheep I have, which are not of this fold : them also I must bring, and they shall hear My voice ; and there shall be one flock and one Shepherd." This is the flock of the *new* Fold. The fold is not to be new in the sense of being separated wholly from the old, but new in quality, because it is created and quickened by the Holy Spirit. New in the sense that the soil which is actually taken up into the life of the plant is new. New in the sense that if any man be " in Christ " he is a " new creation."

The New Fold is the ancient fold regenerated, born anew into a wider fellowship, but not losing its own particular character, the character stamped upon it for good.

We can see a parable of this every day in any of the Church huts which we build in new centres of evangelistic work in South Africa. The square, iron building, which, perforce, is so often erected for church or school, may be a necessary evil on the settled mission station ; but, amongst the heathen, where the work is just beginning, it absolutely refuses to blend with its surroundings. It is new in the wrong sense ; it has no link with the past. On the contrary, it seems frankly to disown any relation to the old life. It stands there apparently disdainful and speaking only of all that is alien and unsympathetic.

The Church *hut*, on the contrary, is obviously friendly of aspect. It is new, but clearly it is not alien to the old. It is higher, and wider, and stronger, and better than the old ; but there are the same dear old sods of mother earth, the same sun-dried thatch reaped from the banks of the stream which flows in the valley below, the same earth floor, beaten and rolled into a smooth surface by cunning hands.

It is true that fifty years ago no one dreamed of such a hut, but unmistakably it belongs to the veld. The New Fold may have much that is surprising and unexpected, but it must be reminiscent of the familiar ancient fold which, to every one of our people, is rich and dear in associations.

This does not mean, of course, that we are to attempt to model the New Fold according to the pattern of the old. It does mean that, as we seek faithfully to build the New Fold, we shall certainly see a fulfilment rather than a destruction of the old. Within the New Fold—the Catholic Church—the convert is to find all of good that was suggested by the old fold. There is to be " not one lost good."

Is not this what our Lord meant when He said, " I came not to destroy but to fulfil " ? Surely these words need not be confined exclusively to Judaism. We may believe that our Lord would have sought to fulfil all that is good, all that tends towards righteousness, all that suggests the working of the Spirit of God amongst the backward peoples of darkest Africa and elsewhere. It is probable that no other saying of our Lord has been so strongly emphasised in the mission field during the last twenty years. It is not easy to " fulfil," but it is exceedingly easy to destroy. The way of destruction is always the smooth and wide road. The little herd boy who drops a match into the dry veld on a windy day lets loose an almost unimaginable power of destruction. In a few minutes the whole country is ablaze. And how impossible it is to repair the damage ! Huts, perhaps, may be rebuilt and rethatched ; but who will call back to life the flowers and the bushes and the little birds and the sheep and the goats ?

Europe has come to Africa with gifts in her hands —some of them very precious and excellent gifts—but she has been guilty of dropping matches and lighting fires which have carried destruction far and wide.

Many ancient and good customs, which did much to secure the welfare of the people, have perished. But, worse than that, some of the best characteristics of the people, mental and moral, have been seriously injured by the impact of civilisation. In many directions to-day we see an effort to undo the damage, but the way of recovery is always difficult, and it calls for heroic endurance to persevere along that way.

Have we missionaries had any share in the disintegration and the destruction which are so evident ? Have we been careful not to destroy but to fulfil ? It would be quite unfair to suggest that missionaries generally have been unsympathetic towards the past history of the people to whom they were sent. On the contrary, many of them took infinite pains to study with great thoroughness the language, customs, and folk-lore of the people. To-day we are reaping the fruit of their labours. But, perhaps, it is not unfair to say that missionaries often failed to see the moral values fostered and conserved in the very constitution of the social life of the people. They failed to see that there had been a real preparation for the Gospel of the kingdom. They failed to see that the " Word which lighteth every man as he cometh into the world " had been speaking amongst these people. The reason of this failure will become more apparent later.

To-day we are learning a new attitude of approach. To some extent this is independent of the newly awakened vision of Catholic unity. An Indian leader is reported to have said, " When missionaries bring their truth to a strange land, unless they bring it in the form of homage it is not accepted and should not be. The manner of offering it to you must not be at all discordant with your own national thought and self-respect." [1]

Another Indian leader probably meant much the same when he said to a missionary, " We want you if you will come to us in the right way." [2] In another recent book on India we are told that the sense of nationalism is so strong that " the question asked in religion was not, is it true, is it morally uplifting ? but is it Indian ? " [3] It is significant that these words are pressed upon our attention by European missionaries themselves. In Africa we are far behind India in intellectual outlook, but African leaders are beginning to say very similar words.

We do not want to foster an exaggerated and exclusive nationalism whether it be in India, or Africa, or England,

---

[1] E. Stanley Jones, *The Christ of the Indian Road*, p. 35.
[2] *Op. cit.*, p. 28.
[3] W. E. S. Holland, *The Indian Outlook*, p. 104.

but we do want eyes to see and to respect all that in the social order has served to create and foster moral values. Primitive order is to find itself anew in the order of the Catholic Church. The primitive order may, and does, contain much that is fatal to the development of character in the individual. It may foster a singular lack of personal responsibility. But it is the home of much that cannot be spared, much that is wanted to be brought within the new order of the kingdom, into which all are invited to find a place of eternal security.

It may seem strange to some to speak at all of *order* in connexion with such people as the backward native tribes of Africa. To the stranger who comes to the African knowing nothing of their ways it may seem, at first sight, as if all were disorder.

How can there be order, he thinks, when there is nothing in black and white, when there are no written laws, no deeds of agreement, no fences to mark off adjacent properties, no charts to define boundaries, no hedges to apportion pasturage ! How can there be order when there are no grammars, no written records, no stability of expression !

Just at first all appears capricious and chaotic.

The stranger goes on to learn that those early impressions are singularly mistaken. He goes on to find, not chaos, but a subtle harmony.

Look at that party of men and women hoeing in the lands. Look at the regular movement of the bodies as they sway backwards and forwards. Look at the measured time of the arms as they lift the hoes in unison, ready for the downward stroke. Listen to the strange monotonous chant which beats an accompaniment to the muscular movements. There has been no formal drilling. There is no sergeant-major. There are no prescribed rules, no penalties for discord. But there is concerted action. You realise you are looking, not at just a group of individuals engaged in manual exercises, but at the members of a body.

You are looking at something which is typical of the old fold. And yet it is not achieved by plan, by rule, by method. It is something imbedded in the very soul of the people.

That same impulse which impels those people to hoe the ground in unison impels them also to do a great many

other things in unison.   Little by little you find out that
the whole life is lived in obedience to common custom.
Custom does not represent merely our word fashion.
It is, on the whole, higher and less fickle than fashion ; it
is a more reasoned and reasonable thing.   It has a higher
pedigree, a more ancient birth, a more honourable
tradition.

"Custom," says Wordsworth, "is almost as deep as
life."

Above all things, custom is intended to impress upon
the mind of the native his membership in the body.

Custom which binds the units together into a community is, indeed, in many ways a real power for good, a lever
which may be used to prize up the downward tendencies
of individual caprice and self-pleasing.   But custom may
easily become a prison in which freedom and progress are
lost.   We see this over and over again.   The custom of
paying dowry for a bride is essentially a case in point.
There is value in the custom.   It tends to deepen the
sense of family ties and of mutual obligation.   It tends
to check hasty impulse and selfish self-pleasing.   But it
tends also, in a very serious way, to lessen the rights of
the individual and to diminish the sense of personal
responsibility.   The bride becomes so much a member of
her husband's family that she loses any real sense of
personal liberty.

Obviously the first necessity seems to be to inform the
conscience of the individual, to flash upon it the light
of the New Fold.   A corporate conscience may be useful,
but only so far as it does not hinder the exercise of personal
responsibility.

In some sense we are bound to make *rebels*.   "Every
man who possesses real vitality can be seen as the resultant
of two forces.   He is, first, the child of a particular age,
society, convention ; of what we may call in one word a
tradition.   He is, secondly, in one degree or another, a
rebel against that tradition." [1]

We want freedom, but it is to be not the freedom from
all corporate responsibility, but the freedom to recognise
and to live up to new ideals of corporate responsibility.

It is here that we reach the dangerous stage.   It is
just when the individual finds that the tribal custom is

[1] Quoted by A. Chandler in *The English Church and Reunion*.

N

not the last word that we are confronted with elements, not only of hope, but also of fear.

Hope, because at last the gate of real progress is opened. Fear, because that gate opens upon a road full of danger and littered with the wrecks of many a brave venture.

" For, brethren," says the great missionary apostle, " ye have been called unto liberty; only use not your liberty for an occasion to the flesh."

II. The Task of the Catholic Missionary.—Missionaries in the past have seen the essential need of freedom from the heavy constraint of social custom. They have seen that no progress was possible until they created " rebels " who would refuse to be bound by the iron bands of social custom when that custom was in conflict with the true Light. But they failed to capture that strong *esprit de corps* which belonged to the primitive order because they failed to present an adequate ideal to which it could respond. They had themselves lost the ideal of the Catholic Church, visibly one, gathering into itself peoples of all nations. They failed to see the beauty and the power of that ideal, and therefore they failed to communicate it to their converts.

In this volume of essays we are chiefly concerned with the missions of the English Church, and, in particular, with those missions which are working under the inspiration of a Catholic ideal. It is the missionary who has that ideal before him who will be quick to see the great opportunity of the past, and in the *esprit de corps* generated therein a real preparation for Catholic teaching and order. It is he who will see, with something like agony of soul, how terribly we have lost our opportunity. On all sides he will see the devastation and destruction of certain moral values.

As we look upon the religion of to-day, whether amongst the white people or amongst the large population of natives; as we look at the various places of worship —each with a rival call; as we listen to the discord of contending interests, we are obliged to say that " the name of it is called Babel."

Our Lord calls us to a visible unity, " that the world may know that Thou hast sent Me, and hast loved them as Thou hast loved Me." Instead of the visible unity for which He prayed, instead of the "one heart and one soul" of Pentecost, we see the confusion of Babel.

It is, of course, true that it is quite possible to have a real comity of missions, but we know that we are required to seek nothing short of the visible unity and cohesion of the Catholic Church. "We think of the Church as 'no mere outcome of the natural instinct of association; no expedient afterthought for the promotion of Christian progress in devout living and spiritual fellowship and godly knowledge'! We argue that 'the test of the true faith unto salvation is the existence of faith unto unification. Faith supplies every defect of every Christian Communion, except the fundamental defect of resting content in isolation, discord, disunion and schism.' We can confess sincerely that, 'To us, on the Catholic side, the unity of the Church appeals as a great prior fact. The individual finds a place in it: it ministers to him, or rather he lives in it.' However blurred our vision of it may be, we do believe that it is God's will to have it actualised on earth. But the rub with Protestantism comes there. Many of its leading writers plead for a federation of Christian bodies instead of organic unity. That point admits for us no possible compromise. The intention behind it, so far as we see, is not the will towards unity, but the will towards mutual toleration of schism. If we impugn such an intention, it is with no idea of censuring those who hold it; but we ask them to believe that our conviction of the Church's organic unity is part of our most intimate experience of Christ and of His Spirit; and we cannot pretend that it is actualised simply because warring sects have ceased to war."[1]

If only we were more alive to the meaning of the unity of the Church, and to the glorious triumphs of such unity, we should see enough, day by day, to rend our hearts. The shame of it is ever present, the burden of it is intolerable.

Behind us, in this country, is the work of a century —work full of so much that is good and splendid, but work largely frustrated and ruined by our grievous fault. If we did not see it twenty years ago, surely we cannot fail to see it to-day! In the past people may perhaps

[1] "The Church and Unity," by E. Gordon Selwyn in *Church Quarterly Review*, January 1917.

have been blinded by the numerical strength, by the power of organisation, by the intellectual fitness, by the strong moral appeal of the various Christian bodies, and they were content to think that the unity which our Lord said was *essential* might, after all, be at best desirable. They lost the great and happy vision of a visible Brotherhood —the One, Holy, Catholic Church.

In the presence of this sad confusion we may at least hear the call of penitence, the call to bend down before the grievous sight of innumerable divisions, and to say " by our fault, by our own most grievous fault we have sinned." And we can at least ask God for grace that we may " seriously lay to heart the great danger we are in by our unhappy divisions." Penitence is needed, but penitence calls for more than expressions of sorrow. It calls for the solid effort of amendment. It calls for the hopeful glad endeavour to recover our heritage. "Arise, let us go hence " to meet the new call and the new opportunity. We want to go forward with a new spirit of venture, less tied to what is purely English, or even European, in our presentation of the Gospel of Jesus Christ. We must be prepared to run risks, prepared to give responsibility to our people, prepared to see them make mistakes. Ultimately, we realise that the only security for the treasure which we bring is not in the strong walls of outward protection, but in the hearts of the people.

III. **Three Outstanding Qualities developed in the Primitive Order which are to find Fulfilment in the Order of the Catholic Church.**—A. *Respect for Authority.*—The great positive commandment of the primitive order was to "honour thy father and mother." But among the natives of Africa every child has many fathers and many mothers, and all have to be honoured with a very practical obedience. In fact, in old days a child was taught to obey all his elders to some extent. Disrespect was one of the most serious offences of the moral code. It should be remembered that childhood, in the sense of submission to parental authority, did not by any means end at the age of twenty-one, nor even at twice twenty-one. This respect for authority cannot, of course, be dissociated from membership in a body. It is because of this strong sense of membership in a body, and because of the *esprit* *de corps* which results from that sense that the African sets so high a value upon respect for authority. He learns it as a child in a family. When he is initiated into manhood he carries it into his relationship, first to the clan, and then to the whole tribe. He becomes a citizen, and if he would find the privileges of citizenship, he must also bear the responsibilities. Behind the parental authority, behind the authority of the heads of the clan, is the authority of the chief. If we think of the tribe as the fold (kraal), the chief is the door or gate. He is the guarantee of the unity of the fold. He it is, ultimately, who shuts and opens. He has the keys and he binds and looses. It is very significant, in this respect, that when the chief dies he is buried at the entrance, or door, of the fold and the fold is then abandoned. Although it is abandoned it remains a sacred place, and it is watched for many years.

It is the chief who owns the tribe, but it is also true that the tribe owns him. On occasions the tribe, generally so subservient, may remind the chief very forcibly that he is owned by them. They will ask him to remember that his mother was *their* wife—the particular wife of his father for whom the tribe paid dowry. Gladly they acknowledge that they belong to him, but he must not altogether forget that he belongs to them. The chief in the exercise of his authority was scrupulously careful to rule according to precedent and custom. I was listening one day at Evensong to a preacher who was reading in Si-Xosa the sixty-first chapter of the prophet Isaiah. I felt, as he read the eighth verse, how wonderfully the words would commend themselves to the minds of our native people. In the English we read " I the Lord love judgment," but the Xosa equivalent is " I the Lord love *that which is according to custom.*" Every single chief would gladly make the words of the prophet his own. He rules, but he rules " according to custom," and that is one great reason why he commands respect for his authority.

It is just such characteristics which must be captured for the new order of the Catholic Church.

Our Lord is the Chief of the new tribe. He is not only the Chief who owns the tribe, but He is also the Chief who is owned by the tribe. He is " our Lord," " my Lord." As Chief He is not only the Shepherd who rules, and guides, and guards, and feeds the flock. He is also the Door of the Fold, the guarantee of unity, the entrance and the closure of the Fold. The thief who comes to kill and to destroy does not come in by the door, he breaks through some other way. He chooses no legitimate authority. He defies authority. The convert who is admitted to the New Fold sees all this, not just as something past, once presented to view in the days of the Incarnate life of our Lord. He sees it as something present, as something rich in meaning in the order of the Catholic Church. He sees that our Lord as the Chief of the new tribe, the redeemed family, exercises His office not only of Shepherd, but also of the Door of the Fold through the Episcopate—the Apostolate of to-day.

When we take the diocese, which is the Church in a certain locality, the Door is the single bishop, or rather our Lord Himself in the bishop. Our Lord exercises His Office of the *Door* through the bishop. The door then, in the person of the bishop, is the guarantee of unity in the New Fold, just as, in the person of the chief, it was the guarantee of unity in the ancient fold, the tribe. The shepherd who enters by it is the shepherd of the flock.

To the Catholic Christian this thought is absolutely familiar. No man would venture to enter the Fold as shepherd except through the bishop of due succession. Without the grace and authority of such ordination the acts of the shepherd are not merely invalid, they are the acts of one who " climbeth up some other way."

It is, then, only through the bishop, the door of the New Fold, that the shepherds enter, and it is to the shepherds that the stewardship of the Word and Sacraments is committed.

It is interesting to remember that the messenger of the chief in the ancient fold, who came in the name of the chief, carried as warrant of his authority and the credentials of his office the *umsila*, the tail (of a leopard). In the same way, at his ordination by the bishop, the priest receives the stole round his neck, and comes to the people in the administration of the sacraments wearing his visible symbol of authority. The stole speaks of the authority given to him at his ordination by the bishop to enter the kraal as shepherd of the flock, to call the sheep, to lead them and to feed them.

It is in this way that the bishop is the door which guarantees the unity of the local Church, while the collective Episcopate guarantees the unity of the whole Church.

To the bishop is committed the power of the Keys; and he not only opens, but he also shuts. He not only looses, but he also binds. Excommunication is ultimately his act just as in a sense Baptism and Absolution are ultimately his acts.

To the native the thoughts of *shutting*, of binding, of excommunication are not new. He has known excommunication (*ukuhlamba*) in the family life of the ancient fold, when a son has, perhaps, so long and so obstinately refused obedience that at last the father, in the presence of relations, disinherits him by a ritual act. He rinses his mouth with a mouthful of milk, into which some blood of a dog's ear has been dropped, and spits it forcibly out. Perhaps even here it is true to say that the excommunication is ultimately the act of the chief who owns the people.

I have never heard or read of any ritual of restoration in the ancient fold if the excommunicated person desires to return. In the New Fold there are few things so touching and so speaking as the public restoration of those who have been publicly excommunicated.

In such ways we are able to lead the African convert along a road which is not wholly strange. He finds in the Catholic Church certain characteristics which have long been familiar to him.

The ultimate aim in the mission field must be, of course, a native Episcopate. The difficulties are naturally great, but towards that aim we must steadily press forward. At least we must never allow the difficulty of a colour prejudice to check the valid aspirations of the native people.

While the Church is bearing a brave witness in opposing parliamentary legislation which is largely based upon colour prejudice, she herself must take care that she is not influenced by a similar prejudice.

It would be a great opportunity for English Catholics to bear witness to the reality of their faith in the grace of the Episcopate if they were given an opportunity of serving under an African bishop, and of receiving sacramental grace

at his hands.   Nothing would do more to demonstrate that
the kingdom of God is not of this world.

B. *Reverence.*—Reverence is not quite the same as
respect.   Is it not true to say that, both in its derivation
and in its use, we associate something of awe with reverence,
and perhaps it is this which differentiates it slightly from
respect ?   Among the Africans we find not only respect
for authority, but a strongly developed sense of reverence.
Before I speak of the reverence towards the unseen and
the spiritual I must say something of the reverence
towards man, the reverence which expresses itself in
manners.

The African is by nature a courteous person.   He
certainly does not express his courtesy in quite the same
way that we do.   Indeed some of his manners are singularly irritating to the European.   The native considers it
quite polite when he meets a stranger to bombard him
with a whole catechism of questions.   " Where do you
come from ? "   " Where are you going to ? "   " What is
your business when you get there ? "   " When will you
be coming back ? " . . . To the white man such questions
are the very reverse of good manners—they sound imper-
tinent—but he goes on to find that they belong to the
courtesies of life on the veld.   To the African it shows
interest in a man to ask where he is going to and where
he comes from.   It would be wanting in good manners
to be indifferent.   Such matters are not merely his private
concern just because man is not a " private concern."
A man belongs to a family, to a clan, to a tribe, to a
people, to humanity.   The native does not ask such
questions like a sentry who is on the look out for a foe,
nor like a policeman who requires every man to have his
credentials.   He asks as the member of a community who
is interested in his fellow members.

Again, the native must find it difficult to understand
the words " To beg I am ashamed."   Why should a man
be ashamed of begging !   If he begs from you a pinch of
tobacco is he not treating you in a filial way and will he
not say, when you have unlocked your pouch, " *Bawo* "
(my Father) ?   He may also add an expression of thanks
which to us sounds the reverse of polite, " *Ungadinwa
nengomso* " (Don't be tired—do the same to-morrow) !
Not only is it polite to beg, it is also equally polite to

borrow, and both in begging and borrowing the native is a master of courtesy.

It would be a simple matter if space allowed to elaborate the account of the manners on the veld, but I have said enough to show that the African is naturally in his own way a person of courteous manners. Further than this, his manners are good in the sense that they are not only good in themselves, but also rightly directed. He does not respect what we should call Mammon—the outward accidents of wealth—but humanity (*ubuntu*). He may indeed look no further in thought than the man of to-day. He may fail to look beyond man to man, and beyond man to his Maker, but his instinct is right in giving respect to manhood. The manners of a people are sacred to those people. Our task is not to treat them with disrespect because they may differ from our own, but to point to Christianity as the fulfilment of all that is good in manners.

Far more depends upon our attitude towards others than we are apt to remember. The peace of the world has often been endangered by a superior or contemptuous attitude. " Trouble does not arise among individuals because one is superior to the others, but because one tells the other so loudly. So it is with races." A recent writer has said that " there has been created a social mentality which discourages humanity in individuals. The courtesy produced by natural feeling disappears, and in its place comes a behaviour which shows entire indifference, even though it is decked out more or less thoroughly in a code of manners. Our society has ceased to allow to all men, as such, a human value and a human dignity." One great task in front of Christianity is to rescue the sense of reverence, and nowhere ought it to find so real a home and opportunity of fulfilment as in the Catholic Church.

The true school of reverence is that lowly place once occupied by Mary of Bethany. It is at the Feet of our Lord that manners are to be learnt. It is He who has taught us the real value of humanity. It is He who urges us to look below the superficial, the world-trodden surface which hides the treasure for which He seeks. It is He who teaches us to look beyond the man as he is to the man as he is to be. The inspiration of all manners is in His word : " Inasmuch as ye did it unto one of the least

of these my brethren ye did it unto Me." Social convention may require difference in the mode of expression, but
the man who sees by faith Christ hidden in the humanity
of all will never fail to see "holy ground" and to do
reverence. The Church, wherever she is true to her Head,
is the home of reverence. Manners at their best are the
direct outcome of the Catholic Faith. They are nourished
by a religion which is sacramental.

"A sacramental religion has a natural influence upon the
manners. For by bringing our bodies into constant connexion with spiritual realities, it naturally affects our
behaviour. . . . behaviour has a more powerful reaction upon
character than men often suppose. True there may be great
social polish on the surface of a corrupt society, behind which a
man may 'smile and smile and be a villain,' hard of heart and
coarse of thought ; a politeness which makes life easier by
robbing it of its grossness, and is justly therefore suspect.
But Christian good manners are the converse of this ; they work
from within outwards, and are the external reflection of interior
truth and love. And such manners are intimately connected
with the reverence which gathers round a sacramental system.
. . . the bodies of Christians are living sacraments, temples of
the Holy Ghost, manifestations of the indwelling Spirit of the
Word made flesh." [1]

Reverence amongst the Africans is not confined to their
attitude and manners towards their fellow-men. "To the
primitive," says Levy-Bruhl, speaking of the primitives
generally, "the surrounding world is the language of
spirits speaking to a spirit." That is very true of the
African primitive. "Il ne faut jamais oublier quand on
étudie la mentalité des noirs que, pour eux, la monde des
esprits est très proche."

This characteristic is so well known that it need not be
dwelt upon. The African is at least prepared to believe
in a supreme Spirit, the fountain of all life. He is at least
prepared to reverence Him. He also believes not only in
the continual existence of the departed, but in their
influence upon the living. The African is wholly removed
from the materialist, and it is in the Catholic Church that
his spiritual aspirations are destined to find their fulfilment
and their expression.

C. *Fellowship.*—The word used in Si-Xosa to translate

[1] Illingworth, *Christian Character.*

fellowship is, as would be expected, a word which means eating together—partaking of a common meal. I fully expect that this is the case in other African languages.

There is, perhaps, no word more dear to the Xosa-speaking African than *ubudlelane* [1] (fellowship), and hidden in this word, as the very heart and root of its meaning, is (*uku*) *dla* (to eat). Eating is a social concern. Amongst the natives no man eats alone. To eat alone is to challenge suspicion. Why should a man eat alone unless he is isolating himself from the family and from the community, unless he is regarding his own interests in a private and exclusive way. Such a man is a person to be avoided. He is the sort of man who does not share his food with others. He is guilty of the unpardonable sin of grudging, and, if he persists in walking along that path, he is likely to bring upon himself the charge of sorcery.

The native regards the land which produces the food as communal property. It is true that, by a figure of speech, the chief is the owner of the land, but each man has a right to his portion. It is his and yet it is not his. It is his only so long as he is a member of the community —the tribe—and fulfils his obligations as such. With this proviso the land is his and the fruits of the land are his. But, just as he only ploughs the land as a member of a community, so he only eats the fruits as a member of a community. They are his, but they are his to share with others—to share primarily with his own family and his friends, but not to be exclusive of the guest and the wayfarer and the hungry. To eat *together* is obviously the outward expression of the links which bind men together in a body. It is the outward and visible sign of a natural sacrament of fellowship. This outward sign may be further emphasised by ritual acts of a closer covenant. The eating together may be, not just the partaking of ordinary food, but the sharing of a sacrificial meal—of meat offered in sacrifice to propitiate ancestors. In such cases the bond which unites men together in a body is seen to transcend the limitations of this life and to link together the living and the departed.

In some tribes the covenant of friendship may be even further emphasised and strengthened by ceremonies connected with blood-brotherhood. In this case each of the

[1] Literally the word means " eating together."

contracting parties makes a slight incision in the arm of the other and mixes a drop of the blood with food. These are the natural sacraments of fellowship among the African people. What a profound significance they have when they are seen in the light of the great Christian and Catholic sacrament of fellowship! "This is My Body." "Take, eat." At last the word for eating has entered the sanctuary. It finds there the fulfilment of its long history. It is true that we have yet to learn all the implications of that eating. What we so dimly conceive as we feed upon the Bread of Life is to be realised to the full hereafter. At least we see this, that the sharing of this Bread is intended to be a bond which breaks down all barriers and binds together into one all the diverse elements of the human family. It is in this way that the word for fellowship speaks to the African of the goal of the long journey of humanity—to be gathered together into the oneness and the perfection of the Body of Christ. It speaks not only of a real fellowship with all fellow members of the Body here in this world. It speaks also of the Communion of Saints in the wider sense of fellowship with all who have departed this life in the Faith of Christ. It reminds the convert of the link with his own friends, and it reminds him of the succours of grace which flow from a living fellowship with Blessed Mary, the Apostles, Martyrs, and the Saints of all ages.

Conclusion.—Is it allowable to read a slightly different meaning into Browning's " Saul " ? May we for a moment think of Saul as he is there presented to us, in his dark mood of despair, as representing humanity in its social order, broken in upon by forces which rob it of its strength and vigour and leave it a prey to a thousand malignant influences ? May we go further and think of Browning's conception of Saul as the picture of many an African tribe robbed of the security of its primitive order and spoiled of the qualities which were dependent upon that order ? May we think of David the musician as the Catholic idealist who sees, and grieves and prays, and longs to redeem ?

Think of the scene in this light. More and more as he looks upon the moral wreck the heart of the musician goes out in deepening love to the pathetic figure of the stricken king. He longs to be able to give freely. He sees vast possibilities—all the purposes of creation—in the figure before him. He longs to see all realised. Gladly he would give—gladly he would sacrifice himself. And then, suddenly, he sees what his love means, and his eager desire. They are a prophecy.

If he can love thus and can so desire to give, what about God from whom all love comes ?

" Would I fain in my impotent yearning do all for this man,
And dare doubt He alone shall not help him, who yet alone can ? "

If he would sacrifice himself to rescue Saul, the mistake, the failure, from ruin, surely God would do more !

" 'Tis not what man does which exalts him, but what man would do !
See the King—I would help him but cannot, the wishes fall through."

And then follows the magnificent prophecy of the coming Christ.

" O Saul, it shall be
A Face like my face that receives thee ; a Man like to me
Thou shalt love and be loved by, for ever : a Hand like this hand
Shall throw open the gates of new life to thee !   See the Christ stand ! "

Here is a great truth. David finds, not only in the revealed word of God, in the voices of the prophets, promises of the Incarnation. He finds the promise in his own nature, in the love of his own heart, in his own longing to save, in his own pity, and in his own helplessness and inability.

God who gave such longing must Himself come to save, come to set His own children free from the tyranny of sin and disorder.

The Catholic missionary faces the facts. He sees the grave difficulties of race relationship. He sees the social and moral disorder. He sees it as a wreck and ruin of a great promise. But the promise itself is not wholly forfeited. Before him he sees the possibilities. He sees " the Christ stand." He sees the gates of a new kingdom thrown open. He sees the vision of an ultimate fulfilment. He sees by faith

" that great city, the holy Jerusalem, descending out of heaven from God . . . and the wall of the city had twelve foundations,

and in them the names of the twelve Apostles of the Lamb . . .
and the city had no need of the sun, neither of the moon to
shine in it : for the glory of God did lighten it and the Lamb
is the Light thereof.   And the nations of them which are saved
shall walk in the light of it : and the kings of the earth do
bring their glory and honour into it.   And the gates of it shall
not be shut at all by day : for there shall be no night there.
And they shall bring the glory and honour of the nations into
it." [1]

NOTE.—For further study on these lines the reader is referred to
Autour du problème de l'Adaptation, Report of the Louvain Conference
(R.C.) on Missionary Work, 1926.   The writer was not acquainted with
the Report when he wrote the essay.

[1] Rev. xxi. 10, 22–26.

X

THE DEVELOPMENT OF
THE NATIVE CHURCH IN WORSHIP

BY M. N. TROLLOPE, BISHOP IN COREA

SYNOPSIS

I. The Rationale of Christian Worship.

Worship a vital element in religion ; but the end rather than the beginning of Christian life and experience, its natural outcome and expression.

II. The Tradition of Christian Worship.

Right and wrong appeal to tradition.
Principles of universal application underlying the Catholic tradition of Christian worship.

    (1) Worship as self-oblation to God the Father through the Son.
    (2) The *corporate* character of Catholic worship.
    (3) The demand on the individual worshipper.
    (4) The Holy Eucharist.
    (5) The Divine Office.
    (6) Litanies and Processions.

III. Worship on the Mission Field. Practical Considerations.

The diocese the normal unit of Church life.
Consequent necessity for a Cathedral Church :

    (*a*) To set a standard of worship.
    (*b*) To maintain the cycle of worship through the Church's year.

Problem of scattered groups of Christians.
Difficulty of observing Sunday and days of obligation in countries where the seven-day week is not customary.
" The bad habit of translating the Prayer Book."
Need of elasticity with firm adherence to principle.

THE DEVELOPMENT OF THE NATIVE CHURCH IN WORSHIP

I. The Rationale of Christian Worship.—Professor Whitehead, in his recently published lecture on the present-day relations between Religion and Science,[1] after pointing out how seriously the just claims of religion have too often been compromised by widespread and obstinately held misconceptions as to its character and function, closes his survey by the following remarkable statement as to what he conceives to be the " essential character of the religious spirit."

" Religion " (he says) " is the vision of something which stands beyond, behind, and within the passing flux of immediate things ; something which is real, and yet waiting to be realised ; something which is a remote possibility, and yet the greatest of present facts ; something that gives meaning to all that passes, and yet eludes apprehension ; something whose possession is the final good, and yet is beyond all reach ; something which is the ultimate ideal, and the hopeless quest. The immediate reaction of human nature to the religious vision is worship. . . . The vision claims nothing but worship ; and worship is the surrender to the claim for assimilation, urged with the motive force of mutual love. . . . That religion is strong which in its ritual and its modes of thought evokes an apprehension of the commanding vision. The worship of God is not a rule of safety—it is an adventure of the spirit, a flight after the unattainable. The death of religion comes with the repression of the high hope of adventure."

This high appreciation of the place rightly occupied by " worship " in religion, emanating as it does from a source so little tinged with ecclesiasticism, becomes the more remarkable when we remember the rather marked way in

---

[1] *Science and the Modern World*, Lowell Lectures, 1925, by Alfred North Whitehead, F.R.S., Sc.D, chap. xii. " Religion and Science " (especially pp. 269–76).

which the subject of "worship" has been excluded (*exempli gratiâ*) from the various "quadrilateral" and other proposals for the reunion of Christendom issuing from the Lambeth Conferences, including that of 1920. The Scriptures, the Creeds, the two Sacraments of the Gospel, and the Apostolic Ministry are recognised as necessary ingredients in any reunited Church of the future. But except so far as it is covered by the "Administration of the Lord's Supper" (which may after all be, as indeed it is in most Protestant communities, a very occasional function), no stress whatever is laid on the necessity of the faithful regularly assembling themselves together for λειτουργία, the Church's corporate worship of the living God.

And yet it is surely not too much to say that no Catholic—whether Anglican, Roman, or Eastern Orthodox —could ever give his assent to any scheme of "reunion," or his allegiance to any "reunited Church," in which "the Lord's Service on the Lord's Day" was not presupposed as the norm of Christian worship, coupled with some observance of that agelong round of Fast and Festival to which we give the name of the Christian Year. For from one point of view at least—though this must of course not be over-emphasised at the expense of other aspects— we are surely justified in affirming that the Holy Catholic Church here on earth is essentially an organisation for the purpose of λειτουργία—a school of worship, wherein souls are trained for that corporate approach to the vision of the Living God, which is to be the joy and the glory of heaven, and of which we are given a foretaste in the book of the Revelation of St. John the Divine. The rites and cere- monies in which Catholic worship finds its expression here on earth do but represent our desire and our effort, based on intimations contained in Holy Writ and prompted doubtless by that Holy Spirit who is ever present to "help our infirmities" in this respect, to associate ourselves with the worship offered by the great concourse of the redeemed in the courts of heaven to "our God which sitteth upon the throne and to the Lamb."

While, however, we claim this paramount position for "worship" in the life of the Church, we must be on our guard against presenting the Christian religion to the inquirer, the catechumen or neophyte convert, under the guise of a mere round of ceremonial observances, or suggesting that the conversion to Christianity from Hinduism, Buddhism, Confucianism or any of the other old ethnic religious systems (most of them very "ritualistic") amounts to no more than the exchange of one set of ceremonial observances for another. Worship is the end rather than the beginning of Christian life and experience, and participation in the Church's corporate acts of worship is the privilege of the regenerate, and certainly ought not to be used either as a bait to attract the outsider or as a test of his conversion. To begin, whether at home or abroad, by urging those whose conversion we have in view to " come to Church " is surely a putting of the cart before the horse. Conversion and instruction in the faith must come first, and these are individual matters. The joy and the glory of the Church's worship should remain as the coveted prerogative of those who have been through the various stages, by which men become " members of Christ, children of God, and inheritors of the kingdom of heaven."

It would be strange indeed if the Christian neophyte, enthralled by "the glorious Gospel of the blessed God," conscious of his redemption, regeneration and incorporation into the Body of Christ, quickened by the indwelling presence of the Holy Spirit, fed on the Bread of Life, and avid of the promise of his eternal inheritance, did not, with the scheme of worship provided for him in the closing chapters of the New Testament, seek frequent occasion to join with his brethren in those mingled strains of doxology, eucharist, penitence, and supplication to which we give the name of "liturgy," and thus find an outlet for the faith, hope, and love within him—and that even though there were no precise commandment, no compelling tradition to guide his thoughts and footsteps thitherward.

And so " worship " emerges as the normal and natural outcome and expression of Christian life and experience— its end rather than its beginning, and we are brought back to the position familiar to us from the oft-recited words of that confession of our Christian Faith commonly called the Creed of St. Athanasius : " The Catholic Faith is this : that we worship one God in Trinity and Trinity in Unity."

II. The Tradition of Christian Worship.—Liturgical worship is then part of the indefeasible inheritance of the children of God. For guidance as to the matter and manner thereof we must look to the agelong tradition of

Holy Church. And the appeal to tradition has, as we are reminded over and over again in the pages both of the Old and New Testaments, its very great difficulties and dangers. If there is (as of course there is) such a thing as making the commandment of God of no effect through our traditions, it must on the other hand be remembered that the obstinate refusal to " hear the Church " in such matters lands one in a very quagmire.

Those Christian bodies which base their religion on " the Bible and the Bible only " are sore put to it to defend such traditional practices as infant baptism against the Baptists, or the observance of the first day of the week as " the Lord's Day " against the criticism of the Seventh Day Adventists. On the other hand the path of the traditionalist is for ever beset by that difficulty of keeping " the mean between the two extremes of too much stiffness in refusing and too much easiness in admitting " rites and ceremonies, which is so impartially set forth in that master-piece of incisive and humorous English, the Preface to the Book of Common Prayer. And moreover, inasmuch as tradition governs matters of both great and little moment, and all men are not possessed of a sense of discretion and proportion, there is always the risk of the worship of God being smothered under a heap of worthless traditions, often of quite recent origin, while those of great weight and antiquity are set on one side.

We find ourselves then in this position, that, whereas we are bound to look to tradition for guidance both as to the matter and manner of the Church's liturgical worship, its rites and ceremonies (for without *some* rites and cere-monies public and common worship would be impossible), we are bound also to recognise that there are traditions and traditions, and to discriminate between those of which it may fairly be said that " the keeping or omitting of a ceremony, in itself considered, is but a small thing," and those of which the neglect would be really " of dangerous consequence, as secretly striking at some established doctrine or laudable practice of the whole Catholic Church of Christ."

It is therefore of the first importance that those who are face to face with the task of training babes in Christ in the art of Christian worship should form some intelli-gent conception of the fundamental principles of universal application underlying the Catholic tradition in this matter, and learn to discriminate between the rites and ceremonies which give expression to these, and those others of which it may be said that " every country should use those ceremonies as they shall think best to the setting forth of God's honour and glory."

(1) Among the fundamental principles underlying the Catholic tradition of Christian worship, we surely cannot be far wrong if we place first and foremost the fact that worship is before all things an approach in humble self-oblation to God our Father in heaven, through the mediation of the Eternal Son of God, for us men and for our salvation made man, and that, in the power of the Holy Ghost, consubstantial and co-eternal with both Father and Son and shed forth upon us as the result of our Risen and Ascended Lord's activities.   The fact that Christian worship is an approach to God through Him who said " No man cometh to the Father but by Me " may seem a truism.   But it none the less needs emphasising nowadays in view of the " spiritual exercises " which too often usurp the name of " worship " amongst those who profess and call themselves Christians.   Even Mattins and Evensong (when said in their entirety) do at least provide us with lections from the New Testament as well as the Old (both read in the ordered scheme), allow us to escape from the tyranny of the extempore prayers, and associate ourselves with the saints of old in psalm and canticle, creed and collect, though even these features are too often obscured by the prominence given to the inevitable sermon and equally inevitable hymns.   But no one with any historic sense (one might almost add, with any sense of humour) could for a moment compare the Divine Office (even at its best) with the magnificent drama of the Mass, which, while including the aforesaid elements of scripture lesson, psalm and canticle, creed and collect, gathers within its embrace the whole of the Church triumphant, expectant, and militant, and sweeps us and all our aspirations up, in company with angels and archangels, and all the company of heaven, to the very throne of God and the Lamb.   It is the Mass, too, which provides the best corrective to that tendency, so prevalent nowadays in Catholic and Protestant circles alike, to concentrate all worship almost exclusively on the adorable Person of our Incarnate Saviour, the second

Person of the Blessed Trinity, a tendency which, after making every allowance for all that may quite justifiably be said in its defence, ought certainly not to be allowed to oust the old Catholic ideal of the approach to the Father through the Son.

(2) After the Fatherhood of God—the brotherhood of man. Here again we shall surely not be far wrong in asserting that the *corporate* character of Catholic worship is one of its main characteristic features—as against the modern tendency to claim that religion is a purely personal and individual matter, calling for no " common " or public expression. Nor will Catholicism allow us to limit our fellowship in worship to that part of the Church Catholic which is still militant here on earth. Every act of Catholic worship presupposes the " Communion of Saints "—our fellowship, that is, with the " blessed company of all faithful people." Over and above the angelic hosts, we are surrounded by the great cloud of witnesses—the vast company of those men and women who have gone before us in the Faith, the saints in glory and our brethren and sisters still awaiting their perfect consummation and bliss in the intermediate state.

In emphasising this aspect, however, of the Communion of Saints, we must be careful not to lose sight of that other aspect which lays stress on the brotherhood of Christians here upon earth, and be greatly on our guard against allowing anything in our arrangements for worship, which would seem to give the Church's sanction to class distinction or racial discrimination. Linguistic difficulties and social customs (such as sitting on seats rather than on the floor) no doubt necessitate a certain amount of segregation or grouping of worshippers. But no pains should be spared to minimise this as far as possible by providing (where this can be done) opportunities of worship at different hours or in separate chapels within the same building, by insisting on the use of a common Baptismal Font, instead of erecting a Font in every little mission chapel,[1] and by emphasising the importance of joint acts of worship on as many occasions as possible year by year.

Closely allied with the emphasis laid on the *corporate*

[1] It should be remembered that the old custom of the Catholic Church (still in force in Florence, Parma, and other cities of Italy) allowed only one Font and Baptistery in each city, and that in the Bishop's Cathedral Church.

character of Catholic worship must be the frank recognition
of the place occupied, within the fellowship, of the sacred
ministry, which involves, as has been so often pointed out,
no infringement of the privileges of the whole body of the
faithful, but provides the indispensable organ through
which the priesthood of that body finds expression. The
Catholic Church is an eminently sacerdotal and hierarchic
body, the representative here on earth of that heavenly
High Priest whose activities are so luminously portrayed
for us in the Epistle to the Hebrews. And the history of the
" anti-sacerdotal " reactions within the various Protestant
bodies which have split off from the unity of the Church
during the last four centuries shows that the endeavour to
exalt the " priesthood of the laity " at the expense of the
official priesthood of the Church does in fact defeat its own
ends. Any attempt to deny or belittle the specific priesthood of the Christian ministry ends in oblivion or denial
of the priestly character of the Church as a whole (if not of
the High Priesthood of Christ Himself), and results in that
ultimate disappearance of all capacity for " worship "
which is one of the marked features of modern Protestantism, and a source of distress to not a few of its leaders.[1]

(3) Next surely to its insistence on the observance of
a due attitude towards God as the object of our worship,
and towards our fellow-creatures as our fellow-worshippers,

---

[1] It is surely disastrous that in so many vernacular renderings of the
Book of Common Prayer in use in the mission field, the word " Priest "
should have been so deliberately excluded in favour of some equivalent
for " Presbyter " or " Elder." The practice of the Church in Japan,
e.g., is peculiarly unfortunate. Discarding the familiar terms used for the
Ministry by the Roman Catholic and Russian Orthodox missions, the
Nippon Sei Ko Kwai (Anglican Church in Japan) has taken for " Bishop "
the term used by the widely extended Methodist missions to describe
their "Superintendents," and for " Priest " that used by the Presbyterians
to describe their " Elders," while for deacon the term used is that adopted
by all the Protestant bodies for an official whose duties have singularly
little in common with the " office of a Deacon " as described in the Ordinal.
It is true that transliterations of the Greek words Episcopos, Presbyteros,
and Diaconos, are printed side by side with these unsatisfactory terms, but
in practice they are never used. And in any case the word " Priest," so
sedulously preserved with all its associations in the English Prayer Book,
has entirely disappeared, although all versions of the Scriptures possess
a quite adequate word to denote the priesthood of our Lord and the
priesthood of the faithful, and one would have thought it was common
ground that the special priesthood of the Christian ministry must come
somewhere between these two. It would be interesting to know how far
this betrayal of the principles of the English Church—hidden in the
obscurity of unknown tongues—has been carried in other quarters of the
mission field.

must rank in importance the demand which Catholicism makes on the individual worshipper. That demand is for nothing less than all that he is and all that he has, and cuts at the root of all those false theories which would exalt the importance of man's body at the expense of his soul (and *vice versa*), or which would suggest that he may compound for the absence of spiritual effort by external ceremonial and the lavish offering of his worldly goods or conversely secure immunity in the selfish enjoyment of these goods by an empty display of " spiritual " fervour. That " whole spirit and soul and body " of ours, for which St. Paul prays that they may be " preserved blameless unto the coming of our Lord Jesus Christ," must be consecrated to the worship of the living God ; nor can any act of worship which leaves any one of these out of count rely on being accepted by Him.

While, therefore, " Lift up your hearts " is the trumpet-sound which rings in our ears as we approach the Holy of Holies, the true test of the extent to which we have really entered into the spirit of the Holy Sacrifice therein offered will always be found in our willingness (or our refusal) to " offer and present ourselves, our souls and bodies to be a reasonable holy and lively sacrifice " unto Almighty God. So long as man's spirit is cabined and confined within a bodily frame, and so long as he is called upon to pass the time of his sojourning here under conditions of time and space, so long there must be a local, temporal and material, as well as a transcendental, side to Christian worship. And the wisdom of the Church lies in maintaining the due proportion and balance between these various elements, and in using things external and material so as to express and not obscure the essentially spiritual character of Christian worship. She must have her times and places of worship, her rites and ceremonies. She must be free to surround her spiritual realities with the appropriate material accessories of art, music, and the like, and will feel it her duty to offer to her Lord, together with the bodies, souls, and spirits of His faithful worshippers, some tithe at least of that wealth of beautiful things wherewith He has surrounded us in this Universe of His creation. The Wise Men of the East with their threefold offering of gold and frankincense and myrrh to the Infant Christ provide a useful object-lesson as to the way in which we should offer to God in worship " all that we have and all that we are."

(4) These, then, are the three fundamental principles on which the Catholic Church must insist as she envisages the subject of worship. Fortunately she has not been left to her own devices to discover how God may be acceptably worshipped in accordance with these principles. From the outset she has felt that in the events which took place in the Upper Room on the first Maundy Thursday she has the germ of that great act of public worship in which God would have His children of the Holy Catholic Church unite throughout the world and until the end of all time. The setting, the surroundings, the accessories may vary in different climes and at different stages of the Church's history, but in and through them all, in the matter of offering acceptable worship to Almighty God, it is the Divine Liturgy, the Holy Eucharist, the Mass that " matters." Any other acts of worship shine as much with a borrowed light as do the moon and stars with light borrowed from the sun.

(5) Next to the Holy Sacrifice of the Altar—*sed longo intervallo*—must come, if any heed is to be paid to Catholic precedent, that ordered and regular recitation of the Psalter, interspersed with Evangelical Canticles and lessons from the other books of Holy Writ, to which the Church has given the name of the Divine Office, and of which St. Benedict thought so highly that he called it the *Opus Dei*. Nor should we allow the false prominence given to these " Choir Offices " at certain periods of the Church's history to prejudice their due claim on the Church's children. And yet, monastic as they were in origin, and involving as they do a high degree of literacy and training in devotional habits in the worshipper, they must remain always to a large extent the possession of that inner circle of God's people to whom the name of " religious " is specifically applied. In the mission field particularly, the literary and musical effort involved in the due recitation of the Choir Office would alone suffice to prevent its ever taking its full place in popular religion. And yet a Church which leaves this side of Catholic worship altogether out of its make-up will only present a maimed ideal of what that worship should be.

(6) Outside the Divine Liturgy and the Divine Office

there remain litanies and processions which have always played so prominent a part in the Church's liturgical activities, and those special liturgical observances with which the Church has loved to mark her holy feasts and seasons; and last, but not least, those extra liturgical devotions, whether centering round the Blessed Sacrament or used—as in the case of the Christmas Crib and the Stations of the Cross—to concentrate attention on certain pages of the Gospel story, which have played so prominent a part in the religion of Western Europe during recent centuries, but which are in any case quite subsidiary to the main current of Christian worship, and which considerations of space prevent our dealing with here.

III. **Worship in the Mission Field: Practical Considerations.**—Assuming therefore, as we surely may, the acceptance of the above fundamental principles, as necessarily underlying the development of Christian worship in the mission field, it remains to draw out in some detail their application in practice to the circumstances in which missionaries find themselves placed in the great continents of Asia and Africa and " the islands of the sea."

And in so doing it does seem of the first importance to recognise the fact that, in liturgical as in other matters, the diocese is the normal " unit " of Church life—not the nation, nor even the province, and certainly not the individual parish or mission station. This is hard doctrine, especially for Anglicans—partly in consequence of the stress laid on the rights of " national churches " from the earliest days of the conflict which led to the separation of the " Church of England " from the rest of Western Christendom, and partly in consequence of the party strife developed within that Church as a result of the peculiar comprehensiveness which is both its boast and its infirmity.

The example set by the " Church of England " in thus correlating Church and State has been so widely copied, and the cool assumption that it represents the mind of Christ and the practice of the Early Church is so universally made, that it seems worth while to recall the fact that the recognition of " national " divisions within the Church hardly dates farther back in Church history than the Council of Constance (A.D. 1415–17), and is singularly difficult to justify on any principles known to the New

Testament; and, further, that it almost inevitably brings two serious evils in its train. One is the gradual enslavement of the Church to the purely secular ideals of nationalism, patriotism (so-called) and imperialism, and her consequent entanglement in political affairs; and the other is the creation of a cumbrous and unwieldy machinery of organisation which is fatal to the elasticity and freedom of the Church, and inevitably provokes reaction in the direction of licence and disorder. Whether or no in the sixteenth century the authorities of the "Church of England" which in those days, even with the inclusion of the "Town of Berwick-upon-Tweed," covered only a small area—were wise in their endeavour to do away with the "great diversity in saying and singing in Churches within this Realm; some following Salisbury Use, some Hereford Use, and some the Use of Bangor, some of York, some of Lincoln," and in their insistence that "from henceforth all this whole Realm shall have but one Use," it is surely ludicrous to hamper the activity of such gigantic units as the "Church of the United States of America" or "the Church of China" by trying to fix them to any such Procrustean bed. For instance, in the "Church of Japan," as in the "Protestant Episcopal Church of the United States of America," no jot or tittle in the liturgical standards may be lawfully altered or departed from without the approval of the general convention, which meets only for three or four crowded days once in three years. The result of so much stiffness and lack of elasticity is simply to stimulate and stereotype that lamentable and disorderly "parochialism" or "congregationalism" which seems to be now regarded almost as an "inseparable accident" of Churches of the Anglican Communion, but which it is wholly impossible to defend on any Catholic principles. In the mission field, at any rate, there is surely everything to be said for the recognition of the diocese as the normal and characteristic unit of Catholic life and worship, tempered of course by reference to the practice of neighbouring dioceses; and, further, by reference to that "Congregation of Rites" in the home Church, the establishment of which is so long overdue.[1]

---

[1] Plainly there must be some reference to the home Church on such matters, if only to prevent churches in the mission field from taking up a position of intolerable diversity from the home Church, on whose alms and prayers they depend.

Upon the recognition of the " diocese " as the normal unit of Church life in liturgical matters follows, as a corollary, the necessity of establishing from the outset a cathedral or pro-cathedral Church which shall set and maintain the due standard of divine worship throughout the diocese. A " cathedral " or " pro-cathedral " does not of course necessarily imply a large or elaborate structure. It is the church in which the Bishop's *cathedra* is set, and in which (among his other prerogatives) he primarily exercises his *jus liturgicum*, being surrounded by such a clerical staff as will enable the worship of God to be performed with due solemnity. Such a cathedral or central church has indeed, from the liturgical point of view, a double value. By setting a standard of public worship, it will prevent too great " diversity of saying and singing," and should act as a check on slovenliness and other indesirable tendencies throughout the churches of the diocese. And, secondly, in view of the fact that most of these outlying mission churches and chapels are inevitably so widely scattered and poorly equipped and served with such difficulty and infrequency that the solemn celebration of the Holy Eucharist on Sundays and Feasts and the due observance of the proper ceremonies connected with the holy seasons of the Church's Year are practically out of the question, the ordered round of worship in the " cathedral " will at least ensure that the infant Church does not lose sight of the ideal altogether. It was probably with some such thought as this, at least partly, in his mind that that great ecclesiastical statesman Archbishop Benson, in founding the Mission to Corea nearly forty years ago, strongly urged the first bishop to devote himself rather to the task of creating " white-hot centres " than to that of developing the " sporadic pastorate."

But, sound as the principle is, it is not always easy to adhere to it—partly because the Spirit has a disconcerting way of blowing where it listeth, and partly because the type of energetic man who volunteers for the mission field is apt to be of the restless "gyrovagus" type (to use St. Benedict's word), which lays more stress on the duty of " sowing beside all waters " than of that of " gathering the wheat into garners." It must be remembered also that far the larger part of the population, in most parts of Asia and Africa where missionaries are at work, is engaged in agriculture and other rural pursuits, and therefore lives scattered all over the country-side, whereas only a very small proportion live in towns.   And it is in dealing with these scattered Christians (trying to hold their own in an atmosphere which is wholly pagan) that the Church finds herself face to face with a real problem.   How is the duty and privilege of habitual worship, even on Sundays and Feasts, to be made a reality to those hundreds of scattered "worshippers"—probably amounting to not less than three-fourths of the total number of communicants—who live five, ten, fifteen miles or more from the equivalent of their "parish church "?   With an effort, if the weather be not unpropitious—and the present writer's annual experience includes winter temperatures below zero and tropical heat, rains, and floods in the summer—these isolated Christians, or some members from each family (for houses cannot be left empty), may find their way for the Great Festivals to the central Church, where however, if they come in large numbers, their housing and feeding becomes a difficulty.   But otherwise there seems nothing for it— poor as is the accommodation in most of these villages— but for these isolated Christians, when they cannot attend the central Church, either to worship separately, family by family, or else to assemble in one another's houses for the purpose, both when the priest arrives at longer or shorter intervals to say Mass and also on those many Sundays and Feasts when no priest is available.   The question then arises as to what is the most suitable form of worship to be used under such conditions.   The ordinary Anglican plan of falling back on " Mattins " (if there be anyone who can lead it) eked out with hymns and address (if there be anyone to give one) would seem to be the worst possible solution of the difficulty.   Surely the best course is to provide these isolated worshippers with some very simple form of *Missa sicca*, ending with an act of Spiritual Communion which will enable them to asso-ciate themselves in spirit with that offering of the Holy Sacrifice in which their more fortunate brethren in the towns are engaged, but at which they themselves are unable to put in a bodily appearance.   Next to this the most desirable form of devotion would seem to be some-thing of the Litany or Rosary type—or like the Way of the Cross—which brings the facts of the Gospel Story and the Creed vividly before the minds of worshippers and enables them to appropriate these, as the basis for their prayers and praises, by the repetition of simple formulae known even to the most illiterate.

It is of course this difficulty of providing for regular worship and administration of the Sacraments in outlying and scattered communities which has called forth in certain quarters the rather wild suggestion that picked Christians should, after a minimum of *ad hoc* instruction, be " ordained elders in every church," with a commission simply to say Mass and administer the Sacraments, while pursuing their usual daily avocation and making their own independent living. Whether or not the advice subsequently given in the Pastoral Epistles on the subject of ordination is evidence that St. Paul had seen reason to recede from the position he had taken up twenty years earlier at the beginning of his missionary career, it is certain that the experience of the Catholic Church has led her to legislate quite definitely against the practice. And, as a matter of practical politics, the present writer is convinced that any such lowering of the priestly standard— involving as it must the separation of the teaching from the liturgical office of the priest, and a good deal of confusion about the administration of the Sacraments of Penance and Baptism (at least to adults)—would really fail of its purpose. The worthy priest-cobbler or priest-farmer would almost inevitably be found often absent from his post, hawking his shoes or marketing his grain, just at the very moment when he was urgently needed for his priestly ministrations in his parish.

It is not, however, merely the *place* of worship—or its absence—nor the lack of ministers which stands in the way of due provision being made for worship in the mission field. The category of *time* also contributes its quota of difficulties. The missionary priest will naturally be anxious from the outset to impress upon his flock (or so much of it as lives within reach of the altar) the duty of observing the Lord's Day, and such other Feasts as are specified in the diocesan calendar as being " of obligation," by the hearing of Mass and resting from servile work.[1]

[1] Feasts of obligation, other than Sundays, have of course varied greatly in number at different periods of the Church's history, and at the present time vary still, even in the various churches of the Roman Communion. In reading what follows, it will be interesting to remember

But a society which has been organised—as society, *e.g.*, in the Far East has—from time immemorial on the basis of the *lunar* calendar, and which is ignorant of the hebdomadal division of time, is apt to make things very difficult for the members of a Church which has built up its round of Fast and Festival on the *solar* calendar which she borrowed from the Roman Empire, and on the *seven-day* week which she borrowed from the Jews. The two systems clash at every point. And although the adoption of the Gregorian Calendar and the Western " week " during the last sixty years has to some extent eased the situation in countries like Japan—schools, government offices, banks, and other large places of business being closed on Sundays—there is even there no general observance of Sunday as a day of rest. Indeed, in such countries it tends to become more and more the day for which every sort of public function, from a State funeral to school sports, is fixed, in order to avoid encroaching on the working days of the week ; while in a country like Corea, as throughout China, the weekly division of time is popularly ignored, all the economic life of the country-side centring round the local " market day," which recurs every *fifth day*, filling a place in the peoples' lives and making demands on their attention which form a very serious obstacle to the Church's rules as to public worship. A further and analogous difficulty arises from the fact that in most missionary lands, certainly in Eastern Asia, the farming which is the occupation of the bulk of the population is carried on on " communal " lines rather than on those individualistic lines with which we are familiar in the West. In other words, certain operations which require a large amount of concentrated labour—such as planting out, weeding, and reaping of crops—are carried out by *all* the farmers working *all* together over *all* the fields. Obviously there are almost insuperable difficulties in the way of one or more of their number claiming exemption from the common task on the ground that they are under obligation to " hear Mass and abstain from servile works." The only solution of these and kindred difficulties would seem—

that St. Francis Xavier was so impressed with the difficulty of observing Lent during the spring season in India that he petitioned the Pope to transfer it to the autumn !

pending the time when the Church is strong enough to impose her own customs on the country-side—to lie in fixing the hour of worship so early as to enable the faithful to present themselves at Mass and Communion before " man goeth forth to his work and to his labour until the evening." Fortunately it is only in the *soi-disant* " civilised " countries that early rising (like fasting) seems to be a difficulty. The " sacred hour of eleven " therefore does not possess in most quarters of the mission field the attraction which it still appears to exercise in England.

When we get away from the environment of Christian worship to its subject-matter, we find ourselves face to face with a double problem. The first is the question of a vernacular liturgy; the second that of the text which ought to underly such liturgical translations as are put forth. To take the latter point first. Thirty or forty years ago it was dealt with in the following way. Any bishop who desired a grant from one of the recognised societies, to help him in the production of a liturgy, was provided with a questionaire in parallel columns. In one of these columns was set forth in numbered order every detail in the English Prayer Book of 1662 as usually published by the King's Printers, beginning with the " title page " and ending with the " XXXIX Articles " and the " Table of kindred and affinity." The other column contained a corresponding number of blank spaces under the heading, " How do you propose to treat this ? " And it is only with an effort that missionary bishops have more or less succeeded in shaking themselves free of this intolerable tyranny, some of the more inconvenient features of which were pointed out by the present Bishop of Southampton (then Bishop of Tokyo) in an article in *The East and the West*, which he had the courage to place under the heading " The Bad Habit of Translating the Prayer Book."

It is indeed a relief to turn from these " stuffy " ideals to the sensible Resolutions on the subject formally adopted by the Lambeth Conference of 1920. They are as follows :

" While maintaining the authority of the Book of Common Prayer as the Anglican standard of doctrine and practice, we consider that liturgical uniformity should not be regarded as a necessity throughout the Churches of the Anglican Communion. The conditions of the Church in many parts of the mission field render inapplicable the retention of that book as the one fixed liturgical model."

" Although the inherent right of a Diocesan Bishop to put forth or sanction liturgical forms is subject to such limitations as may be imposed by higher synodical authority, it is desirable that such authority should not be too rigidly exercised so long as those features are retained which are essential to the safeguarding of the unity of the Anglican Communion."

" The Conference recommends the appointment of a Committee of students of liturgical questions which would be ready to advise any Diocese or Province on the Form and Matter of services proposed for adoption, and requests the Archbishop of Canterbury to take such steps as he deems best to give early effect to this resolution." [1]

In full accordance with, and in the exercise of the liberty conceded by, these resolutions the present writer would be strongly in favour of the adoption—with whatever variations in detail—of a simple form, such as that provided by the 1549 Prayer Book, as the basis for the Eucharistic Liturgy in the mission field. This is not the place to sing the praises of that book. Suffice it to say that most Liturgical scholars are agreed that it is the most satisfactory of the Anglican group of Liturgies, preserving in a clearly recognisable form the structure and main features of the ancient Liturgies, without too great elaboration of detail.

With reference to the use of the vernacular in Liturgical worship, the question is not so simple as it appears

---

[1] [The foreign prayer books, published by S.P.C.K., are produced under the auspices of the Foreign Literature Committee, which is appointed not by the members of the Society, but by the Archbishop of Canterbury. In the production of translations it works under the direction of the Archbishop. No other course would be consistent with Church Order. The regulations in the past have been strict. Overseas bishops were bound by them only in so far as they sought financial aid from the Society ; they have always been at liberty to produce their books independently of the S.P.C.K. The purpose of the regulations was to ensure that a book purporting to be a translation of the Book of Common Prayer was what it purported to be. The Society has gladly helped in the provision of Diocesan Service books. But it has certainly stood in the way of the growth of an indefinite number of local liturgies.

Of recent years the position has changed completely. The Archbishop of Canterbury raises no objection to the Society's printing any prayer book which has *provincial* sanction. Isolated dioceses, which are still in a measure responsible to Canterbury, and indeed draw upon the Church of England for supplies of men and money, if they wish to make substantial deviations from the English Prayer Book in a vernacular version to be published with the S.P.C.K. imprint, are referred to the Liturgical Committee of the Lambeth Conference.—ED.]

P

at the first blush. It is indeed easy (though not so easy now as in the seventeenth century) to be eloquent on the folly of having " public prayer in the Church—in a tongue not understanded of the people " ; and so far as the Choir Offices are concerned, if they are to bulk at all largely in congregational worship, it is obvious that vernacular service books are a necessity. But with regard to the Eucharistic Liturgy, it must be remembered that the Roman Catholic Church—which is the greatest and most successful missionary body in the world—has carried on its missions everywhere under this handicap, if it is a handicap. And though it is true that the Eastern Orthodox Church in its great Asiatic missions has adhered firmly to the principle of a vernacular Liturgy, it must be remembered that a great part of the Liturgy is performed inside the closed Holy Doors, and much of what the priest has to say is uttered μυστικῶς. And quite apart from questions of Church traditions, the practical difficulties in the way of insisting that we are all entitled to hear Mass "in our own tongue wherein we were born " are becoming insuper- able, owing to the rapid disappearance of national bound- aries and the mutual interfiltration of all the races of the world.   Unreasoning insistence on the vernacular simply results in providing excuses for that racial segregation and discrimination, of which something has been already said and which is so fatally untrue to the spirit of Catholicism. And if the vernacular is not insisted on, it would seem only reasonable to resort to the use of one or other of the great traditional Liturgical languages of the Church, at least as an alternative to the " tongue understanded of the people." [1]

Analogous to the question of a vernacular Liturgy is the further problem as to how far it is wise or possible to adopt local custom or colour in the accessories of Christian worship—architecture, music, shape and colour of vest- ments, ornaments, and so forth.   This question of "adapt- ation " has been faithfully dealt with by a missionary of

---

[1] Those magnificent missionaries of the Society of Jesus—Matteo Ricci and his companions and followers who did such a great work in China from the sixteenth to the eighteenth centuries—tried hard to get permission from Rome to say Mass in Chinese, but without success.   On the other hand, the Liturgies of St. John Chrysostom and St. Basil have been translated into and are in regular use in the Chinese, Japanese, Corean, and doubtless other Asiatic languages.

great experience in the very last number of *The East and the West*, to which readers are referred, as space will not permit of our dealing with it in detail here.[1] Suffice it to say that most of us arrive in the mission field full of the fascinating idea that the Catholic religion should be presented in " native dress " to every nation under heaven, and that most of us find reason to modify our opinion in the light of experience. We require far greater knowledge than most of us possess of the agelong philosophy or deeply rooted associations lying behind the use of particular forms, colours, melodies, and bodily actions by Indians, Africans, Chinese, Coreans or Japanese, to justify us in being certain that these can be incorporated into the Christian tradition.

The sum of the whole matter is this that, in the mission field as elsewhere, we need to be always putting first things first, and while leaving plenty of room for elasticity and free play in subsidiary and accessory matters, to be clear and definite in our assertion of fundamental principles, and unflinching in our determination at all costs to abide by St. Paul's injunction to Timothy :

τὴν παραθήκην φύλαξον.

[1] " L'adaptation," by the Rev. W. F. France (formerly a missionary in Japan), in *The East and the West* for October 1927 : " Some local customs the Church has had perforce to adopt or tolerate for a time, such as in China and Corea the keeping of the head covered by men during worship, the baring of the head in the presence of a superior being a sign of gross disrespect. But the gradual disappearance of the old native headdress everywhere has solved this difficulty."

XI

THE DEVELOPMENT OF
THE NATIVE CHURCH IN WITNESS

BY W. J. CLISSOLD

SYNOPSIS

" Christianity flourishes through its saints."

It is for churches and individuals with longer experience to hand on the torch to others.

Our Aim must be to foster the development of Christian character, the supreme means of witness and evangelisation.

This character is

(1) supernatural.

A "religion of morality" not enough. Man's search for God must be fulfilled through his instinct for the supernatural. Value of sacramental religion as a means to this end.

To claim that Christianity is the orientation of the religious instinct towards Christ is not to deny either the reality of grace and the need of new birth, or the need of a moral life. Grace does not destroy nature but fulfils it. Christian character is the fruit of Christian faith.

(2) expressed corporately as well as individually.

To an African the tribeless man is of all men the most miserable. The Church is the great Christian tribe.

Our Method must be that of God in the Incarnation, its patience, and its risks. We must begin by trying to create a right environment for spiritual growth, and end by effacing ourselves and letting the young Church take its own risks. To this end :

(1) The missionary must see to his own personal life.

(2) The Church of the mission station must be a home of worship.

(3) Instruction must be given on the meaning of incorporation into Christ through the Church.

(4) The missionary must learn to stand aside and risk lesser failures for the sake of real success.

True and false self-development, and means to its accomplishment.

Hindrances to native development arising from failure of Europeans in practical Christian brotherhood.

THE DEVELOPMENT OF THE NATIVE
CHURCH IN WITNESS

THE writer ought to begin this essay by confessing that
he has no qualifications, either through experience or study,
enabling him to deal with this subject in a general historical
way. He proposes therefore to put before the reader the
view which has been forced upon him by the circumstances
of a very limited ministry among the Bantu during the
last fifteen years.

The late Baron von Hügel, recalling an address delivered
in Oxford in 1920, has written the following thought-
provoking passage :

"I have still vividly before me the sea of eager youthful
countenances upturned in welcome to the substance of this
paper. . . . It then struck me once more with a wistful delight
that in very deed *Christianity flourishes through its saints, and
that the surest way to rob it of its congenital attraction is to shrink
from its heroic heights*. And further it struck me afresh that
this great fact, and the apprehension and presentation of
religion with this great fact maintained, as its very life-blood
throughout it : that these are visions and utterances which
youth must not be expected of itself to see and to proclaim
steadily and whole. *It is for the trained and experienced seniors
to hand on this steadily flaming torch of life and love to the as
yet fitful juniors*. If Lucretius was right to see the successive
generations of mankind transmitting each to the next, the light
and warmth of civilisation, in a sort of gigantic torch race :
still more applicable is this noble simile to the history of
heroism and holiness.

"Now let us observe that not only young individuals but
also young nations, and with them every at all pure democracy,
are not likely of themselves to perceive the full costliness of the
deepest life and richest wisdom. The arduousness, the rarity,
the straightened circumstances in and for this our earthly life,
of all things greatly beautiful : this can hardly be felt very
widely by young countries, still less by materially prosperous

need purification since they are mingled with much that is foolish and sinful ; granted that they are often divorced from morality and sometimes actively fruitful in evil ; yet in spite of this they witness at their best to a pathetic striving after light and at their worst to a corruption of what is true, and not to essential falsehood. So far from the existence of parallels between heathenism and Catholicism being an argument for the falsehood of the latter, it is the strongest possible argument for its truth. It means in fact that Catholicism alone can fulfil what is elemental in human nature, what strives to find fulfilment even amid the blight of ignorance and sin.

In this connexion the harm that has been done by the exclusion of sacramental religion from native life in the towns is immense. Divorced from tribal tradition and out of touch with Christianity, the unfortunate African loses the one force which has unified and sustained his life. For here is precisely the practical value of what we may call " the instinct for the supernatural," to unify by control the lesser instincts for surrender to a force which is at once both immanent and transcendent, for incorporation into a tradition, for stimulus and emotion which shall give relief from the fetters of self. The man who has lost this control is like the man in the parable whose " last state was worse than the first." When the devil who had previously diverted his religion to " superstition " has gone out, the impulses towards surrender and stimulus will not die, but will return in fatal shapes, such as uncontrolled submission to the passions, drink, immorality, social revolt. Hence the tremendous need that Christianity should be presented in such a way as not to stultify, but to develop and purify the instinct for the supernatural and all the associations which centre round it.

At this point I am sure that two objections will arise in the mind of the reader. They are these : If this is so, if Christianity is but the orientation of the religious instinct towards Christ, the development of something which heathen men possess, what becomes of our Lord's words about the " new birth " and the apostolic insistence upon repentance ? I answer that birth, though a crisis, is really a development, and that repentance, instantaneous as it may seem, is never unrelated to a long process which has gone before. Even in the classic and unusual case of

St. Paul, this may be shown to be so.   St. Paul was a good Christian because he had been a good Jew, and the greatness of his repentance was determined by the force with which for long he had " kicked against the pricks." If you object that this theory seems to leave no room for that very supernatural element upon which we have just insisted, I answer that, while it does indeed exclude the idea of God's working without respect for human law and limitation, it greatly increases our apprehension of His wisdom, and tenderness and patience in the co-operation of divine grace with human effort.   How God loves to work through humanity ! This thought, if you come to dwell upon it, is the basis of the Catholic idea of saintship and of the devotion to the Sacred Heart itself.   Christ Incarnate, St. Stephen's prayers, St. Paul's efforts, all the media of God's power!   And remember that when our Lord became man, He espoused not only the external Church, but the whole of humanity as His Bride.   Do we not find here the source from which flows His healing grace through the jungles and deserts of heathen lands ?

I am very anxious not to be misunderstood with regard to this, which is really, as I take it, the fundamental of orthodoxy ; I mean that I have no thought of denying the gift of grace as a thing absolutely above and beyond the reach of unaided nature, a free and entirely new and supreme gift.   In this sense Christianity is a new life, a fresh beginning so immeasurably above the old, that it has often been regarded as obliterating or eclipsing it.   It is only against this latter mistake that I wish to protest, for the glory of salvation lies uniquely in the fact that grace never destroys or eclipses but *lifts* and *fulfils* and *purifies* the natural life which, in its order, is as much as grace the gift of God.

The other objection is concerned with the relation of religion to morality.   Would it not be best, it has been urged, to make the heathen moral before encouraging him in Catholic practices and ideas which might end, apart from morality, in barren superstition, as has in fact actually happened at times ?   To this we must answer, " Do you expect fruit without seed ? " True it is that Christian life is of paramount importance, but to walk in the way of the Commandments man must have a Guide and Strengthener, and to ask him to do so without is both foolish and cruel. As a matter of historical fact, Christian character is the fruit of Christian Faith. It was only when his eyes were fixed on Christ that Peter walked and did not sink amidst the stormy waters. And all the cults and practices of Catholicism are but means of fixing men's eyes on Christ. Because some use these means and do not walk, we must not imagine that they can walk without them.

Before we leave this point of the necessity of the supernatural element in Christian character as a witness and evangelising power, I should like to illustrate it from examples I have known. " Ye are the light of the world," said our Lord to His disciples, and in our own personal experience has not each of us found that what has strengthened his religion most has been the friendship of those in whose life has shone the evidence that they have " been with Jesus." Is it not just this intensely human, yet intensely supernatural, character which gave missionary power to St. Francis, to Fr. Stanton, to Fr. Dolling ?

I well remember the contemptuous tone in which an African spoke of certain missionaries in whose work the industrial took apparent precedence of the spiritual : " Father, they are farmers, not priests at all." I recall, too, the wonderfully attractive power of some native catechists in Southern Rhodesia whose intellectual and administrative abilities were much smaller than those of others. There was an indefinable sense of spiritual influence about the little mud churches where these catechists worked. " Cases " at their villages would not take the usual form of wrangles about Church dues or external breaches of discipline. Rather they would result in numbers of confessions, or visits from inquirers perplexed as to dreams, conduct, the Bible, or the meaning of the Church. Above all, I see now that same light shining in the eyes of the newly baptised beside an African river which I had seen in the eyes of the newly initiated after the heathen sacrament of tribal initiation, only now intensified and purified. It was a light that spoke of faith in the unseen, of new birth, of corporate sharing in a supreme mystery, of passionate loyalty to a Chief and to a great Tradition. In all these instances it was the mystical element which dominated and had been fulfilled. The African has no use for a " rationalised " religion at all.

" We have become accustomed," writes Canon A. W. Robinson,[1] " to the phrase ' reduced Christianity,' and the expression aptly describes a great deal of what is now prevalent among us. The type will be recognised as soon as its characteristics are described. It is ethical rather than spiritual, not wanting in moral earnestness, but laying little stress upon the fact of sin. It disdains dogma, is unfavourable to worship, and dislikes the suggestion of discipline. The supernatural for it is reduced almost to vanishing point. There is no insistence upon the means of grace. We are not uncharitable when we say that there is in it little assurance or vision ; and up to the present it has failed to excite any great missionary enthusiasm. It is certainly not the faith that once overcame the world."

(2) This supernatural Christian character must have its corporate and not only its individual side.[2] Protestantism has failed lamentably in this abroad as at home. In the case of the Bantu the failure is all the more pitiable, since the very substance of their conscious life is the sharing in a common tribal unity. I make bold to say that to the average African it is not so much the great thought of individual salvation which makes the chief appeal in Christianity, but the thought of incorporation into the Church, the great Christian tribe, and if he often lacks in some measure a sense of deep individual devotion to our Saviour, who shall say that this is a greater defect than the total lack of comprehension among many Europeans that the Church, considered as the Household of God, is immeasurably superior to the individual ? To an African a tribeless man is of all men the most miserable. He well-nigh worships his chief as head and embodiment of the tribe. These ideas will readily be seen to be in line with Catholic teaching on the Church, with the theology of St. Paul as to Christ's Body, and the mystical teaching of our Lord as to the Vine and the branches. Canon Robinson, in the same little book from which I have already quoted, points out that to the early believer a Christian was not so much a " follower of Christ " as a member of His Body. We Catholics have here another immense asset in the mission field. We shall wantonly

---

[1] *Christ and the Church*, p. 30.
[2] Our Lord desired not only individuals, but also His Church, the " City set upon a hill," to be His witness.

throw it away if we fail to uphold the idea of the grandeur, the mystery, the richness, the strength, of the Church as the Bride of Christ, the City of God, the Army terrible with banners. Do not make the mistake of imagining that these conceptions are useless because beyond the comprehension of "primitive peoples." Ideas so small as to be capable of complete comprehension (if there be such) would be powerless to uplift and inspire. And God has designed His deepest mysteries, not for the "wise and prudent," but for "babes." [1]

Perhaps, too, it is possible to suggest that we who are in communion with Canterbury have a special appeal to make in this respect. Africans at all events unite in many tribes strong reverence for authority with a strong sense of the rights of the society, and insist that an authority which disregards the latter is *ipso facto* in that respect dissolved. They would not find it difficult to reconcile the idea of a constitutional papacy with the idea of the Headship of Christ which it represents in the ecclesiastical sphere much as the chief represents God in the civil. But they are fully alive to the dangers accruing to blind obedience, and they recognise at once that there may be cases where to disobey the letter is to obey the reality.

Our Method.—We now come to the more practical part of our consideration, the method by which the development of this supernatural Christian character, individual and corporate, may best be fostered as a witness and a power in evangelisation. Before we begin to construct a theory it will be well to clear the ground of one particular misapprehension—I mean the idea that the conditions of the Early Church will furnish our model in details. The conditions of the Early Church were not normal and called for abnormal methods. For instance, there were then comparatively few to carry on the immense work of evangelisation, and in consequence it was quite impossible for the apostles to stay long in one place. Again, the apostles were dealing mostly with highly civilised nations. The theology of the Church had not yet become explicit in the manner in which history has since made it so. "The gift of miracles" and other similarly striking gifts appear

---

[1] A friend who has long lived in South Africa makes the following comment : "The Bantu, unused as he may be to European custom, has none the less a sensitiveness of imagination and a subtlety of thought which exceed that of many a European."

to have been granted temporarily in order to compel attention and faith in a manner which has been superseded
by the continual miracle of the existence and progress of
the Church as we see it, through all the ups and downs
of history. Means of transport, though efficient, were
comparatively elementary. Human ideas—geographical,
scientific, psychological—were very much less developed.
Eschatology especially needed the correction of experience.
In short, though the spirit of the apostles is our model for
all ages, their method was adapted to their own age rather
than to ours.

A much deeper pattern is the method of God in the
Incarnation. If we consider this with attention we shall
be struck first with God's marvellous *patience,* and then
with the risks He was willing to take in order to guard the
freedom of man's will. For ages of ages the loving Father
waited and suffered before the Incarnation till He had
prepared the right environment for the divine seed. Even
in this preparation He would not work without the co-operation of men. First a chosen race, then a chosen family,
lastly a chosen individual, arose and responded amid failure
and sin. Then at the very instant when this response had
become perfect, the Eternal Word leaped down. Mary's
Fiat marks the marriage of earth's need with heaven's
fulfilment. A new era in redemption had begun.

Now notice the stages of the development of the Christian seed—that seed through which the supernatural life
of God unites with, purifies, re-energises, and uplifts the
natural life of men. During the incarnate life of our Lord
a long preparation, external guidance, teaching, example,
preserved as it were the soil in which alone the tender
growth could flourish. But soon that external guidance
was to give place to something of even greater importance
to the mature and sturdy plant. " It is expedient for you
that I go away : for if I go not away, the Comforter will
not come unto you." The principle of external guidance
was to make way for the principle of internal assimilation.
In this new process personality, human co-operation, effort
through failure, the development of every human gift and
faculty, such as organising power, philosophy, material
wealth, were to find fulfilment in a gradual and grand
struggle to seize hold of divine grace. Salvation in one
sense is the sole act of God. In another, we " work out

our own salvation," for the supreme paradox of life lies in this, that only in surrender to God can man find freedom.

If we apply these ideas to our own missionary method, we shall learn then to be patient ; to concentrate every effort at first towards the creation of a right environment ; to watch with tender care over the early stages of the growth of that seed which we have sown not without the pangs of death. Then, last of all, to withdraw in later stages too close and rigid an external influence, and rather to encourage " independence " or " self-determination," taking great risks and suffering, both in ourselves and in those we are evangelising, in the process.

We shall find that modern psychology supports to the hilt this programme. Psychologists are laying more and more stress on the importance of *beginnings* in the life of the child or people. No less do they stress the evil of unbalanced external repression of individuality in the life of the growing boy or growing nation. The only thing in which they sometimes seem blind is forgetfulness of the supreme power of supernatural influence, and the attempt to account for all phenomena on a purely natural basis. After what we have seen with regard to the importance of the supernatural, we shall be in little danger of falling into this error. But we do need to open our eyes to the new light which psychology gives us. We ought to give up expecting results without causes and " miraculous " instantaneous conversions, where patient tending of gradual growth is God's normal method.

And now to be severely practical. How can we best apply these methods ? Von Hügel writes : " Not only young individuals but also young nations . . . are not likely of themselves to perceive the full costliness of the deepest life and richest wisdom." " It is for the trained and experienced seniors to hand on this steadily flaming torch of life and love to the as yet fitful juniors." Yes, and the first necessity, therefore, for those seniors, is to see that the fire of the supernatural is burning in their own lives, otherwise they will be quite unable to pass it on. " For their sakes I sanctify myself." As well expect to get fire from water as a supernatural atmosphere in a mission where the priest himself is not living the supernatural life. I do not say " where the priest is not a perfect priest," for if that were the condition we had best give up trying to evangelise others. No, I say, where the priest is not living in the constant realisation and strength of the supernatural, amid all his weakness and failure. And that implies a full use of the Catholic system—the daily Mass (the native will derive his idea of its value very largely from the pains the priest takes to say it well and regularly), frequent confession, private prayer and meditation, before the Reserved Sacrament if possible ; great reverence in outward things within the church, and scrupulous care for all that concerns its worship, especially the Blessed Sacrament ; a certain expectancy of supernatural happenings, such as answer to prayer, or guidance through circumstances, in his own life and that of his people ; the practice of meditation and Bible-reading ; these and many other similar things will have far greater influence upon his flock than anything else in handing on the torch of the supernatural. I think as I write these words of one missionary well known in South Africa, a member of a religious order, of whom it was said to me, " Just to be in the same room with him makes you feel better even if he never speaks a word." In this case I believe that the power of the supernatural had largely found expression through patient suffering. And to suffer patiently with Christ is perhaps the supreme means of evangelisation. Is not this the central teaching of the Cross, and the explanation of the old saying that " the blood of the martyrs is the seed of the Church " ? I am certain that primitive peoples, like young children, are specially alive to such subtle indefinable influences in personal relations. An old Mochuana said to me the other day, " We became Christians in the time of Dr. Livingstone because we saw the power of Christianity in his life. Now the heathen do not want Christianity because of the evil example of unbelieving white men." David Livingstone was not technically a Catholic, and consequently he lost immensely in the lack of that sense of authority and awe which our commission as officers of the Catholic Church, that marvellous Personality so far transcending our own, can give. Yet in so far as he belonged to the soul of the Church, in so far as he lived abidingly in the sense of Christ's presence, to that extent he was a great and effective missionary.

Next to the personal life of the missionary comes the

Q

place occupied by the actual building of the church. If the altar is felt and seen to be the very centre and power-house of every activity on the mission, then it will become what it is meant to be, a door into the spiritual. Here again I think of an actual example, a church in S. Rhodesia. I remember how, when newly arrived from England, as I approached the mission I feared the strangeness and loneliness I should find. And then when I entered this great thatched sanctuary, so unmistakably the heart of all, and saw the dark kneeling figures before the shrines and altars, the dim lamp in the chapel of the Blessed Sacrament, the six tall candles of the High Altar, I knew that I had but just come home once more. And every day on that mission confirmed that conviction. It is the Catholic Church which makes the whole world a home. And along with the Church, of course, we must include the services ; and here in the mission field, as elsewhere, " it is the Mass which matters." Of course the Mass must be frequent, grand, simple, mysterious, sublime, the root and crown of every activity ; and of course it must be rendered with faithfulness in detail as well as entire devotion in spirit. Leave theorists to say that ritual details are unimportant. Who does not feel the difference in visiting a mission where there is a daily Mass, and another mission where the Holy Mysteries are infrequently celebrated without the loving outward signs of reverence which to a Catholic are so precious just because of their association with what is so holy ? And next to the Mass come the other Sacraments, Reservation, statues, holy water, the pictures of the way of the Cross, and all the time-honoured aids to Catholic worship ; for these things are the windows through which the infinite heavens look down on finite men ; or, as was said above, the means by which we fix our eyes on Christ amid earth's tempests.

As with the personal life of the priest, so with the atmosphere of the Church ; I have known many cases in which it has been a great evangelising influence in the true, the supernatural significance. The hush of awe, the reverence, the astonishment, which such a church will produce even upon the raw heathen, is evidence of this. I have known myself Africans brought up in Protestantism immensely impressed and attracted when they entered our little church at Molepolole. To the end of time it will

be true that loving souls are drawn to Christ through the
healing beauty of His Bride.

And after these things we must place methods of instruction. Sometimes people are surprised that we do
not " begin with the gospels " ; some indeed, as we have
remarked above, wish us to begin with the teaching of the
Ten Commandments. But surely since we live after the
gift of the Incarnation, this would be entirely the wrong
order. First teach the supernatural power and glory of
incorporation into the living and victorious Saviour through
the Church which is His Body. Then all the rest will fall
into its right position. There will be no fear of a purely
"rationalised" religion—a religion of "following Christ"
which has not first learnt to " abide in Him." And the
Ten Commandments will then be no hard, cruel law, impossible of observance and most often honoured in the
breach by a hypocritical convention, but the path on which
our Captain leads us and which He gives us strength
gradually to traverse with Him. As Canon Robinson
points out, the Prayer Book does not insist that we should
" walk in His commandments " till we remember that
we are " Members of His Body." That is the right, the
supernatural order. And we need to note that morality
is a wonderful fruit of slow and difficult growth. Great
harm has been done by missionary literature which leads
people at home to look for heroic virtue as a matter of
course in the newly baptised.

But after we have provided for this right environment,
how shall we provide for that freedom for self-development
which we have seen to be so necessary ? There is a type
of mission where all seems in apple-pie order, where discipline seems perfect, and respect for authority is marked,
and yet the one thing needful is absent—that is, the
sturdiness, the beauty, the supernatural growth, which
only freedom can give. There are other missions over
which the disciplinarian and government official sometimes shakes his head, where no rows of respectful natives
shout " Nkosi " as their betters pass, no brand-new buildings and brand-new methods delight the inspector's heart!
Only there seems about the people a delightful sense of
being at home. Yet in these last I think sometimes the
angels find their greatest pleasure. I am quite sure
which type the natives themselves count best. The wise

missionary will not be deceived by outward success in order and discipline. What he must aim at is creating the discipline of the heart. And that will not be created unless he himself is willing at times to stand aside, to resist the obsession of his own importance, to risk lesser failures for the real success. He must be ready to work with imperfect human instruments, as God worked in the Incarnation, rather than secure a specious perfection with the loss of that freedom which is indeed divine.

I have used the term " self-development," and after all that has gone before I think I can do so without fear of misunderstanding. There is a type of " self-development " and " self-support " which is really uncatholic ; I mean the type which refuses all interchange of ideas and helps between nations on the ground that they are " not native." People obsessed with this idea will not suffer any European ornament in an African church, and sometimes desire even to substitute a " native liturgy " for the liturgical riches stored up in the Church throughout the ages. They are so eager for an entirely native ministry that they even suggest that a mission is a failure unless Europeans can clear away from it after a period of five years! But all history and all psychology teach that God's Church is not built up like this ; nor would it be desirable, even if it were possible, that a local church should be in this insular sense " self-supporting."

Experience seems to point out that in Africa (I have no first-hand knowledge of other parts of the mission field) the wisest way to secure true " self-development " is for the European teacher to invite the advice of the native, without, for a long period, giving him authority to act independently. The reason for this is contained in the extract from von Hügel with which we began : " The arduousness, the rarity, the straitened circumstances in and for this our earthly life, of all things greatly beautiful : this can hardly be felt very widely by young countries." Watch any native in a European store and you will soon prove to yourself the truth of these words, for, left to himself, he will almost invariably choose the most worthless trash he can find. What is needed is that the European, from his greater experience and opportunity, should guide and educate native choice of all that is good, both in his own native culture and in the culture of his new teachers, thus restraining the tendency to throw over everything, both good and bad, in the reaction against the old heathen life, or, on the other hand, to adopt nothing new simply on the score that it is foreign. When this right choice has been educated, then, and not till then, may independent authority be gradually allowed. To grant it earlier is to put a cruel power of self-injury into the hands of inexperience.

I have found that a good practical way to carry out this principle is to arrange that certain members of the Church Council should be elected, others appointed by the priest, and that from these the priest should choose a few as counsellors. If " cases " are judged as a matter of course by native councils as a whole, they are apt to degenerate into entertainments for the discussion of scandal. One runs the risk of appearing too autocratic by the other method, but I have found this a lesser risk than the latter.

In matters of worship much may be done to encourage the congregation in taking an active part, but here again native initiative needs careful educating. It is a good plan to choose a few of the wisest and best to join, first in a prayer-circle in a private house, before beginning in public as prayer-leaders. In this way the priest can point out the pitfalls awaiting public informal extempore prayer, such as pride, dwelling on the sins of others, or the use of conventional phrases. It may be wise to give each member a subject for prayer, so that he may think it over beforehand, and then to call upon members by name at the meeting, to ensure greater order. Besides extempore prayer, the present writer suggests that the people should be encouraged to lead such devotions as the " Stations," the Rosary, or even Public Offices and Occasional Prayers.

Finally, let the European remember that consultation is as much for his own education as that of his people. His native advisers will be able gradually to open his eyes to all that is best in native custom, and perhaps to suggest ways in which this may be incorporated into Christianity, as, for instance, with regard to marriage custom or the " initiation " rites. I say " gradually," for we have seen that only little by little can the natives themselves come to realise true values, and only by continual effort can the European win sufficient confidence from his people to allow free communication of their inmost thoughts, and the power to recognise in these, even when most unfamiliar, what comes from God.

The law of the apprehension of grace demands, in this fallen world, effort and suffering ; man apprehends his salvation by using it, as the child learns to walk through walking.

The next stage, then, for the missionary, after sowing the seed of the supernatural and watched over its development in a suitable environment, is to stand aside and give it a chance of developing itself ; only so can it really become strong. The Christian convert is now in the position of a rider on a spirited horse, who needs by running a race to learn assurance. To pursue this homely image a little further : even in his heathen days he had possessed a horse (the libido or " urge " of psychology), but it was a vicious animal at times, and he himself was often like a child carried at random with a broken bridle by which he could not control the power beneath him. Our Lord by His example and grace has now given the Christian instruction in the art of horsemanship, and a bridle and rein by which he may translate precept into practice. In a sense we may now compare the control of the horse to the will, formerly inactive through despair following upon repeated failure, but now revived by the consciousness of the new power which the Christian Faith has given, the new means by which he can direct the deep forces within him. In psychological term, this renewed bridle, received and put into use, is the faculty of right " suggestion " which, once received from Christ, is controlled by will, and sends continual beneficent messages to the " unconscious " ; this, like the horse, in turn reacts upon its master by carrying him without his conscious effort towards his ideal.

Now let us note the effect which this new attitude to life has upon all life's associations. What to the aimless child was before an obstacle becomes to the jockey but a chance for greater glory. Hurdles are no longer hindrances ; that is, the difficulties of life—suffering, human weakness, even sin—are no longer insurmountable, but the very opportunities which make for greater glory. And as to the jockey everything he meets will be invested with fresh significance, as to the lover every faculty will now be exercised towards the making of a home for his beloved, so to the Christian nothing will be too small to find glory and purpose from the sunshine of Christianity. One so often meets in the mission-field with this renaissance of the whole man under the gracious influence of conversion.

If the reader has been disappointed that this essay has not dealt at greater length with the details of Christian activity, the reason will now perhaps occur to him. It is because all these activities are really dependent on the ability to apprehend and direct aright man's faculty for the supernatural, and therefore the development of witness is really the development of this great faculty. Where it is found, all the lovely fruits of Christianity flourish, such as pure family affection, truth, upright political aim, the religious life in its technical sense, and so on. Without it heathen life is ineffective, and still more the lives of those who have no system of religion, because of their inability to overcome obstacles—untruthfulness, impurity, pride, and all that makes for disintegration. " The truth shall make you free."

What can be more " worth while " to the missionary, who should be that greatest of all artists—an " artist in souls "—than to watch the gradual development of this divine life within the personalities of those whom God has given him to sow it in. The writer thinks of some youth, trained on the mission in habits of prayer and sacramental response, sent out for the first time into a heathen village, and building up there, through many weaknesses, another little centre of supernatural influence. One such congregation he was told of by a brother missionary. Here both catechist and people had often failed most grievously. Yet when once after a long enforced absence in war-time the priest visited again this place in the desert, he found that every one of those weak Christians had laid down their lives for their Faith and been burnt alive, rather than return, as their enemies wished, to their old superstition. If one may say so reverently, it is such experiences as these which seem to reflect what our Lord must have felt in heaven when He witnessed the triumph of His first young martyr, St. Stephen.

Perhaps before I close I shall be expected to say something of the thorny question of " discipline." Space fails, so I will but suggest that great laxity spells licence, and that great severity will end in the expulsion of love by fear.

In public discipline the wise missionary will steer a middle course between them.

But I cannot close without referring to the great hindrance to the development of witness among " natives " ; I mean the utter failure of " white Christians " to exhibit the witness of Christian brotherhood. As long as the " native sees that the average white Christian will not allow him in his religious buildings, will not receive communion from a black priest, will not count him really as a brother at all, so long he will be unable to receive from him the flame of supernatural love, and so long he will suspect him of utter insincerity. The influence of one act such as that of the Prince of Wales when he made his Communion with natives at the hand of a West African priest, does more than a thousand sermons to clear away this hindrance. Would that such acts were common ! Other hindrances are, of course, the absorption of the white man in the material to the exclusion of the spiritual, and the schisms of Christendom.

I have left myself no space to dwell on the importance of teaching from the start that the Christian life is given, not so much for our own sake, but as a trust to hand on to others. The lack of the realisation of this truth is a fruitful source of failure in missionary enthusiasm in native churches. Nor can I dwell on the self-evident fact that our position as teachers does not imply for a moment a pharisaical assumption that we are " better " than our pupils, any more than the position of a father as the teacher of his son implies such an assumption. In most cases I should think we might hold the reverse. But I want to end with an encouragement and a challenge. An encouragement because the Church of which we are such unworthy instruments, in spite of our failure, goes on, still captivates the imagination, still raises and heals and triumphs in heathen lands. A challenge, because this miracle calls to-day, as ever, for our keener co-operation, our deeper faith, our more generous abandonment to the supreme Adventure. And who knows ? It may be that by the renewed faith of child-nations even our own decadence may find purification and renewal !

XII

MISSIONARY VOCATION AND TRAINING

BY E. R. MORGAN

SYNOPSIS

VOCATION.

John the Baptist's training of his disciples for the call of Christ characterised by definiteness and detachment.

There must be the same definiteness and detachment in all who have to prepare the young for the call of Christ.

Three stages in this call :

(1) " Master where dwellest thou ? " " Come and ye shall see."
(2) " Follow me."
(3) " As the Father hath sent me, even so send I you."

We are called, chosen, sent.

THE TESTING OF VOCATION.

God tests the individual through human society, circumstances, the Church, using special groups to test special vocations. Possibility of mistakes and self-deception.

TRAINING.

The demand made on missionaries by the present world-situation, and the increase of knowledge.

The real problem of training, the adjustment of the study of an enormous and ever-enlarging field of " subjects " to the training of character.

The stages in the training of a missionary correspond with the steps in the development of vocation.

I. General Christian training such as will prepare the young to hear and respond to the call of God.

II. Training in (i) the understanding of the Christian revelation. Need for a new orientation of the curriculum of all theological colleges. (ii) the capacity to receive. Necessity for the element of " retreat " in missionary training.

III. Special training for the special sphere to which the missionary is sent.

MISSIONARY VOCATION AND TRAINING

Vocation.—Discipleship in the school of John the Baptist fostered the expectancy of great events to be embodied in the coming of a Person, of One who was to bear and heal the sorrows of the world, who, led as a lamb to the slaughter, was to see the travail of His soul and be satisfied. It was an expectancy of mingled hope and godly fear, involving a discontent with conventional religion, a preparation of prayer, fasting, and repentance ; a repentance interpreted by John himself in the words of the prophet of the exile as a great road-making enterprise, a straightening out of men's lives, giving them aim and direction, a smoothing out of rough places and a cutting through of mountains—the making of a highway for our God.

It was in this school that Andrew and John and other disciples were prepared to make their first venture of acquaintance with Jesus. When they met Him as He walked, they began following because their hearts were made ready to recognise Him.

Everyone must find Christ for himself ; but everyone must be put in the way of being found by Him. The kind of home and schooling he has had will help or hinder him in his quest. Enshrined in the vivid stories with which the Gospels open is to be found a treasury of teaching about vocation and the way in which it is fostered and developed by God. To the disciples it would seem at first almost accidental that they had come across Jesus, but as they looked back in after years they would understand how, through the circumstances of home and work and teaching, God in His Providence had been suggesting and making plain the direction of their lives, either negatively by thwarting their efforts to go one way, or positively by encouraging them to go another, until Jesus met them and they met Jesus on the road.

Of the early home life and circumstances of the disciples

we know next to nothing, though we can be sure of some of them that they were country-bred in a life of sturdy craftsmanship. Of John the Baptist himself we know that he came of a priestly family, and that his birth was heralded by divine visitation and joyful and wondering response. As of more than one of the earlier prophets, we are assured that while he was yet in the womb of his mother he was " lent to the Lord," [1] so of this last and greatest of the prophets we may believe that from the time of his conception his was a dedicated life.

In John the Baptist's training of his disciples for the coming of Christ, there is a fundamental principle to guide us in the task of fostering Christian vocation in home and school and parish. His whole mission is consummated in the words : " There cometh One that is mightier than I " : " He must increase, but I must decrease." There is splendid objectivity and detachment in the attitude which points others definitely to the Person of Christ as the goal of their attachment, and yet leaves them free to find Him for themselves. John had attached disciples to himself in order that they might be led through him to that Other. There is a whole philosophy of influence here. There must be these two qualities of definiteness and detachment in the influence of parents and spiritual pastors and masters if the boys and girls whom they serve are to find in Christ their heart's final attachment.

It is a truism to say that the aim of every Christian home and school and parish in relation to their children must be : " Behold the Lamb of God : He must increase, but we must decrease." But how often is so-called Christian education lacking either in definiteness or detachment.

There are never lacking in any generation parents who, from a love of power or from a selfish and exacting affection which passes for anxious solicitude, so dominate the spiritual development of their children as to demand a blind obedience which makes them either cowards or rebels. " It is difficult," says George Meredith, in *Richard Feverel,* " for those who think very earnestly for their children to know when their children are thinking on their own account. The exercise of their volition we construe as revolt. Our love does not like to be invalided and deposed from its

---

[1] 1 Sam. i. 11 ; *cf.* Jer. i. 5.

command, and here I think yonder old thrush on the lawn, who has just kicked the last of her lank offspring out of the nest to go shift for itself, much the kinder of the two, though sentimental people do shrug their shoulders at these unsentimental acts of the creatures who never wander from nature."

In the same way, though domination is far less severe in modern school life than it has been in the past, there is often enough lacking in schools that spirit of detachment which is content to keep itself in the background to the point of allowing boys and girls to be themselves, and see and hear for themselves; there are sometimes a school tradition and a school *esprit de corps* which make the individual so afraid or even ashamed of himself as to lead him to shelter behind tradition and privilege, and consequently sap his courage and daunt his moral initiative.

On the other hand there is little to be said in favour of those parents who, either because they do not care, make little or no attempt to bring their children to the knowledge of God, or deliberately adopt a policy of *laissez-faire* in the mistaken idea that this will give their children spiritual freedom.

And there are many schools on a Christian foundation in which there is too little definite or coherent unity of outlook upon the world, in which in the minds and characters of the teachers and pupils there persists, perhaps unperceived, the old battle between a man-centred and a God-centred view of life, manifesting itself now in the conflict between Hellenism and Christianity, now in different approaches to historical study presented as mutually antagonistic, now in the supposed incompatibility of science and religion. Many Christian educationists have not made up their minds whether their last word to their pupils is to be " Behold the speech of Pericles," or " Behold the *Élan Vital*," or " Behold the Lamb of God "; or if they are to proclaim the truth of all, how they are to be reconciled.[1]

It goes without saying that what is here said of Christian homes and schools applies with equal force to the training of children in the parish. The parish priest will be missing priceless opportunities unless he is constantly

---

[1] *Cf.* Dr. Streeter's notable attempt to reconcile the scientific, philosophical, aesthetic and religious approaches to Reality in *Reality.*

trying to understand more and more clearly the meaning of vocation, and to foster it in the children and young people committed to his care.

In so far as Christian homes and schools and parishes are combining definiteness and detachment in the sense suggested above, they will be training spiritual listeners, fostering a temper of healthy expectancy, and inevitably also of repentance ; for the sense of the coming of our God evokes the desire to prepare a highway for His coming. In so far as they fail to do this, there is bred in those they train a world-weariness and a slackness of moral fibre only too easily recognisable in every class of society in the West.

The notes incorporated in the first chapter of St. John's Gospel [1] are true to life as a record of the initial stage of Christ's call to His disciples. Through their home life and their schooling, through human influences and outward circumstances, God in His Providence had been making plain to them the direction of their life. They were led to Christ and welcomed as His friends. So in every age the wishes and claims of our parents, books, and friends, natural gifts, incalculable hindrances or opportunities are used by God to bring us where He would have us to be.

But our acceptance of the Providence of God must not close our minds to the more direct ordering of our life which follows. Jesus came into Galilee preaching the gospel of God,[2] and found by the lake shore Simon and Andrew at their work. Following up the acquaintance already made, He gave them a clear and definite call to follow Him, with the promise that He would make them fishers of men. They heard the call, and though they cannot possibly have guessed at all that was involved in it, responded in un-questioning obedience. They were therefore henceforward chosen men, but not yet sent. Jesus promised that if they obeyed He would *make them to become* fishers of men.

Upon this stage of vocation more light is thrown in the records of the ministry and teaching of our Lord. Simon and Andrew and the other disciples were called and chosen. But many are called, and few are chosen. The called are not chosen because when God speaks they do not hear or heed. They either refuse or presume upon the invitation.[3] Some offer before they are called.[4] Their offer is not

[1] John i. 19–51.   [2] Mark i. 14.
[3] Matt. xxii. 1–14.   [4] Luke ix. 57.

refused, but it is not encouraged. Some respond to the call upon conditions.[1] In each case unconditional surrender is demanded.

At this stage something fuller is revealed of God than His benevolent Providence. He is shown exercising an active will and purpose. He desires that His children should be all that they have it in them to become; but there is in Him a deliberate initiative, and a definite, purposeful and unchanging activity in relation to the need of the world, a redemptive plan in which men are called to share, and chosen to share if they will trust themselves utterly to Him. Nothing less than the adventure of offering our lives completely to Him will suffice. Though there are clearly in Scripture calls from God which can only be regarded as special calls, there is nothing to warrant any idea of a demand for whole-hearted self-giving from some and for partial self-giving from others. Utter surrender, as Father Benson of Cowley was never tired of teaching, belongs to ordinary Christianity.[2] And it is surrender to a Person, and not primarily to a task or to a Church. And because it is surrender to a Person, obviously we cannot see at once all that is involved in our response; what we can do is to set ourselves deliberately to conform our lives to that Person's will and purpose.

The third stage is illustrated in the record of the activity of the Apostolic Church commissioned by the Risen Lord in the words : " As the Father hath sent Me, even so send I you." God's sending of His messengers to the uttermost parts of the earth, though it is obviously in order that all men may have the chance of knowing Him, is not primarily geographical but spiritual. The outward mission to every continent and island is sacramental of the universality of His love. The fare to the place to which God sends us may be £60 or it may be 1s. 6d., but it is equally true in either case that we are sent " into all the world." If we are called and chosen, we are always sent, but not always to the place that we expected. The apostles called and chosen were sent by the Risen Christ to their different spheres and missions : James the brother of John to an early martydom ; Thomas, perhaps to missionary work in India ; James, the Lord's brother, to the presidency over the Church in Jerusalem ;

[1] Luke ix. 59–62. [2] See Father Benson's *Letters.*

Peter and Paul to the work of travelling missionaries ; the beloved disciple to that activity which is the fruit of contemplation. So in every age, when the Church is prompted to stir up the gift of the Spirit who indwells her, the divine life flowers out in a rich complexity of manifold vocation. And in every age it is true that the choice of God falls not so often upon those that are " wise after the flesh," but upon the " unlearned " and those of humble birth and simple faith. These are responding generously to God's call to-day, and God forbid that the Church should deny them the opportunity of fulfilling their vocation.

God is at this stage revealed not only as Providence, not only in His purposeful and unchanging activity of redemption, but as at work in relation to particular needs of a particular time in history, as, so to speak, the Director of a great campaign, moving His men now here, now there, with consistent plan but changing tactics.[1] He has called His messengers and chosen them, and after training them He sends them to special spheres of work, and to specialised work within those spheres, to lifelong dedication, as, for example, in ordination, the " religious " life, or marriage, or to changing work in view of changing needs ; some to be vessels of lesser honour, some of greater honour ; some to serve in one part of the vineyard, some in another.

A serious problem will here occur to the reader as to the relation between life in the ordinary spheres of duty and life in the special spheres of apostolic and pastoral activity. In what sense is God's call to one to be a master-mariner or a cowman's wife similar to or different from His call to another to be a priest or a " religious " ?

Popular language tends to confuse us. If we are faithful, God calls and chooses and sends every one of us in precisely the same sense, albeit apparently sometimes with special clearness. Always the call of God is primarily to attachment to Himself. In so far as we respond to Him, He sends us to fulfil His purpose according to the diversity of the gifts with which He has endowed us, in the home, the laboratory, the office, or the sanctuary ; on the land, in teaching, or in art. Variously we are sent to serve the kingdom of God in creative activity, in maintaining and enriching what He has made, and in redeeming

---

[1] *Cf.* Dr. Temple, *Christus Veritas*, pp. 97–101.

it from evil. Some are sent to share generally in His purpose, others in some special part of it. Some special missions in life have attached to them a degree of responsibility which demands special assurance of commission, and special discipline and training, lest pain and loss should occur instead of health and salvation.

Missionary work overseas is one of the special tasks to which God sends His children, subsequently to their response to His call to follow Him whithersoever He goeth. That there are special difficulties associated with such work demanding abundant gifts of patience, endurance, and single-hearted devotion, no one would be foolish enough to deny ; and the willingness to go is in a real sense the acid test of Christian sincerity. But to *every* Christian Christ says, " He that loveth father or mother more than Me is not worthy of Me ; and he that loveth son or daughter more than Me is not worthy of Me. And he that doth not take up his cross daily and follow after Me is not worthy of Me." [1] It will help us to clearer thinking about missionary service if we bear in mind first, that there is no such thing as special sacrifice in Christianity, and consequently, though in a popular sense it may be true, strictly speaking it is erroneous and misleading to speak of missionary work as involving a " call to special sacrifice " ; secondly, that God does not call us to our work ; He calls us to Himself and sends us to our work ; and, thirdly, that God can and does use the lure of a special kind of work to draw us to Himself, and may or may not subsequently send us to that work. Our response to the adventure and romance of missionary service may be one of the means by which God draws us to Himself. When we have committed ourselves to Him, He may send us overseas. If He does not, God forbid that we should either call Him unfaithful or think that our interest in the overseas work of the Church was a mistake, or imagine that it is not He that is sending us to the other work that we undertake.

However partial and inadequate a description that may be of the way in which God calls and chooses and sends us to share in His creative, redemptive and sanctifying purposes, it will be sufficiently clear that though the development of vocation may, like biological development, be both resultant and emergent—both " by slide and by

[1] Matt. x. 37 ; Luke ix. 23.

R

jump "—it is an orderly process in the sense that God reveals Himself progressively, and at each stage demands and invites an appropriate response.

The Testing of Vocation.—Though my vocation is in a real sense, and is felt to be, the intimate concern of God and myself, yet God is all the time fostering and testing the vocation of the individual through human society and circumstances, the doctrine and ordinances and authority of His Body corporate, and the faith and love and insight of its members, to encourage the individual and to challenge him to the act of surrender, to test its genuineness and clarify its meaning. He uses special groups within the Body to encourage and develop and test us in relation to our mission. The architect, the chemist, the navigator, people of all sorts and kinds of trades and professions have groups of experts to encourage and develop and test their ability for their particular work : the medical school and hospital test the doctor and the nurse ; the religious community the postulant ; the theological college the ordinand ; the missionary society, through its committee and its colleges, the missionary. Wherever there seem indications evident and persistent that God means to send us to a particular work, such indications must be tested in the light of our own insight and experience and that of others. And herein we shall be guided by certain considerations.

Positively we can be encouraged to believe in the reality of the guidance as divine according to " the aspect which it presents to unbiassed observers of spiritual mind, . . . and the degree of its persistence under adverse conditions. . . . When such considerations coincide with and confirm the outward guidance of our circumstances, and the inward attraction which we believe to be Divine, we may go forward in the hope that the Lord is with us." [1]

On the other hand we must be on our guard against those popular misunderstandings of the nature of vocation to which reference has already been made, and remember that, if a vocation to missionary work is thwarted, an alternative career is not to be accepted as a *pis aller* or the " mere negative qualification of unfitness for other things," [2] but rather to be embraced as God's plan for us, about which we were previously mistaken ; nor must we

---

[1] Illingworth, " Vocation," in *Cathedral and University Sermons.*
[2] *Ibid.*

forget that vocation is God's call not to a piece of work, but to attachment to Himself, the fruit of which is that a piece of work is given us to do.

It is further to be observed that an offer of service may be made before God's call has come, or after we have been called, but before we have made that response which enables God to choose us. God is drawing us perhaps by means of the attraction which a special kind of work has for us, and we respond to the work before we have responded to Him. It is here that the teaching of psychology about unconscious motives is illuminating. It is a disturbing fact that we may in reality be actuated by motives diametrically opposite from those which we sincerely believe to be our motives : to be acting, for example, from selfish motives precisely at the point where we sincerely think ourselves most altruistic. We are fatally prone to claim as divine persistence what is only the persistent obstinacy of our own desire. Most easily are we deceived by such unconscious motives where the ministry and missionary work are concerned, because these are careers which afford obvious compensations against inferiority, a certain position and importance and publicity, and the opportunity of showing the stuff of which we are made, and because missionary work overseas affords a manner of escape from temptation and the difficulties which lie near home, which not merely covers our defeat but wins approbation from religious people. The desire to become a missionary may be in point of fact the wish to rise up " to flee unto Tarshish from the presence of the Lord." [1]

The teaching of psychology in regard to unconscious motives is sufficiently disquieting to rouse us to deeper self-knowledge and humbler self-scrutiny; but it must be remembered that all human motives are more or less mixed, and that there is a real distinction between an offer (the motive of which is hidden from the candidate) which precedes the call of God, and an offer inspired by a genuine call but obscured by an unusual complication of motive. If the true motive is laid bare in the former case, there can hardly be an impulse to go forward unless and until the true call comes ; in the latter, the knowledge is received with relief and gratitude and godly fear.

[1] Jonah i. 3.

Finally, it is not strictly true to speak either of God calling and the Church sending, or of God calling and the Church testing. The truth is subtler. God calls and chooses and sends, at every point using the authority and encouragement and judgment of His Church. Nor is the whole truth expressed in saying that the Church tests God's call to the individual. The individual also tests for himself, and the Church not only tests but is tested by every call of God to the individual. Just as the Church tested and was tested by God's call to Joan of Arc, so the Candidates' Committee and the Training College test and are tested by every missionary candidate committed to their consideration and care. It is extraordinarily easy for committees and colleges to expect of missionary candidates a standard of spiritual life and discipline which it does not occur to them to apply to themselves. Yet there are not two Christian standards. We can only dare to judge of the reality of acts of self-offering believed to be in response to the call of God in proportion as we are ourselves trying daily to offer all that we have and are.[1]

Training.—It is obvious that the present state of the world makes a demand on those who are called to be missionaries which no one, humanly speaking, can possibly satisfy.

All the difficulties associated with problems of race, caste, and class, with the rise of nationalist movements in all parts of the world, with the new sympathies and antipathies between East and West, make such a demand. And no less far-reaching developments in scientific knowledge, in the comparative study of religion, psychology, anthropology, tropical medicine, and the science of language, make bewildering and clamorous appeal to the missionary student. We cannot ignore new knowledge that has been given to us, for we know that the self that has even in a small degree come to terms with these

[1] There is at present far too little opportunity for young men and women who offer for missionary service to test their vocation. The plan at St. Boniface College, Warminster, and St. Augustine's, Canterbury, by which men become resident members of the College before going to the University, and prepare for matriculation, and then return to College after taking their degree, is undoubtedly valuable ; and the Preparation Unions working under the aegis of the missionary societies for those who aspire to be missionaries are to some extent a testing ground. But more carefully thought-out and correlated plans are obviously required if the need is to be met.

sciences is a richer and a fuller self, and therefore a less unworthy minister and witness than the self which is either ignorant or wilfully neglectful of them.

And yet it is alike impossible and undesirable that the modern missionary should be a walking encyclopaedia in these ever-widening realms of knowledge.

Moreover, the present trend of missionary development is based on the realisation that whatever pioneers in the past were called to do in laying the foundations of civilisation as well as Christianity, to attempt to cover the whole surface of the earth with foreign missionaries is chimerical. Governments are more and more alive to the task of building civilised life; and though missionaries will for many years to come be called upon to take their share in general civilising work, they will increasingly be required to concentrate their energy on the work of training native ministers and witnesses, and in making such experiments in educational, medical and welfare work as governments can watch and assist and develop. For such responsibilities missionaries of outstanding quality and training are needed.

Seen against the background of the modern world-situation, the problem of missionary training presents an acute form of the problem of all modern education; the problem of the adjustment of the study of an enormous and ever-enlarging field of " subjects " to the training of character. At one extreme a hundred subjects might be included in the curriculum of a Missionary Training College; at the other, the whole time and energy of training might be given to the building and discipline of the interior life. As between these two extremes the true rhythm between interior discipline and a large and generous culture and outlook must be found. The former divorced from the latter will induce a forced and narrow intensity; the latter without the former lies open to the disaster of a distracted and dissipated life, busy on its circumference but impoverished at its centre. The missionary must know " how to be in want and how to abound," and a proportionate place must be given in training to each element, so that each is embraced not as antagonistic, but as complementary to the other.

The stages in the training of a missionary correspond with the steps in the development of vocation. Vocation

Colleges nor " Home " Theological Colleges ought to attempt to multiply the subjects of their curriculum, but all the teaching given at all Theological Colleges, not merely those training missionaries for work overseas, needs to be orientated with a view to drawing out, by comparison with other attempts to come to terms with Reality, the essential uniqueness and power of Christianity as the way of salvation for the whole world. This will be done, not by the addition of new subjects of study, but by relating Bible study and the study of Christian doctrine, worship, and ethics to the comparative study of religion, psychology, anthropology, and sociology ; and the history and principles of missions with the New Testament and Church history.

It is only possible briefly to indicate how this may be done by three examples :

(a) The Old Testament can be studied in such a way as to lead to the understanding of the motives, instincts, fears, attitudes, aspirations, which lie at the basis of all religion in its mystical, prophetic and institutional aspects : problems of synthesis, syncretism, adaptation and the like confronted the Hebrews in much the same way as they beset not only the modern missionary, but the thoughtful parish priest at home. The Scriptures are found to serve as the best introduction to a comparative study of religion which will give both a sympathetic understanding in the presentation of the Gospel and a sense of the fullness and uniqueness of the appeal and claim of Christ.

(b) A problem which seems on the surface to be most immediately related to psychology and social anthropology arises in regard to sexual customs. The demand for the enlightenment of all Christian workers both at home and abroad upon this subject is at the present time insistent. Students must be made ready to face and understand the sexual customs and aberrations which will inevitably confront them. They will be able to deal with problems that arise in proportion as their own attitude to sex is healthy. The time of training must test this attitude, and be so devised as to test it ; the observations of the staff, the corporate College life, lectures, and discussions will all contribute to this end. Special lectures dealing exclusively with moral hygiene can do something ; but far more desirable and effective is the discussion of such problems in the light of larger psychological, theological, and missionary principles.

(c) Church history can be presented as the story of the *Gesta Christi per orbem*, and will thus elucidate and clarify the eternal principles whereby He is subduing all things to Himself. Misunderstandings, friction, disillusionment, and the sense of isolation from a familiar heritage too often mar the life of the missionary, and this may be partly due to sheer ignorance and neglect of the story of the growth of the Catholic Church, with its increasing triumphs won out of defeat and disaster. Blessed is the man in whom there is inbred that historic sense which moulds the mind to appreciate great events and to enter into the desires and struggles of other men. The bitterness of present trials is sweetened if he can see them in their true perspective ; the sting of prejudice is drawn as he fights his way through the conflicts of the past. He can draw deep of the wells of ancient achievement and find refreshment for the present. He can find encouragement and inspiration in the lives of confessors, martyrs, and saints.[1]

2. *Training in Capacity to receive.*—The strain of an unfamiliar, and often tropical, climate makes a demand on the self-control of the missionary, on his temper, and on his mental and spiritual energy. The forces of evil in a country where Christ is little known press upon him in their naked strength. There is probably no long heritage of Christian history and experience to support him : often he is deprived, for long periods, of the normal means of grace, and must live in isolation. He has to face continual disappointment, continual criticism, and " a constant sense, if he is a person of imagination, of vast opportunities barely grasped." He must have endurance, a quiet mind, a sense of humour, a genius for friendship, a capacity for enlargement, and that long-heartedness which finds its expression in courteous forbearance.

Grace to live such a life is to be sought and found in a time of withdrawal of the nature of an extended retreat.

The essential inward purpose of missionary training will be identical with that of a retreat—" to be alone with the living God," " to hearken to what He will say concerning us," " to be cleansed by His word abiding in us, that we may bear more fruit."

[1] *Cf.* G. M. Trevelyan, *Clio, a Muse.*

Christ was content to wait in His home in Nazareth until He was over thirty years old before beginning His public ministry. All the silent years He was about His Father's business, training Himself to depend upon the Father's will. After His Baptism He was alone in the wilderness for forty days, fasting, thinking, praying out the principles which were to govern His work on earth. The source and spring of His activity was His constant communion with God.

So missionary training is centred in the College Chapel, in eucharistic worship and oblation, the Divine Office, the daily exercise of prayer and meditation, and self-examination. Only the Vision of God and a lively and increasing sense of what Christ has done and is doing for us can show us and help us to get rid of the sin which so easily besets us, and empower us for service in the Missionary Fellowship, the Mystical Body offered for the life of the world.

III. As the sense of being called and chosen is deepened and clarified, there grows the awareness of being sent. And though we are sent " into all the world," we are sent to a particular sphere of work. For those whose mission is to peoples other than their own, special training becomes necessary, training which involves studies determined by the country and district to which they are sent—the study of a particular language, of the manners and customs obtaining in a particular locality, and possibly some technical knowledge which may include activities as various as stock-breeding, poultry keeping, gardening, building, weaving, dyeing, printing, or some special aspect of educational work such as the teaching of defectives or the blind.

Circumstances will determine how much specialist study can be undertaken before going overseas. But seeing that owing to " the exigencies of the service " very few missionaries know whither they are going until a few months before they sail, and therefore cannot specialise in advance, and that there is obviously much that can only be learnt on the spot, there is value in the suggestion recently made by Dr. Timothy Lew that all missionaries during their first term of service should be called student-missionaries.

Just as the vicar who gives a man his title knows that he is responsible for continuing that man's training, so senior missionaries recognise that much time and thought and sympathy must be expended upon those who have just come out if the splendid qualities of courage and sincerity and the capacity for responsible work inherent in missionary candidates of the present day are to be disciplined and developed.

As training homes for native women workers develop in India, Africa, and the Far East, it will be possible for women missionaries to spend six months or a year living with them, learning the language, and becoming acquainted with the social customs of their district. It is further to be hoped that a first furlough course will be normally required of all missionaries in subjects such as language, anthropology, the comparative study of religion, and such technical subjects as are seen to be necessary.

A single illustration must suffice in order to show how specialised missionary studies may be apportioned, and this shall be drawn from language study.

1. Philology and the comparative study of language have elucidated principles of language structure ; linguistics, a science based on the hypothesis that the human mind tends to work in the same way all the world over,[1] has enunciated principles governing the intellectual approach to language study ; and phonetics, based on the hypothesis that the human vocal organs operate more or less uniformly, is dealing with the physiological aspect.

Such study, together with some work on the grammar of a particular language, may be begun before going overseas.

2. The chief task of acquiring the vernacular of the people among whom the missionary is to work must obviously be undertaken on the field during the first period of service.

3. Further investigation of principles, a corrective course in the vernacular, and work upon the literature, allied languages, and classical languages on which the vernaculars are in some cases based, should ideally be undertaken on first furlough.

It remains to make mention of the training of advanced experts in some particular religion or branch of missionary

---

[1] The difference between the mentality of one race and another is said to be much less significant than the difference in mentality as between individuals, whether belonging to one race or different races.

work. The Canons of St. George's Cathedral, Jerusalem, are all trained specialists of this kind. The S.P.G. has recently provided money for the training of a missionary of experience for the advanced study of Islamics. The future will probably see colleges of such specialists established in different countries.

The Church is awakening to the urgent need of missionary training. It is to be hoped that the subject of preparation for all kinds of Christian ministry will find a foremost place in the prayer and thought of the Home Church, and lead to a richer offering of sacrificial service.

XIII
THE SPIRITUAL LIFE OF THE MISSIONARY (A)
BY MOTHER EDITH, O.M.S.E.

drawn to Him who lived it, and then He said : " If any man would come after Me "—would live on earth the perfect life that the Father wills His true sons to live—" let him deny himself and take up his cross daily and follow Me." How strongly our Lord put the continual self-sacrifice required for living the life of love, when He described it as the daily taking up of the cross, the symbol to a Jew of the most painful, humiliating, and abhorred form of death! But this willing readiness to bear pain and humiliation for love's sake is the first requisite for living the life of the kingdom of heaven ; self-sacrifice is the preliminary, negative side of the new kingdom's one great law—the law of love to God and man.

Even after the kingdom was founded men still needed to have this truth kept vividly before them. So our Lord called for volunteers within His Church, who should be through the ages a visible reminder of that absolutely self-emptying side of His life, which not even the most beautiful Christian family life could represent. He invited those who were " able to receive it " to live unmarried for His sake and the Gospel's ; to join in this Him who emptied Himself wholly that He might give Himself wholly to the doing of the Father's will. They had to be volunteers, for it must be done through pure love alone. Here lies the origin of the Religious Life. Christ called the Religious to be standard-bearers, as it were, to the great host who follow Him by the path of self-denial, the way of the Cross ; and one great effect of their existence in all ages has been to keep before men's consciousness the remembrance of the extremely strong element of self-denial in our Blessed Lord's own life and in all true Christian life. Dr. Gore has said lately : " I believe it to be true that the normal life of Christians, as married people or good citizens, requires for its maintenance on any really Christian level the concurrent witness of actual renunciation—the Religious Life—side by side with it."

To-day, when the study of the science of conduct is interesting so many minds, we are being told, quite apart from religion, as a new discovery of science, that no man can attain a high personal character unless he cultivates certain of the primary instincts at the expense, so to speak, of the rest of them ; and that a highly civilised state of society can only be attained when men are willing to give

up many individual personal advantages for the sake of the
whole body ; while for the whole world to become *morally*
good, willing self-denial on the part of all the human beings
in it would be necessary.

Now that our Lord's teaching of self-denial is being so
strongly reinforced by these discoveries made by man's
own observation and reasoning powers, we may expect men
to look with new interest and understanding at the history
of the Religious Life through the ages. It is a history as
varied as that of the great Church herself, but always one
definite purpose runs through it ; for it is the response of
men of all the centuries and of many races to our Lord's
invitation to come after Him, and learn by denying self
and taking up the cross daily, to share in His life of oblation
for the redemption of the world. Fresh study will surely
lead on to new gallant ventures of faith, for, as Bishop
Westcott said, " it seems impossible to doubt that in the
great types of disciplined life God still shows us by earlier
victories what new blessings He has yet in store for absolute
self-sacrifice." Whenever this ideal of denying self for
the direct purpose of union with Christ in the life that
gives all for love has been raised on high and set before
men, as by the hermits, for instance, St. Francis and
St. Vincent de Paul, and all other leaders in ways of self-
sacrificing love, we know how that spark of divine self-
giving, which is in man because he is created in God's
image, has been kindled into fresh flame, and the noblest
sons and daughters of each generation have responded with
glad hearts to the invitation of the perfect Son of God to
follow Him in giving absolutely all in love to the Father
for the doing of His will.

II

All Christian life is one, for Christian life can be nothing
else than the following of our Blessed Lord. The spiritual
life of a Religious is one with the life of all Christ's followers,
only it is that life lived under simpler conditions and
in a more concentrated form. A great many of Christ's
followers—all the married, for instance, and all owners of
property, and all rulers—have to study our Lord's example
and His teaching, and live by His principles as applied
to an altogether different condition of life ; whereas

S

every teaching of our Lord applies directly and literally to the Religious, since he has taken the Religious vows of Poverty, Chastity, and Obedience in order that all his *time*, all his *desire*, and all his *energy* may be devoted without distraction to the sole object of following our Lord in His devotion to the Father's will.

Just as a Christian father prays feeling himself in a special relation to the Father of whom all fatherhood in heaven and on earth is named, a Christian doctor in a special relation to the Good Physician, and a priest of the Church to the great High-Priest, so the prayer-life of a Religious is largely conditioned by the spiritual relationship to our Blessed Lord, and through Him to the Father and to mankind, into which he enters at his Profession. Religious Profession has always been considered closely parallel to our Blessed Lord's Baptism. Our Lord came to His ministry acknowledged by the Voice from heaven to be God's beloved, His unique Son, the first of the human race wholly devoted to the doing of the Father's will; and after the Temptation in the wilderness, the time of testing motives of action to their root, He was recognised and proclaimed by the herald-prophet as the Lamb of God, which taketh away the sin of the world. He who is called to the Religious Life, after a novitiate spent in tracing out and disciplining under the Counsels the inner springs of all his action, is publicly dedicated in the Church at his Profession to the life of oblation, and places himself in prayer at the feet of the Lamb of God ; with his Lord he says : " Lo, I am come to do Thy will, O my God ; I delight to do it, yea, Thy law is within my heart " ; and he asks to be taken up into His perfect life of self-sacrifice, that taught of Him he may be given the utmost share possible in the thoughts, the prayers, the longings, and the work of the Lamb of God.

As our Lord at His Baptism saw the heavens opened—the eternal verities of Being disclosed—and the Spirit descending to abide upon Him, so the Religious lifts his eyes to greet from afar the revealed end, the day of the marriage of the Lamb. He sees with the eyes of faith redeemed humanity, the great Church of every nation and tongue and people, made ready in the end of the days as a bride adorned for her husband ; when He who loved her and gave Himself up for her, and washed her from her sins

in His own blood, having made her at last free from spot
or wrinkle, all glorious within, will bring her to the Father
as His bride. Then the Church will become in truth spirit
of her Lord's spirit, even as Eve was flesh of Adam's
flesh ; since she is taken into that wholly perfect sharing
of all that is her Bridegroom's, that oneness with Himself
of which marriage is the earthly type ; redeemed humanity
will become in that day wholly Christ's, wholly in Him ;
in God at last, according to her Lord's prayer, even as the
Father is in the Son, and the Son in the Father. This is
that end surely coming, when the Son will deliver up
the kingdom to the Father—the kingdom of Love over all
human wills—and God will be all in all.

This vision of the end (as far as it is for us to know),
and of the purpose of the oblation of the Lamb, fills the
Religious with new realisation of the majesty and love of
God—how sure a salvation we have ; and of the oneness
of all mankind.

What God is in Himself, and the thoughts of God for the
other worlds of His vast universe, lie beyond human thinking. But for this world, one of the least of them all (is
His tender love the more perhaps for its very littleness ?),
the Father's revealed will is that all men should be saved
and come to the knowledge of the truth, and that man
should be made partaker of His own divine nature. He
so loves the world that for this He gave His only begotten
Son. And the Son gave Himself for the redemption of the
whole world ; He has shown us that nothing less than
the finding and saving of His last lost sheep can satisfy
the heart of the Good Shepherd. It is into oneness with
Christ in longing for, and working for, and giving Himself
for the fulfilling of the Father's will by bringing to Him
all humanity to be His true child that the followers of the
Lamb are lifted up.

By the absolute surrender of self, soul and body, for
ever to the will of God, which a Religious makes at his
Profession, he is not only putting into the Father's hands
a tiny oblation which He can use as part of our Lord's self-
oblation for the salvation of the world, but through it he
also becomes himself more wholly than ever before his
heavenly Father's child ; a first-fruit to Him, so to speak,
of those human children wholly His own for whom the
Father's heart has been longing ever since He made the

and perfect the union with Christ, which Christ effects through Holy Communion. His intercessions both public and private are those of one who is united with his Lord in communion, and therefore dares to claim a wonderful fulfilment of His promise : " If ye abide in Me and My words abide in you, ask whatsoever ye will and it shall be done unto you." The difficulties of his work and daily struggle against temptation he will feel as opportunities for the exercise of the strength received in Communion and as signs of the necessity of renewing that strength. He will strive so to " pray without ceasing " that none of his activities may impair the life of communion with his Lord to which he is called ; therefore he makes all arrangements for work in the light of Christ's words, " He that abideth in Me and I in him the same beareth much fruit, for apart from Me ye can do nothing : as the branch cannot bear fruit of itself except it abide in the vine, so neither can ye except ye abide in Me " ; and he never forgets how constant is the temptation to substitute some less important activity for prayer.

Christ's gift of Himself in the Eucharist fills his life with abiding thankfulness and joy, both on account of the present union with his Lord which is thus made possible, and of the hope of the Beatific Vision of which the Eucharistic gift is a pledge ; and this leads to that distinctive feature in the spiritual life of Religious, the recitation of the Divine Office, the renewal of Eucharistic adoration and oblation, at the seven canonical hours of prayer.

" For their sakes I consecrate myself." In the Body of Christ it has always been the function of those dedicated to God under Religious vows to offer to God this sacrifice of praise on behalf of and as representatives of the whole Church. For Religious the bell for an Office means ideally that the hour of oblation has come, the Altar is ready, the angel has taken his censer, and the Church in heaven and on earth waits for them to fulfil their ministry of upraising to God from on earth the song of the Bride, rejoicing in the perfections of her heavenly Bridegroom, whose law is her delight, whose statutes are her songs in the house of her pilgrimage, and whose testimonies are the very joy of her heart.

This way of prayer is a sacrificial act, an act of homage

to God. It does not depend on the *feelings* of the Religious at the time, for by quiet resolute persistence in making the oblation in the midst of all difficulties he pays even more honour to God than if he found such service always easy ; it is an oblation made by his will. St. Benedict calls saying the Office " our divine duty," " the work of God," and he puts it between self-discipline and labour as one of the three chief things to be learnt in the monastery regarded as " a school of the service of God," a pre-eminent means of training men's souls for God. For adoration is the final and eternal form of prayer ; the one prayer of heaven, where God is seen as He is, and everything in His temple saith " Glory."

In making this oblation of adoration as representatives of the whole Church on earth—for all whose work leaves them little time for formal prayer, as well as for the many who do not yet give worship its proper place in their spiritual life—Religious in the mission field have the glad privilege of offering it specially " in advance," as it were, for all the heathen around them, who do not yet know God their Father.

This sacrificial life of adoration is sustained by another distinctive feature of the Religious Life, its times of silence.

No one can study the record of our Lord's life on earth without being deeply conscious that it has two sides : on the one hand, His life of love to men as He went about among them doing good, accessible to all, seeing with eyes of sympathy all their need and supplying it, giving them, as it were, all His attention. Yet on the other side His life was entirely given to God, in devotion to and dependence on the Father, without whom the Son could do nothing, for His very meat, what He lived by, was to do the Father's will. His short ministry not only began with the long withdrawal into the wilderness, but there were nights of special prayer, times alone, and the going out from the city into silence by night after teaching by day, in order to wait upon God and be sure of the Father's will, so that He might in all things follow that, and not His own human will.

And so the Religious, who want to share completely in their Lord's life of oblation, and carry on His work on earth in His own way, make careful provision for such silence in their lives. Besides Retreats and special days of quite different kind; it is the grateful, adoring love of one who receives; not, like His, the love of one who gives. Only in earnestly striving to use the life given us in communion for loving our brethren can we really learn, not merely in theory but—what is a very different thing—by practice, to love as God loves, with love that gives and forgives, bears and forbears. In constant effort to love others in this way with protecting self-sacrificing love, like parental love, whatever their conduct towards us may be, we grow like our Father, and really begin to live His life, loving in the *same way* that He loves. And in doing this we gain wonderful new insight into His character, and a new understanding of all He is doing for us His children, so that our love for God Himself is at the same time profoundly deepened.

Our Lord invites the Religious, taken up into His own life of oblation, to learn to share His mind and think His thoughts, especially through the discipline of the three vows.

He who though He was rich yet for our sakes became poor, that we through His poverty might become rich, invites the Religious to share His own poverty of spirit by having a mind entirely free from desire for, or endeavour to get or keep for self, wealth, comforts, possessions, or any other earthly good; not even spiritual privileges are to be grasped for self, but used for others' good. This is a condition of utmost freedom, for in it God's child lives in such joyous, trustful dependence on his Father that he is truly free to seek first God's kingdom and His righteousness, and to give the whole of his time and thought to the fulfilling of his Father's will. Pouring himself out for others, he lives as poor yet making many rich, as having nothing and yet possessing all things.

And Christ invites the Religious to follow Him in the unmarried state, not that they may love less, but that their hearts may be so wholly given to Himself that they may be able to love with His love all with whom He brings them into relation. Above all, He longs to bring them with and in Himself to centre their whole desire on the Father and the doing of His will. In her Lord the soul is to learn to say, " Whom have I in heaven but Thee; and there is none upon earth that I desire in comparison of Thee; my heart and my flesh rejoice in the living God." It is thus " in

Christ " that the Religious says the Divine Office, using in the Psalms the very words of prayer that Christ Himself used on earth.

And Christ became obedient even as far as death.   The obedient-mindedness which the Son of God learnt and manifested under the conditions of earthly life was a spirit in which love, humility, and obedience were woven into one.   He practised self-surrender in a hidden lowly life till nothing could be asked of Him or taken from Him that He would not willingly give.   It is under this yoke that He invites the Religious to come and learn at His side to be meek and lowly of heart like Himself; ready and desirous to do the will of others rather than their own ; obedient from the heart as unto God and not unto men. Here, close to the side of Him who " pleased not Himself " they shall indeed find rest unto their souls, having every thought brought into captivity to the obedience of Christ.

III

But the Religious is not only an individual who has made over himself, his soul and body, to his Lord for ever ; he also became at his Profession a member of an organised community, which aims at upholding the primitive ideal of the Catholic Church, of which it is written :   " The multitude of them that believed were of one heart and soul : and not one of them said that aught of the things he possessed was his own ; but they had all things common."   Religious therefore consider their Lord's new command and all the exhortations in the New Testament to brotherly love, as having a direct and special reference to them as members of their community ; so that the love for one another to which they attain becomes to them a direct proof that their Lord abides in them and they in Him.   In every prayer the Religious prays and every work he does, he prays and works and lives as a member of a body, with the strength of the whole body supporting him ; for they are all like-minded, joined together by Christ to be one body in love, with all their powers directed to a common end ; and this unity of love fills them with thankfulness and great joy, for it is a foretaste of the perfected joy of the communion of saints.

The Religious in the mission field realises most

poignantly how integral and vital a part of his Lord's kingdom is this corporate unity in Him. His Lord knit together His first disciples in a Body which was to manifest to the world the new life of love, and said, " By this shall all men know that ye are My disciples, if ye have love one to another " ; and as long as those looking at the Christian community could say, " See how these Christians love one another," multitudes were added to the Church, drawn in by the attractive power of a body living the life of divine love. But how painfully different is the situation now. The witness of Christian *corporate* life has been almost lost ever since the nominal conversion of the Roman Empire filled the Church with thousands upon thousands, Christian only in name, all but submerging Christianity by their vast numbers, just as a cup of yeast is swallowed up by a mass of dough. There was no means of reorganising the great empire and all its laws by the rule of Christ's teaching ; civil government went on still being ordered by merely earthly wisdom ; for the law of love cannot be enforced from outside, it can only work gradually from within, changing men's hearts. So war, slavery, lawsuits, vindictive punishment, and all the tyrannies of class separa-tion passed on into the new composite society as part of the established social order ; and " Gentile " ideas of lordship and authority, which our Blessed Lord had so clearly pointed out as the opposite of His own, had an immensely strong reflex influence—stronger than men yet realise—on the organisation and life of the Church itself, leading to division after division ever since.

But Christ has never left Himself without the witness of smaller bodies within the Church living by His prin-ciples, as well as that of the countless Christians who have been His true disciples individually. It was just at the time of the conversion of the empire that Religious Life *in communities* began, for Christ had a new *corporate* work for the Religious to do.

The outward unity of the Church is broken, and cannot be regained till she is renewed in her Lord's own humility and love ; and there has never yet been a nation wholly Christian, taking Christ's laws as the basis of its *corporate* life. But the leaven is at work within the mass. Already the law of love working from within has undermined slavery, and is fast sweeping away vindictive punishment ;

and in the hearts of Christ's people all over the world a longing desire for unity in Christ is growing—a unity that can only be won by a new corporate denying of self, and taking up the cross daily.   Two thousand years are but as yesterday and to-day in the working out of the plans of eternal God.   The Church has not yet nearly attained her full stature.   What may not happen when God's gifts to the East of spirituality and courtesy, and to Africa of the child-like heart, are brought into the Church ?   Can we not imagine some as yet unwon nation turning to Christ with its whole heart, and reinterpreting the Gospel to the world by living *as a community* the divine life of humility and love—willing to love with that greatest love which will lead it *as a body* to lay down its life in martyrdom that others, catching from it the light of truth, may live ? " The blood of the martyrs is the seed of the Church." The way of Christ's true followers in this world can be none other than " the Royal Way of the Holy Cross." The Church's pioneers must be leaders in self-sacrifice. In the mission field the witness to Christ of the life of a Religious Community counts far above the sum-total of the witness of the lives of its individual members.

XIV

THE SPIRITUAL LIFE OF THE MISSIONARY (B)

BY CECIL BOUTFLOWER, BISHOP OF
SOUTHAMPTON

SYNOPSIS

The subject of the essay is the spiritual life as lived under the distinctive conditions of the missionary calling.

Privations and self-sustenance.
  The need of acquiring and maintaining the habit of meditation.

Dangers to self-discipline.
  The need of resilience.
  Temptation to regard initial sacrifice as compounding for [sub-sequent slackness.

Danger to evangelistic hope.'
  The need of zeal to win souls, and of the expectation of conversions, unbaffled by absence of response.

Need of personal experience, supported by Catholic system.

Dangers to faith.
  Amid pressure of non-Christian atmospheres the missionary lives on the prayers of the Church.

Danger of self-importance.
  The missionary *is* an important person, and often possesses much independence of character. Special grace is needed for team-work.

Need of a Catholicism that can face facts.

Need to cultivate spiritual fellowship.

Need of the Communion of Saints.

Need of inward joy.

THE SPIRITUAL LIFE OF THE MISSIONARY (B)

THE spiritual life of the missionary, his life in Christ, is one with that of the ordinary private Christian, lived by the same grace and subject to the same laws, and the truths concerning it that matter most are common to both. The health of the tea-planter in the East is not different in kind from that of his brother in the London office, but in the conditions under which it has to be maintained and the particular work for which it has to fit him. The subject of this essay then is *the spiritual life as lived under conditions of the missionary calling,* and its proper business to discuss the *differentia* only, not the more vital things which are common ground. But those distinctive conditions vary so greatly with land, climate, and circumstances in which that life is lived, and again with the particular work, evangelistic, educational, or medical, and again with the location, isolated or community-shared,[1] that it is not easy to select characteristics true of all. Such selection would be better reached by a symposium. The points that follow are those that have struck the present writer.

Privations and Self-sustenance.—Privation in some spiritual privileges normal at home is, in varying degree, the lot of most missionaries ; in many instances it is extreme. Ability to meet it varies exceedingly with temperament and training. Some are by nature sensitive to surroundings. They feel keenly the absence of the uplift of art, music, and architecture, or of social sympathy in worship. And others have so concentrated their devotion and experiences round the sacrament of the Altar, that nothing but the special grace of God can make up to them for the loss of the old opportunities. Others by temperament or habit are more independent. They have

[1] The spiritual life of the missionary under conditions of Religious Order or Community Rule is dealt with in the preceding essay.

T

never made much use of churches for private purposes, or of priests for spiritual direction. They thrive well in silence and solitude. By upbringing they pray at their own bedside, and ask only that nothing shall rob them of their morning hour with God. Some seem little dependent even on books, beyond their own Bible; and, though perhaps a little underfed mentally, they bear no marks of spiritual starvation. Certainly these latter will be spared much of what others would suffer in many posts of solitary service. An isolated Englishwoman, perchance, in heathen surroundings, with a sacrament once in six weeks, but seemingly robust and cheery on these minimum means of grace, and withal saving souls—this is a brave sight to find; and the visiting priest or bishop, coming from his own central privileges of intercourse and frequent cele-brations, may return humbled and filled with admiration for the grace of God.

It is surely to be desired that the missionary's prepara-tion should take some account of all this, and that what-ever generous provision in spiritual things may for other reasons be profitable in the course of training, he (or she) should be drilled and inured to the grace and habits of self-sustenance in private prayer, and in the cultivated practice of meditation and spiritual communion.

And here may the opinion be added that, when all is said for commentaries, the reader of the New Testament who can really read it in Greek is at a lasting advantage; and therefore for one who, with a good education, is to be so largely dependent on Scripture study and meditation for spiritual growth, some mastery of Greek is peculiarly worth while. Bishop Westcott, father and sender of missionaries, meant something serious when he said, with half a smile, that the whole Gospel may be found in the Greek aorist and the preposition ἐv.

Next to the Book, the lonely or mentally isolated missionary specially owes it to himself to commune with other books helpful to the spiritual life; and home friends specially owe it to him (or her) to supply them.

Dangers to Self-discipline.—These dangers arise from causes without and within. The missionary life is plainly to be lived in unfamiliar and uncertain conditions. Unless it happens to be lived at some fixed spot and under community rule, it is almost certain to be irregular of necessity ; and the worker who is tied by the oppressions of time and inelastic programmes is likely to be not only a trial to fellow-workers, but in the eyes of the timeless East a phenomenon alien to all that they associate with religion and sainthood. Holy men do not have watches. They sit for days, we are told, under a tree, till someone asks them their message. At any rate Nicodemus' visits do not fit into time-tables, and interviews ending in Baptism are missed if Gospel messengers have not time to stroll on desert roads, or if chariots cannot afford to stop. For some of us it demands real vexatious effort to break down our self-centred adherence to acquired rules of life, and our Western impatience with unpunctuality and waste of time. Then in such conditions may come danger to the whole structure of necessary and possible self-discipline. Because we often perforce *cannot* be regular or punctual, we cease to be so where we could. The untempered steel that cannot yield or bend breaks altogether, and there is no restraint left. That spirit of discipline is most precious which can be trusted because it is resilient—faithful in the cramped privacy on board ship or in the noisy inn, as in the quiet rest-house or the church compound. This too should find place for practice in the days of training, and the institution ruled by bells and time-tables is not a sufficient practising ground.

More subtle yet is the danger from within. The missionary may be tempted to regard his initial vocation as in some sort compounding for relaxations of self-discipline in other directions, and may without noticing it go very far. Initial sacrifice there is for most missionaries ; to some it is an ever-present sacrifice, though for the joy that God gives and the deep interest of the work itself, compared with the dreary or superficial pre-occupations of much church work at home, they may resent reference to it as " sacrifice." But this will not debar Satan from suggesting to the soul, almost unconsciously, that the self-offering once made is, if not an atonement for lapses, at least a palliative, or a ground for some indulgences of indiscipline. Against such deadly form of spiritual pride may God steel and defend His missionary servants in their high and perilous calling, as those on whom so much depends, and who remember that the whole burnt-offering must be " without blemish."

Danger to Evangelistic Hope.—The primary hope and purpose of the missionary, of whatever department, is the conversion of men : in St. Paul's language " to open their eyes, to turn them from darkness to light, and from the power of Satan unto God." It should be needless to state this, since it might be assumed that the same hope and purpose will be a large part of the life of any man having cure of souls, the majority of whose flock are not so " turned " or practising any religion whatever. But in a land which is in some vague and traditional sense Christian it is strangely possible for the missionary side of God's " messengers, stewards, and watchmen " to drop out of sight, and that aspect of ministry and the expectation of conversions to be left to the witness of the Salvation Army and the like. There are parishes where seen duties are not neglected, where services are frequent, but where, so to speak, nothing fresh happens. At Confirmation time there are no adult converts, no spiritual histories, though there are plenty of practical heathen all round the church. And the parish priest does not appear to his friend or his bishop to be worried or depressed about it. He is not, as far as one can judge, expecting or working for these things. If in a town parish, he has possibly joined the new school that would rather wait in a vestry to counsel the faithful than go round houses and dockyards after lost sheep. Or perhaps, unsparing of himself, he is seeking by a perpetual galvanism of guilds and personal stimulus to supply the absence of Life from on high, to keep the clock hands moving without the spring. He is too busy to fret if there are no fresh conversions. But not so the missionary. If his gospel is not winning fresh hearts, his occupation is gone. He was not sent to play the settled pastor to ready-made native congregations, even if these exist ; it is not normal or desirable that he should do so. He may profitably be much occupied in teaching and inspiring his native catechists and priests, but if they are failing to win souls, the disappointment is his still at second hand. Yet such experiences of seemingly barren labour over long periods are the lot of the missionary in most lands. Henry Martyn was not the first nor the last who has died without seeing a single convert. " In the three years since we came here," writes one from Africa, " we have found no sign that we were wanted. The soil and climate give them all they need with little trouble. They have few wants. In the South London parish that we left poverty and suffering did at least keep a sort of door open for the messages of the Gospel." Or, by contrast, from one of the districts of India where "most have less than enough to eat," another quotes the remark, "Tell us how to get rice and we will listen. For your other good news we have no hunger. Give up the folly of trying to feed men who are not hungry." The spiritual life which is to face such experiences needs to be sure of its Lord and its mission. In one of his greatest sermons Phillips Brooks discusses St. Paul's vision of the Man of Macedonia. When, in response to the call to come over, St. Paul landed on the quay at Neapolis, there was no Man of Macedonia to greet him; nothing either there or at Philippi to match or justify the vision. Very far from it; not even a synagogue to give him the usual opening; and before long he and Silas found themselves in gaol. What, then, did it all mean? Was the vision a delusion? No, the Man of Macedonia was a reality; but he represented Macedonia's need, not as Macedonia felt it, but as God saw it. The missionary who is nearest to His Lord, who abiding in Him has, in St. Paul's words, "the mind of Christ," will best see and hear the call of mankind's need as God sees and hears it, unbaffled by absence of response; able, if only he is sure God has sent him, to wait in prayer and hope unfading for God's time. There will be a Church of Philippi one day, and its Epistle may prove the happiest reading of all.

Need of Personal Experience, supported by Catholic System.—The last section has assumed that the hope and purpose of the missionary is to convert the hearts and wills of men—*i.e.* to "open their eyes, to turn them from darkness to light." Perhaps the assumption has been made too easily. There are workers to be met with, even in the mission field, who seem too little qualified for that primary work. They might serve usefully in a settled parish at home. They are faithful in what they know. They gladly instruct those who will learn. They help to organise the Church. But they do not make converts, and they seem to have no definite idea of doing it. They do not grapple with men's wills, or lead them to decision, to the great change, the illumination from on high. They do not

" turn men from darkness to light." " Illumination," an opening of eyes from darkness to light, in a non-Christian environment the reality is plainer to see. Such illumination and conversion is the work and prerogative of the Holy Spirit, but so far as human agents are concerned in it, it is generally effected only by means of those who have some living and first-hand experience of their message to offer, in however humble a degree. Otherwise they may serve faithfully in some sides of the priestly and lay Christian life, and not without some witness in the consistency of their lives to our great Redeemer ; but they can hardly be direct missionaries either abroad or at home, because they have no clear message, based on experience, of the transforming light and grace of God. They have only the Church's gospel to give at second hand. They cannot with the Samaritans say to the " woman " the *Ecclesia docens* : " Now we believe, not because of thy word : for we have heard Him ourselves and know that this is the Saviour of the world." How much of this God meant for us all He best knows, but for the missionary some portion of it is needful to his equipment. Only out of this abundance of the heart doth the mouth speak. Often we are rebuked by the zealous spirit of propaganda in the ranks of Spiritualism and " Christian Science." It is natural. These cults, however fantastic or unworthy in their matter, appeal to experience, real or supposed : and the experience makes the missionary. We may settle it with ourselves that the Church which neglects the personal and mystical side of religion will always be lame in missionary propaganda. And not for his own fruition but for the sake of his work and message the missionary may well pray for his portion of the first-hand knowledge of Christ and the power of His resurrection.

But this first-hand experience or realisation of things unseen is not the whole or the staple of Christian life for the individual, in most instances, or for the community. It needs behind it the stability of the Catholic system. That system may be compared to a mighty viaduct, resting indeed on the foundation of experience, from Pentecost to this hour—experiences regenerative, illuminative, eucharistic ; yet an organic structure, which like the spiritual lives of most of us only touches that foundation at certain points, in the experience of its apostles and prophets and its faithful in all ages.   For the individual, and indeed for the Church, there are periods, even long intervals, when vivid experience of things unseen and the powers of the world to come are in abeyance, when prophets are scarce and visibility low in spiritual matters.   (Let none suppose that the missionary, cut off as he is from many corporate and tangible supports, is by special grace spared this trial.)   And then it is that the system comes in to save and carry over, in fixed creed and sacrament and trained habit, the life of the community or of the individual Churchman in one continuous process.   We are not left at the mercy of our fitful moods or herd instincts, or flickering spiritual experiences.   Feverishly to claim and affect these at moments when they are not ours breeds a terrible unreality.   But behind us in our dullest hours is the truth of the Catholic gospel, the communal experience in which we have part, though for the moment realisation fails us.   Blessed be God for the One Life of His Church, wherein our own littleness, the dimness and fickleness of our experience is swallowed up and borne over in the embracing unity of the Body of Christ, of that enduring spiritual structure whose builder and maker is God.   Such truths may seem too general to be proper to this essay, but it is the solitary missionary, thrown in on himself, who has most need to live in the light of them.

Dangers to Faith.—It is not only hope that may suffer, as has been said above, when the power of the gospel fails to be evident ; there is actual danger to personal faith. It is natural to think that when once the surrender is made and we have forsaken all for the gospel's sake we shall surely find our reward at least in a certainty of faith we never knew at home.   And so it has sometimes been, but not always.   Was it that even in our self-offering we were seeking our own spiritual peace and advantage, not simply " losing " ourselves for the gospel's sake ?   Anyhow, no such compensating assurance may be granted ; and this comes as a disappointment to faith which has so much that is hard and strange to try it.   Workers in lands where heathenism is grosser and more degraded speak of the oppressive sense of almost physically breathing its atmosphere.   Satan seems near and real, and they feel even their prayer-life choked by it.   Others, sent to lands like Japan, where what remains of heathenism is picturesque

Living growth and development must needs sweep away the elementary moulds or the scaffolding that served for a beginning, and new exigencies may hasten their removal. The little church we built with our own hands, the system we inaugurated that worked so well, the Western liturgy we laboured to translate, all are outgrown or must give way, sooner perhaps than we are willing to believe. We can but build the best we know ; but the wisest missionary knows not what God may be shaping. That nothing shall be lost we may rest assured, but it is hard to yield up what we have so carefully constructed, to be scrapped and cast into His melting-pot, and be left with nothing of our own making to rejoice in. Yet this is the law of fruitfulness, the corn of wheat that dies ; and herein the worker's baptismal death unto self is most deeply searched.

Need of a Catholicism that can Face Facts.—The first thing to strike the missionary who has not previously travelled much is how very provincial and abnormal is that historic Church of England in which he has been bred ; and further, though by virtue of the world-wide Empire it is far spread, how small as yet is its communion, and the acceptance of its theory as an expression of Catholicism, outside those bounds. He may be convinced that an adaptable and nationalised Catholicism is the way of reason and that which holds the surest missionary promise for mankind ; but as yet this is matter of faith, and as he travels the globe the uncompromising anti-national Catholicism of Rome seems to dwarf the missionary successes, as well as the sacrifices, of his own communion. And the next thing that dawns on him outside Europe— he is aware of it already if he belongs to the American continent—is how fractional is the contribution of all forms of non-Roman Catholicism in the sum-total of missionary effort and fruit to-day. He will do well to think out his particular faith in relation to these facts before he has to meet them, and those who train him, especially in English surroundings, should help him to do so. Certainly he will not best equip himself if he lives in a circle of purring symphonies. His theological shelf should not show only the works of Anglican divines. In a calling where readiness to learn is peculiarly a need of the man who hopes to teach, he is ill-fitted for his adventure if he thinks all things settled and clear, or if he holds his faith after the manner of some of the penny booklets that adorn church book-tables. Attempts to give the Catholic Faith in a nutshell do not as a rule correspond to the vastness and complexity of truth that life in the open reveals. It is of course possible for him to find his mission among a simple people, where the ground is undisputed by other presentations of the gospel, and unvexed for the present by the problems of Christian disunion. If so, and finding his own gospel not without power, he may be undisturbed in his tenets and happy without questionings. But such a position is precarious. And if, as is probable, his experience is otherwise, and he endeavours for sake of faithfulness to his particular religion to ignore all conflicting phenomena, the sacrifice of intellectual candour to loyalty cannot be made without affecting his spiritual life. The God of Truth does not call him to muddle a second- or third-class brain by reading metaphysical theology or higher criticism that he is not learned enough to weigh for himself, but He does call him to face and weigh all the facts of personal experience. He is bound to relate what he holds to the actual ways in which he observes God to work. Reserve in communicating religious instruction is a recognised principle of wisdom in the mission field, but reserve in our own thinking, the spirit of fearfulness in facing all observed truth and following its conclusions, is a condition perilous to the spiritual eye. Only this teachableness must include *all* available resources. One to whom, with no knowledge of Church history and the past, " observed truths " include only those within the limits of his own gaze, or of one generation or century, is in no position to think truly, or to appraise his own Catholic religion in relation to variations from it that for the time may seem equally efficient.

Need to Cultivate Spiritual Fellowship.—The missionary's opportunities of spiritual intercourse with fellow-workers (as distinct from his own flock and disciples) are limited, and in some cases rare. It does not follow that he will always naturally use those he has. To do so may require effort. Some who cross his path are with him workers in the name of Christ, but under another banner, and may have little Christian faith in common with him beyond devotion to the same Lord and the souls He died for. Others may be actually mates in a common work, but mates of whose ways he does not wholly approve. In either case they may be the last persons he would choose as private friends, trying to his temperament, or dull or unsympathetic. The saints have not always been pleasant company. On the other hand, his own nature may be reserved, and slow to speak of sacred things save to a few intimates. The loss to joint work when the atmosphere of spiritual fellowship is cold is not our business here, but the loss to spiritual life—one's own, and possibly still more the other man's—of yielding to this reserve is real. That when chances of joint prayer are scarce, two of Christ's workers should meet, possibly spend a day or night together, and part without any such prayer, or speech together of our Blessed Lord and of His Word, betokens something spiritually wrong on one side or both. It is probable that a sufficient outpouring of the divine love and joy in the Lord—those two first " fruits of the Spirit " —would break through barriers. Certainly we do well, by any effort, to cultivate and keep the atmosphere of united prayer. It is so doubtful if talking over the work will do us or it any good : it is so certain that the prayer of two agreed in the Name will.

This same reserve, if yielded to, on the part of an already isolated worker, may issue in his dropping the use of confession or spiritual counsel that he has found good for his soul's health, and neglecting to share the retreats and conferences where his presence helps others as well as himself. He is ceasing to live healthily in the Body of Christ. Happily this unsocial tendency is exceptional.

Need of the Communion of Saints.—That the Communion of Saints must mean more to one cut off from kith and kin and the stimulating intercourse of teachers at home, is too obvious to dwell on. How much it may mean is partly a matter of spiritual temperament. To some quite simple souls the company of the unseen is wonderfully real and satisfying. But partly also it depends on cultivation, on our resolute seeking to live as conscious members of the One Life of the Head, knit in that one Life to all His other members on this side the veil and that. *Oceano divisi, Eucharistia conjuncti*, is almost too trite a motto to write to a missionary friend now. It has only become so because it is proved so precious a truth. Whatever be the case at home, it is not often that the missionary afield can find his satisfaction in the *visible* fellowship of his communions. And the same faith that bridges distance bridges the barriers of the life beyond.

> Christ of the wayside altar,
>   Lord of the two or three,
> Praise for the great Communion
>   That knits Thy saints to Thee !
>
> All that have loved and suffered,
>   All that have known the fight,
> All that have served unseeing
>   And entered into light,
>
> Lit with th' eternal rapture
>   Are here about our ways,
> Smite through our sunless worship,
>   Shout in our Feast of praise.

It is the isolated missionary who needs and best knows this comfortable truth.

But he needs the Communion of Saints for more than his own comfort. He needs it to help guard his self-respect and stir his zeal. There is singularly little that we can affirm with scriptural confidence about the departed in relation to ourselves, beyond the truths which flow from the faith that they and we are " in Christ." But one thing we may surely infer from the language of Heb. xii. 1—that somehow *they watch us* [1] ; and in the context that thought is used as a stimulus to enduring effort. To be removed from the observation of one's peers and fellows proves a temptation to the missionary, as well as to the planter " east of Suez," in unexpected ways. In the small things of self-respect, in the matter of clothes, it is easy for men or women who would never be untidy or ill-dressed among their own people, to become indifferent when, in a country station, no eye capable of criticism will ever see them from one month's end to another. But the same holds good in much graver ways, and it is a help to live as " watched," in the high company that by our heavenly birthright we belong to. For, while the Christian would desire to be so absorbed in the vision of his Lord that no eye, no presence

---

[1] The *word* " witnesses " (μάρτυρες) does not imply " spectators," but the figure (of the amphitheatre) does. (*Cp.* Westcott's note on Heb. xii. 1.)

but His should matter, the presence and the gaze of his fellow-men does in fact prove an added check or stimulus when he has it ; and in its absence the encompassing " cloud of witnesses " may truly uphold his ways.

[Here may a postscript to general readers be pardoned ? Do those who write (or might write) to missionaries know how much their letters contribute (or might contribute) to this sense of being " watched " in Christ's contest ? The mere getting of them counts for something valuable, even when no direct word is said beyond home news and kindly interest. But—

> When Christmas-kindled fancies glow,
> Faces and hearth-light far away,
> Remember, and give thanks to know
> What high behest thy feet obey :

—when the Christmas mail comes in, will it contain any simple word to suggest that inspiration ? that hearts are " watching the match " and congratulate the (possibly tired) player ? The writer of such a word can little guess how far it may go to rekindle courage and the sense of mission.]

Need of Inward Joy.—This must be the last word, and it is soon said. Joy, like sunlight to their bodily well-being, is good for the spiritual health of all. And joy—not faith or hope—is the second-named " fruit of the Spirit." Joy is not naturally a very stable and portable virtue. More than most graces it is likely to be affected by the external accidents of life—climate, for instance—and to these accidents the missionary is a specially exposed person. Yet the loss of joy is hurtful not only to the loser. It is apt to be reflected—though, please God, we will never knowingly let it be so—in our missionary letters home ; and that chills and disappoints friends who vaguely but rightly believe that missionaries are generally happy people —happy by reason of their work, and by God's special grace given to them. That belief is a bit of their own faith, and we are ashamed of ourselves if we weaken it. And loss of joy, if concealed in our letters, will certainly leak out in our intercourse with fellow-workers and at the conference table, and do as much harm as loss of heart in the councils of the battle-field. But even more simply and immediately has the missionary need of inward joy just because his work *is* missionary, and no advertisement of anything worth having in this world or the next is so potent as joy in its possessors and confident gladness in its heralds. The Salvation Army officials are nothing if not advertisers of their gospel. No testimony to them is commoner among the poor than that they "looked so happy." In some degree every propagandist in Christ's name may covet that passport. In full view of the Cross and in face of tragedy and the work of sin, the prerogative of inward joy may remain.

But if the missionary's need of this is special, his resource is none other than that of us all. For him, as for us, joy must be inward, that it may be immune from changing circumstances and outward conditions. Yet no mere temperamental joy or natural good spirits, however useful, will suffice. Spiritual joy is objective, created by and centred on an Object unchangeable and divine. It is "joy in the Lord," the joy of possession and privilege, of benediction and adoration. But in a different and deeper sense yet, spiritual joy is "in the Lord," because it is St. Paul's "joy in the Holy Ghost"; not ultimately *our* joy at all, but Christ's imparted; not a joy *like Christ's*, but His own absolute Joy derived to His members abiding in Him: "That My joy may remain in you, and that your joy may be full." In this, as indeed in every respect, the spiritual life of the missionary is his life "in Christ." This, first and last, is his Catholic religion, the Faith of the Incarnation.

XV

THE RELIGIOUS COMMUNITY AS A MISSIONARY INSTRUMENT

BY REGINALD TRIBE, DIRECTOR, S.S.M.

U

SYNOPSIS

I. THE HISTORIC RELIGIOUS COMMUNITIES AND THEIR AIMS.

II. ANGLICAN COMMUNITIES TO-DAY ARE HANDMAIDS TO OTHER MISSIONARY BODIES RATHER THAN MISSIONARY BODIES THEMSELVES.

    (a) They are different in this respect from the communities of the Roman Church.

    (b) Anglican communities largely in experimental stage.

    (c) Some modern communal experiments.

III. THE MAIN OBJECT OF THE CHURCH'S WORK IN THE MISSION FIELD IS TO FOUND NATIVE DAUGHTER CHURCHES, AND TO CREATE CHRISTIAN NATIONS.

    Hence it must be a primary aim of missionary work to create—

        (a) A native ministry.

        (b) Schools.

        (c) Centres of intensive Christian thinking and action.

        (d) Centres for the creation and diffusion of Christian literature in the vernacular.

IV. THE BEARING OF THESE AIMS UPON THE COMMUNITY AS A MISSIONARY INSTRUMENT.

    (a) The value of team-work in evangelisation.

    (b) Institutional work best done by members of a community.

    (c) Communities have advantages in experience continuity, and

    (d) Recruitment.

    (e) Special communities existing for missionary work only.

    (f) Dangers and difficulties attending community work.

    (g) The vicariate apostolic of the Roman Church as a means of overcoming them.

    (h) The development of the Religious Life in daughter churches.

V. EXISTING COMMUNITY WORK OF THE ANGLICAN CHURCH IN THE MISSION FIELD.

    (a) The men's communities.

    (b) The sisterhoods.

VI. THE INWARD MEANING AND WORK OF THE RELIGIOUS LIFE.

THE RELIGIOUS COMMUNITY AS A MISSIONARY INSTRUMENT

I

AT the outset it is necessary to get clear a difference in type and object in the historic religious communities. The purpose of the old Orders that grew up in Western Christendom during the Dark Ages and the Early Mediaeval Period was primarily withdraw ıl from a turbulent world for peace and prayer. Their common life lay within the cloister, and their organisation was based upon this fact. Such an object and such an organisation tended naturally to make the religious house a large self-contained unit. It is the great abbeys that are typical of this period.

A day equally divided into prayer, self-supporting work, and sleep was the Benedictine plan. But prayer was the special *Opus Dei*. As the monasteries grew to be financially independent of their labour and the world grew more secure, at the end of the Dark Ages they began to take on other social services and religious works. Thus it was that they became the schools and hospitals, alms-houses and art schools of the Middle Ages. Indirectly, these intensive centres of Christian culture played a big part in the evangelisation of Europe. They had originally been planted down in the uninhabited hills, but there soon grew up round them villages, and even towns, which were naturally favourable centres of evangelisation. Directly the Benedictines were also actual missionaries and pioneers. Indeed, it is to a Benedictine Mission and Settlement that the Anglo-Saxon race owes Augustine and Paulinus, and Scandinavia practically owes its Christianity.

With the coming of the later Middle Ages and the Renaissance Period new types of communities came into being. The mission of the Franciscan was to the outside world, especially to the poor. Later on, the founding of the Jesuits completed the process of change, and the typical community of modern foundation is one with a definite active purpose. The work comes first, and the life of prayer holds a subordinate place. The Rule and the organisation of these later communities show this clearly. The earlier Religious Life was concentrated in the cloister, the later diffused throughout the world. It is convenient to speak of communities of the older foundation as Orders, and of the later as Congregations.

Those who revived the Religious Life in England at the Oxford Movement were never quite clear as to which of these ideals they were following, except in the case of the enclosed communities for women. But it is not necessarily a fault that this was so.

II

The Religious Orders having been swept away, when the English Church came to face seriously its obligation to preach the Gospel in its dominions overseas, about the close of the seventeenth century, there was no instrument to hand to organise and plan the evangelisation. So the first missionary societies, the S.P.C.K. and the S.P.G., came into being to meet the need. Thus these societies have taken over one of the functions of the former religious communities, with the result that to-day the Anglican communities are handmaids to other missionary bodies, rather than missionary bodies themselves.

(a) In the Roman Church the communities, having lived on continuously, are still the main agencies and organisations responsible for finance and policy, though there is, of course, the Congregation of the Propaganda at Rome to direct the missionary strategy of that Church and to supply the staff of the General Headquarters in this warfare. Out of its 8196 European priests engaged in missions to the heathen, and a further 1000 in the missions in the Near East, only about 600 are seculars. Of the 8600 " religious," 3600 belong to the old orders and 5000 to the modern congregations.[1]

It is almost the general custom in Roman missions to find that what corresponds to an Anglican missionary

[1] *Manuel des Missions Catholiques* (Arens, *Louvain*, 1925).

diocese is made the responsibility of one of the great communities as Vicar-Apostolic.

These facts will explain the reason for the wealth that many of the communities have accumulated by bequest. They are the Roman equivalents of the C.M.S. and the U.M.C.A.

(b) But our main concern is with what is actual and what is possible within our own Communion. The number and strength of these communities, using the word " community " in its customary sense, is very small, especially in the case of the men. Although they are doing valuable and good work, in amount it cannot compare for one moment with what is being done by secular missionaries or by the Roman communities.

This means that we have very little experience to draw upon, and that the greater part of this essay must be concerned with more or less speculative ideas of what they might do, as well as of difficulties that lie ahead. There can be no doubt that the call to the Religious Life will become much more common as England grows into a fuller understanding of and capacity for supernatural religion. But it is very necessary that those seeking such a way of life should be on their guard against a merely antiquarian following of its ancient forms, or a copying of what there is to be seen in the Latin countries. The fullness of the Spirit will undoubtedly prompt in the coming centuries fresh forms of dedication to meet the differing needs of God's people. Yet it is not without tears that such developments come to birth. Benedictinism could not understand the aims of St. Francis, but a discerning Pope saved Franciscanism for the world. Nor could the religious world see what St. Ignatius Loyola had in his mind. It needs an open mind free from religious conventionalism to be ready for the new wine of God when it comes to fill the old bottles of the Church.

(c) This consideration naturally leads one to point out the fact that we have in the Bush Brotherhoods a type of community life which is particularly a product of our own age and modern needs, and is doing a most valuable work in the scattered population of the Dominions overseas. The common purse and the celibate state are two of the three conditions which make this a form of community life ; but the lack of the feature of permanence differentiates it missionary work means merely "the preaching of the Gospel," and that this does not include even the teaching of reading and writing. Such is not the conception set forth in this essay, which is wholly based on the contention that salvation means the redemption of the whole man, and not merely of some abstract thing called " the soul."

Schools, therefore, are a necessity for the whole of the new Christian race, and not merely for its prospective sacred ministry.

(c) If the evangelisation of a nation is going to mean the sanctification of all institutions and activities, it is probable that this will come about all the more quickly if there are centres of intensive Christian life. When a minority of Christians is scattered about in a large pagan majority, there is very little chance for the social implications of Christianity to show themselves. The individual virtues of chastity, honesty, soberness, will be there, but the massive corporate effects of the Christian gospel—that is to say, the reform of pagan institutions, such as caste, tribal initiation customs, or industrial conditions—cannot make much headway. It takes a group of men to achieve the transformation of group activities. These groups are best formed round schools, industrial or agricultural settlements.

Moreover, there must also be centres of intensive Christian thinking, since thinking is as important as action. They must be centres in which European and native converts mingle in daily intercourse : the native to bring his knowledge of native customs, the European to bring his experience of a 1800 year-old Christendom.

Both these considerations, the need of Christian action and Christian thinking, point to the desirability of large institutions, and the relation of institutions to communities will be dealt with in the next section of this essay.

(d) With this idea of a corporate Christianity the need of centres for the creation and diffusion of Christian literature in the vernacular will be at once apparent. Missionary experience has already found and met the need for the translation of the Scriptures and the preparation of books for public worship. The need for literature, however, extends far beyond this. Catechisms, books of instruction, and manuals of private prayers are almost a necessity. Moreover, as education spreads, there will be a need for the writing of Christian books, simple exegesis, lives of the saints, and even Christian philosophy for races of more advanced culture.

There are some areas, especially in Africa, which have no literature of any sort, and it is obviously a duty of the Christian Church to produce the beginnings not only of religious but of secular literature for such races, if Christianity is going to include all life within its scope.

All this means team work, and as in the case of institution work, the bearing of this upon the community as a missionary instrument will be considered in the next section.

IV

(a) Although the ultimate aim of any mission is to found a new native Church, it is obvious that the earliest activity of the mission is to make individual converts, and that a large part of the European missionaries' work, until there is a sufficient native priesthood, will be the pastoral care of native Christians. For this work communities, as such, are not particularly well suited. It generally means the isolation of the missionaries in individual work among small scattered groups of Christians; and members of communities are less well fitted than secular priests, both by temperament and by training, to stand isolation. The same is true of women workers, though the circumstances of the mission field make it undesirable for a woman ever to live alone; the Mary Slessors are so few that they ought not to provide precedents.

In the intermediate stages of development, when one expects a fair number of native priests or deacons, but with European priests as directors of mission districts, the same criticism about community priests holds good.

(b) It is when one comes to institutional work that the advantages of a community are most apparent. Every institution is bound to create a tradition of its own, and its success is further dependent upon the existence of a team spirit.

Many institutions in the mission field staffed by secular priests or lay women have developed these necessities most admirably. But, both for the institution itself and for the subsequent recruits to the staff, this is a matter that takes

the present time.   Under (i) it is to be said that there are
undoubtedly many men now at work in the mission field
who would not be there but for their membership of some
community ;   but there are undoubtedly many would-
have-been missionaries kept at home by their community's
needs.   Under (ii) the small size of the communities makes
their desire to fling down mission works here and there at
the strategical points in the heathen world incapable of
achievement, and the missionaries have to be employed
only in the very limited number of places where the
communities are actually at work.

(e) In addition to the communities with their headquarters in England and some of their works overseas,
there are also special communities which exist for missionary
purposes only, and with their headquarters in the mission
field itself. They may be styled *ad hoc* communities, in
that membership of them implies a vocation primarily to
a particular missionary area.   Such, for instance, are the
Oxford Mission to Calcutta for men, with its allied Sisterhood of the Epiphany for women, and the Sisters of the
Sacred Passion in the dioceses of Zanzibar and Masasi.
There are also some Sisterhoods with their headquarters
in the various Dominions overseas.   In most cases they
have strong missionary daughter houses, but, as they do
not engage themselves exclusively in missionary work,
they cannot be reckoned as *ad hoc* communities.

The existence of these latter provides a fine organisation for both men and women who desire the special
dedication of the Religious Life, but are also conscious of
a vocation to the mission field or to a particular mission.

The tactical advantages of such a spearhead for mission
work in any particular diocese or missionary area are
obvious, and it is greatly to be hoped that there will be
a much larger development of them.

(f) It is now time to speak of some of the dangers and
difficulties which may attend community work.   The most
serious are those which come from the competing jurisdic-
tion of the local Bishop, the local Superior, and the Superior
General of the community.   It is, in fact, the problem of
the *imperium in imperio* ;   and it shows itself in matters
of diocesan policy, finance, and the personal discipline of
individuals.

Up to the present, owing to the small size of the community groups working abroad, the community members have worked mostly as individuals and under the individual authority of the Bishop. This has frequently meant friction between the Bishop and the Superior General over the placing in or removal from the mission of community members. Whilst Christian courtesy and a desire to see the other person's point of view have frequently done much to reduce the friction, a certain amount is inevitable owing to the clash of interests.

With the growth in size of the men's communities at work overseas, this type of individual work is now being replaced by corporate works : missionary bishops have entrusted a given work to the community as a community, and the latter's responsibility takes the shape of providing that the work is adequately done rather than that of supplying individual workers for the bishop's disposal. Some examples of this will be found in the next section, which is descriptive of some of the works that communities are actually doing.

In unorganised work the difficulties of the *imperium in imperio* are apparent. So far as the organised work goes, there ought to be no more difficulty than there is between a bishop, a vicar, and the latter's curates, except for its greater extent. But if some of the financial support comes from England, or from community funds, it is quite clear that the Bishop and the Superior at home finding the money are both entitled to have budgets and accounts submitted to them, and to have views upon them. The same is true of buildings and other fixed properties. Or, again, over the appointment and control of the local superior and over the introduction and removal of men, the two authorities may find themselves in conflict.

In a diocese where Seculars and Religious are working side by side, there exists the danger of the community forming an organised *bloc* in synod or diocesan chapter to force decisions in a particular direction. It is true that in theory the community members are free to vote and speak as they like in such assemblies, but the tendency of men who share a common outlook and live together to form a clique is inevitable.

Apart from such questions of practical policy, there are also the questions of doctrinal and liturgical development. These are not due merely to the special conditions of has stations at Bombay and Poona in India, at Cape Town and Tsolo in South Africa. Whilst reproducing the atmosphere of the dedicated and disciplined life of the Mother House at Cowley in these mission stations, the brethren are mostly engaged in the pastoral care of native Christians in these great cities and country stations. The Society has also received into membership a few native Indian clergy. The Community of the Resurrection's chief mission station is at Rosettenville, on the outskirts of Johannesburg. From this centre the brethren do a vast work amongst the native mine-workers on the Rand. Here also are to be found primary and secondary schools, with a theological college for ordinands and catechists. The community has also the mission district of Penhalonga in Southern Rhodesia. Although it is not a mission work, there is also the magnificent public school, St. John's College, at Johannesburg, which the community founded and is still extending. The Society of the Sacred Mission has the greater part of the work amongst natives in the Orange Free State under its care. The provincial house at Modderpoort has, in addition to a large mission area, primary and secondary schools, the latter a boarding school, and a theological college. It is responsible also for a good deal of translation work and the publishing of books in the vernacular.

The Society of the Divine Compassion has a station overseas at Wreningham, Southern Rhodesia, and the Oratory of the Good Shepherd has oratory houses in Northern Rhodesia and Rockhampton. The Order of St. Benedict is responsible for the native theological college in the diocese of Accra at Kumasi.

Then there is the *ad hoc* community of the Oxford Mission to Calcutta, with its first and second orders of men and women. It is almost impossible to exaggerate the importance of the works of this community-mission. It has its mission stations and out-stations, its hostels for Indian boys and men, and the large work of intellectual permeation by means of writings and publications. The reader is referred to the Secretary of the Mission in England, at 8 Dartmouth Street, S.W. 1, for information concerning its manifold enterprises.

Finally, in the Society of the Servants of Christ (Christa Seva Sangh) is the newest venture of the English Church abroad. It consists of a group of young Englishmen, priests and laymen, who have started a community life on the Franciscan model in Poona. They have already several Indian members living in common life with the Europeans, but on the Indian model. The main object of the community is prayer and a life of renunciation, but its members are also engaging in active work.

(b) Out of the fifty-one sisterhoods in England mentioned in the official *Year Book of the Church of England*, eleven have works abroad or in the Dominions.

It is impossible to speak of these works in detail, owing to their number. Generalisation, therefore, is a tribute to their size and importance, and not an evidence of the smallness of the work of the mission work of the communities for women. In general, their work takes the form of schools, hostels, orphanages, hospitals, and pastoral work in almost equal amount. It is to be found in India, Japan, Korea, South Africa and East Africa. In several instances there is further work on behalf of Europeans living in these countries, mostly in the form of schools. Although this is not strictly speaking " mission " work, it ought always to be considered in this connexion, for it has two characteristics which it shares with mission work proper : it has very largely to be recruited and financed from home ; and it is under the direction of bishops, the greater part of whose task is a missionary one.

But to return to missions to native peoples. An interesting feature is the association of the men's Society of St. John the Evangelist with the Sisterhoods of St. Mary, Wantage, and All Saints, St. Albans, in mission work at Poona and Bombay in India, and Kaffraria and Cape Town in South Africa. The same sort of co-operation obtains in the Oxford Mission to Calcutta between the two communities of the Epiphany for men and for women.

In England the Missionary Community of St. Denys at Warminster fulfils a special rôle in its training college for women missionaries ; and it has its own overseas work at Chota Nagpur.

There is an *ad hoc* missionary sisterhood for women in the Community of the Sacred Passion. It was founded by Bishop Weston of Zanzibar, in 1910, for work in the U.M.C.A. in East Africa. The Novice House is at Poplar, in England. Although the Sisters are employed in active

x

work in Africa as nurses and educationists, the labour of prayer and the devotion of life stand as its primary aim. The Bishop gave as the objects of the Community these three aims :

1. To honour our Lord Jesus Christ by exhibiting to Africans the joy and the power of the Passion of Jesus.
2. To offer to God a life of complete poverty, chastity, and obedience in union with the reparation offered to Him by our Lord upon the Cross.
3. To win souls for our Lord Jesus by a life of prayer and missionary work.[1]

This section would be incomplete without a reference to the sisterhoods which exist in the various Dominions. South Africa alone has no less than three communities of women of its own. These naturally have important missionary activities in their own provinces of the Church. Their existence is in itself a sign of great spontaneity and vitality in the Church overseas. But they have an even more important sign of life, for it so happens—and not without good reason—that it is they who are responsible for fostering the beginnings of the dedicated life for native women. In the Zanzibar diocese, the Community of the Sacred Passion is caring for the first East African postulant for the Religious Life ; in South Africa the Community of St. Michael and All Angels is tending the beginnings of a native community for women ; and in India the Sisters of the Epiphany have been the means of starting on their lives the first Indian Sisters.

In all these instances the aim is not to receive the native Sisters into the European communities, but to bring about the foundation of native communities.

VI

So far we have been dealing with communities from the practical point of view, and considering them as instruments of outward activity. That is the scope laid down for this essay. But it would be incomplete, and lacking in its deepest part, if it did not refer to the inward meaning and work of the Religious Life. After all, the task of the

[1] *Frank, Bishop of Zanzibar*, by Maynard Smith, p. 134.

missionary is with the imponderables. The aim of all his external activities is an internal thing : the passing on of a spiritual reality—the Gospel of Redemption. In the divine economy this demands a spiritual energy, and a spiritual price to be paid. Therefore, we cannot omit the special energy of prayer that is to be brought to the missionary work of the Church by the religious communities. There is first of all the prayer of intercession. No one can doubt that the marvellous spread of the Gospel within the past century is due very largely to the spread of the habit of intercession for missions. The prayer meetings, the immense diffusion of intercession leaflets, and the rich offerings of Eucharists are the secret of the forward movements of to-day, and of the hunger for the Gospel, which have created the insistent demand for more and yet more agents in the mission field. We have been taken by surprise in the mission field, and have been caught unprepared in the matter of providing the personnel, because we have never really believed in the efficacy of our own prayer.

In the work of intercession, the missionary can and must bear a peculiar share. He or she is right in the midst of the work for which intercession is being made. He has a special knowledge of detailed needs ; and he has a special emotional passion, because of his close contact with the work and its needs, and because of his own dedication to the work. But beyond intercession, the Religious has in a special degree the higher forms of prayer as his task. There is the Prayer of Reparation, reparation for the sins that Christendom has done against the non-Christian races, and the offering of adoration to God for the heathen who know Him not as yet.

In evangelisation there is an outward work—the organisation of schools, the teaching of catechumens, and the preaching of the Gospel. But there is also work to be done in the unseen world. Those souls who have the capacity of sensing the mystic realities which give shape to the outward things of life will recognise missionary work as a vast arena in which death and life are contending. For them there will be many a conflict in some corner of the arena where Christian pity, love, and long-suffering are locked in a death-grip with the active hate, the sullen sloth, and the sensual degradation inspired of rebellious principalities and powers. We need those contemplatives in the mission field as much or more than we need them at home, to be the storm troops in the warfare of God against that spiritual wickedness in high places which rages almost unchecked in heathendom.

This consideration brings us close to another aspect of the Religious Life in the mission field—namely, the witness it is to certain aspects of life, especially life as inspired by the Gospel. Long centuries of heathenism have produced a weakness of will and subjection to the passions in those who have lived under it. The Religious Life stands for discipline in a peculiar degree, and to give an example of discipline is worth a thousand precepts teaching it by maxim. The particular application in the threefold conditions of the Religious Life has a cogency for the African or Asiatic in that it shows this self-discipline in action. The chastity of celibacy is an answer to the sexual sensuality which the unbridled heathen might think to be the norm of human conduct. The self-limitation which poverty and obedience put upon a man or woman Religious has a teaching for the self-will of the self-indulgent or overbearing Asiatic.

Above all, the Religious Life ought to show a love of God and a devotion to Him that should be eloquent in a way that no preaching or teaching can be. The very heart of the Christian response to the Gospel is surrender to God, and this kind of life is an example of surrender. The very essence of all Christian conduct is forgetfulness of self, and this is one way of showing that dedication of self which rests upon such forgetfulness.

There are many ways of loving God, and there are many forms in which devotion to Him can be expressed. But the witness of this particular way is unmistakable. Our hope should be that it may inspire the races just reborn to bring forth in due time their own particular and new forms of devotion, not only in the religious life but also in the general life of these peoples.

XVI

THE CHURCH AT HOME

(A) A Letter from India
BY PHILIP LOYD, BISHOP

(B) Ad Commensales
BY STACY WADDY

SYNOPSIS

A

1. The passing of the Indian Church Measure, an epoch in the history of the Church in India.
2. If the Church of India is to be a Church with an Indian life lived by Indians, is there still a place for the foreign missionary ?
3. Though some missionaries should probably go, many are still needed for the vast unevangelised areas.
4. There is still room for the missionary who is prepared to live the life of the Indian Church.
5. The diocesan frame gives an opportunity for Indian and foreigner to work happily together in and for the Indian Church.
6. Suggested division of responsibility as between the native Church and the foreign mission.
7. Further evidence of the need of the foreign missionary. His impartiality in regard to native problems. He can help to solve the problem of the Anglo-Indian community.
8. He can witness to the Catholicity of the Church, and help to safeguard the young Church against the dangers of nationalism and heresy. He can hand on the heritage of Catholic devotion.
9. He can develop Community life.
10. The older Church which sends the missionary must have a generous confidence in the younger Church to which he is sent.
11. The kind of missionaries needed.

B

The Catholicity of the Gospel demands adaptability in the Church. The problems of a young Church are the concern of all.

Native Christian communities are beginning to realise that God is calling them to be the soul of their nation.

In order to become so they must be united into one Church ; hence proposals for Christian reunion are a feature of the Christian world to-day.

To this movement towards unity Anglicans must contribute their witness to the Catholic elements in the Faith, and a truly Catholic spirit.

A Bishop overseas called to guide new movements and to proclaim Catholic principles needs from the Church at home the most gracious and constructive expositions of these principles : he asks for clear thinking in brotherly love, and, above all, for men and women to live by these principles overseas.

A Catholic revival is needed in the Church at home, with "Hallowed be Thy Name " as its motto.

THE CHURCH AT HOME

A

THE passing of the Indian Church Measure at the end of 1927 marked an important epoch in the history of the Church in India. It represented a stage which has now been reached, not only by the Church of the Anglican Communion, but also by many Christian bodies which belong to the Free Churches. In fact, it is hardly too much to say that it signalises the birth of the real Indian Church.

Hitherto the Indian Christians who, apart from the ancient Syrian Church and the long-established Roman Catholic communities, have been found scattered up and down that vast country have existed as groups gathered round those who have been responsible for their evangelisation and conversion. The foreign missionaries converted them, and they still clung round them and faced towards them, being dependent upon those missionaries for guidance, discipline, and unity. But of late years the situation has been changing, and there have been plentiful signs of the dawning of a new era. The Indian Christian has begun to feel that he is not only a Christian, but also an Indian. He has ceased to look at his Christianity as a refuge from a dark and baneful heritage, and has begun to regard his national life and tradition as a mould into which his Christianity must be poured if it is to find its fullest and truest expression. The Christianity which he wants is not to serve him just as an ambulance wagon for the wounded, but as a chariot for an invader and conqueror. He has found a religion which has a mission for the Indians as a nation, which can give them unity and strength. And for that there must be, not groups of Christian converts, but one living and growing Church of India.

This Church of India must be a Church with an Indian life lived by Indians. At once this raises the question

Can any live this Indian life save Indians ? Above all, Can any guide and mould this life save the Indians themselves ? In other words, Is there still a place for the foreign missionary in this new-born Church of India ?

This is not a merely academic question. We missionaries have been told of late, and not without emphasis, that we are no longer wanted, and that our continued stay in the country is actually harmful. We are bound to consider the matter when it is so put to us. I propose to deal with it in this letter, partly because I think that an answer from the missionary's point of view is worth making, and partly because such an answer will serve as a convenient peg on which to hang what I have to say.

But before I proceed to offer any reply I should like to mention the two chief sources of this cry of " missionaries not wanted," so far as I am able to discern them.

One source is the growing nationalist feeling. Indians want India for the Indians, and they feel that Indians should be free to develop and control things Indian. It is, of course, only the educated Indian who has attained as yet in any great degree to this national consciousness. He is himself fully aware that his numbers are few compared with the whole population of India ; and when he looks round him to see what forces and what leadership he can muster he sees at once that a not inconsiderable portion of educated Indians are markedly European in their sympathies and way of life. These are the Indian Christians. The Indian Nationalist regards them as traitors to his country and her cause. He may be unfair in doing so, but he cannot be called particularly unreasonable. As a matter of fact, the young educated Indian Christian of to-day is becoming very proud of being an Indian. The English or American missionary is by no means to him a person to be imitated in every respect. In fact it is the modern educated Indian Christian who is the other source from which the no-missionary cry comes. He feels that he is being " bossed " too much, and is impatient of missionary control. He thinks that he is being " run " by a foreign bureau, and even hates the money which has educated him, as being the price of his liberty and self-respect. Here again we must admit that he is far from being merely ungrateful and unreasonable. The missionary is too often to blame for a certain arrogant hastiness of judgment and lack of sympathy and imagination.

But, if missionaries have erred, it does not necessarily follow that they are not wanted, or that they are inevitably harmful. For one thing, these educated Indians, of what- ever religion, only amount to a very small part of the whole population of India ; and the Christians themselves are but a handful compared with the millions of non-Christians. Even in areas where Christian missions have flourished for half a century or more there are vast tracts of country still entirely unevangelised ; while there are other areas of staggering dimensions in which the name of Christ has never been heard. In the face of these unevangelised areas it would be very hard to maintain that there is no work left for the foreign missionary to do. The harvest is so great, and the labourers so few, that the native Indian Church could simply not be believed if it declared—and after all it is only a few that venture to make such an assertion—that it can quite well dispense with any help from outside in this great enterprise of preaching the Gospel throughout the length and breadth of India.

Nevertheless, if any Indian says to us, " Yes, we admit that we need all the help we can get from anywhere in this gigantic task of evangelising India ; but all the same we are reluctantly forced to say that your presence as mis- sionaries in India is so harmful that we must at all costs get on without you," then he would be entitled to a calm and reasonable hearing. I do not intend to argue the point directly with him in this letter. He may accuse us of being anti-national. He may complain of our hustling Western ways. He may urge that we are pauperising the infant Indian Church. He may point out—the fairest and truest reproach of all—that we have imported our sectarian differences wholesale into a land which has no interest in them, and can only suffer grievously from them. I shall remain dumb. I shall not attempt to defend us or to excuse the many faults of the past and present. I will meet him at least half-way, and admit that there are some of us at least who should go. I will also admit that it is extremely likely that none of us is as indispensable as we like to think.

But, having made these admissions, I shall suggest that, even if it is true that some missionaries should go, that does not necessarily mean that no new missionaries should come. If in the face of the enormous need for evangelistic enterprise there are missionaries who are so harmful that they must be got rid of at all costs, this can only be because they are not living the life that needs to be lived in India to-day. Surely there is room for the missionary who will come and range himself alongside the Indian, and will join him and help him in the absorbing task of discovering, interpreting, and living the life of this new-born Indian Church. Yes, that is the heart of the answer which we must give, and that is the charter which we must put into the hands of the missionaries of the next generation ; namely, that they will make good their standing and prove effectual in their work according as they do or do not succeed in *living the life of the Indian Church.*

Now, this is rather a vague phrase ; and if we cannot make it clearer, we may be accused of merely taking cover behind a smoke-screen. Unfortunately, it is difficult to write in anything more than rather vague and general language ; because this living the life of the Indian Church is a great spiritual venture which has to be explored and attempted by younger and fresher minds than ours. As I have already said, it is *the* great venture which awaits and claims all the energy and enthusiasm of the new generation. But still, something can be attempted in the way of giving a clearer outline to the idea ; and I hope that in making the attempt I shall be able to give some idea of the kind of missionary we hope will come to our help, and of the way in which I believe he should set about his work.

The mould into which the life of the young Indian Church of our communion is being poured is the diocese. The missionary society with its organisation and institutions is only the forerunner of the diocesan life. It must decrease, while the other—the diocesan life—must increase. In the sphere of the missionary institutions the Indian must of necessity be to a large extent in a position of pupilage and subordination ; he can only slowly and painfully win his way to a share of control, and in doing so must be constantly subject to much irksome scrutiny. But in the sphere of the diocese it is quite different. He enters there on an absolute equality of footing with the missionary. The missionary as missionary has no standing or privilege there. So it can be seen at once that in the full development of diocesan life lies the most natural and the happiest solution of any conflicting claims which there may be between the missionary and native Indians. Indeed, I believe that it is due to our diocesan organisation that we are often better able than Christians of other communions to overcome difficulties of this kind.

The Diocesan Council, which represents the heart and mind of the native Church, is to increase, while the Missionary Committee must decrease. More and more the seeing of visions, the conceiving of great enterprises, the making of bold and far-reaching plans, must be done by the Diocesan Council and its evangelistic, educational, and other boards. The Missionary Committee remains for some time yet as the trustee and steward of moneys collected in England and elsewhere outside India. It is good that the native Church should have the discipline and spur to greater self-support which comes from having to ask the Missionary Committees for help in this and that endeavour. But it need not be doubted that the missionary bodies will be only too glad to forsake their own planning and become supporters of the plans which are made by the Diocesan Council in proportion as that Council shows itself to be capable of far-seeing and statesmanlike enterprise.

Here, then, is the line along which the missionary to-day must make his venture. As smaller and more manageable, and also more Indian, dioceses arise, he must cease to think too much in the terms of his own mission. He must throw himself whole-heartedly into the life of the diocese ; and, entering on equal footing with the Indian into its counsels, he must help him to become a more and more efficient and successful planner and organiser. At times it will demand patience and faith on the missionary's part. Schemes which he by a little bit of " bossing " and drive could carry through at once in his own little area will have to wait upon the needs of the diocese as a whole, and will have to win the consent and understanding of the whole Christian community before they can be put on foot. Yes, it will need patience and faith ; but if he is the kind of missionary we want he will know well enough that the life he lives counts more than the work he does or the schemes he engineers.

I hope that this last paragraph may have helped to

show more clearly what is meant by living the life of the Indian Church. It may perhaps help to greater clearness if a word is said about the kinds of work which should be handed over as soon as possible to the Indian Church and those for which the foreign missionary should at present retain at least an equal share of responsibility.

A rough division can be made under three heads— pastoral, evangelistic, and institutional. The *pastoral* work of ministering to the needs of the Indian Christians is already being very largely handed over to the Indians themselves. It is the work which they can most naturally undertake ; and, able as they are to understand their own people better than we can, they can often do it better than we could. It is therefore usually, and rightly, assumed that the first step towards self-support that a Christian community should make ought to be the undertaking of responsibility for the financial support of its clergy and lay workers—at least of those of them who are engaged in pastoral work.

Of course, it is our ideal that every Christian should regard himself as an evangelist ; and, with our Christian communities embedded in whole tracts of pagan life, there can be no hard and fast delimitation of pastoral and evangelistic spheres. But it may well be that, when it comes to *evangelistic* enterprise, there may be a clear call for a missionary society to finance and staff the evangelisation of a new area. This is not because the foreign missionary is necessarily a better evangelist than the Indian. Often he is not ; but sometimes, chiefly owing to caste difficulties, he is. The reason for asking the foreign society to undertake the work is simply that the native Christian resources are not sufficient for all that has to be done. So it will work out that, while the native Church cannot undertake its own pastoral responsibility without automatically taking a greater and greater share in the evangelistic enterprise, yet in this latter field there is likely to be for some time to come plenty of room for the foreign missionary to continue to work on much the same terms as in the past.

When we come to *institutional* work, we come to the sphere in which the foreign missionary will probably longest be wanted—the sphere, therefore, in which the missionary societies can most surely expend money with no fear of " pauperising " the Indian Church. A young and ardent Church at close grips with stubborn and all-pervading heathenism can have little time or strength to devote to the solid educational work which does not give very quick returns and yet is of such great importance. The thorough training of the clergy, the steady raising of the standard of education by means of Normal Schools and well-run High Schools, these are enterprises which are bound to be carried through all the better if missionary societies will come generously to the aid of a comparatively poor and youthful Church. Then, again, there are hospitals, sanatoria, and every kind of medical work—such invaluable object-lessons of the truth and power of Christianity, yet demanding such costly equipment and such expensive training of those who work in them. They are largely beyond the strength and resources of the Indian Church. They are, therefore, a proper field for the missionary society and its agents.

Yet a word of caution must be added with regard to those institutions, whether medical or educational. Those who work in them must not forget our charter—they are to live the life of the Indian Church. Even in the case of these institutions they must remember that in the last resort they are only trustees and stewards. Therefore they must not embark upon, and they must be content not to have, institutions of such magnitude and elaborate efficiency as will for ever be beyond the power of the Indian Church to maintain. There is a real call here for self-denial on the part of the doctor or educationist just out from England. The money is available ; the way is clear ; the man-power is available. But pause and think. Are you twisting a leading-string or forging a fetter ? These fine new white buildings, whom do you mean to be responsible for their overhaul and repair fifty years hence ?

I must be about half-way through my letter ; and let me be frank and confess that I am now coming to the part of it which really interests me, which I really want to write. In this last part I want to indicate what I believe the missionary can do for us in India if he is the right kind of man and will work on the lines which I have so inadequately sketched. And perhaps it is at this point that I can most conveniently say that, though I only use the masculine gender, I am thinking of the woman quite as much as of the man missionary.

Let us look at his influence, first, in the sphere of diocesan life, and then in the Indian Church as a whole.

The foreign missionary is a foreigner, and that is a drawback. He is well aware of the fact ; and, from the time when he sets himself to learn a new language written in strange characters and apparently unpronounceable, to the day some years later when he realises that he knows nothing really of the country and never will, he is never in danger of forgetting for long what a drawback it is to be a foreigner. And yet even drawbacks have their advantages which can be turned to account. For one thing, a foreigner can often be more impartial than the native. I can imagine that it is possible that the natives of England might sometimes find things running more smoothly and reasonably in a Diocesan or even in a Parochial Church Council if there were one or two foreigners present to " keep the ring "! Certainly in India, which is courageously engaged in fighting down and destroying old caste divisions and jealousies, the presence of the impartial foreigner can often be a real help. Again and again the foreigner's impartiality enables him to utter the needed word of that wisdom which is " first pure, then peaceable, gentle, easy to be entreated," and the fact that he is *known* to be impartial by the very nature of the case helps to make that word of wisdom acceptable.

Then again, and still in the sphere of diocesan life for the most part, there is the problem of the Anglo-Indian community, one of the heaviest burdens which this young Church has to shoulder. How is justice to be done to that community ? How is it to find a permanently happy place in the life of the nation ? If the Indian Church cannot help them to find it, no one else can. But there—it is not rash to say it—the missionary is wanted to help the Indian and Anglo-Indian to unite in the task. The missionary is, or should be, able to understand them both. He is also the natural link between them both and the English communities in India. If he as an Englishman nevertheless sets himself whole-heartedly to live the life of the Indian Church, then he can contribute to the solution something which no one else can hope to contribute.

But it is when we consider the life of the Indian Church

as a whole that we can see most clearly the distinctive and most important contribution which the missionary has to make. The Indian Church must be a Catholic Church; it must be a living, conscious part of the universal, Catholic Church. It is not so yet. It is not old enough or big enough to be so yet. This is something into which it must grow up. In the meantime there are two great dangers which beset it, either of which might prevent it from becoming truly Catholic. One is nationalism; the other is heresy. " Swaraj " and " India for the Indians " are cries which to-day are ringing in every Indian's ears. How easily we might have also " The Indian Church for the Indians "! But no, it must be " The Indian Church, not merely for the Indians, but for the world, for all mankind, for Christ." Or, to put it round the other way, it must be not so much the Church for India, as India for the Church, for the Catholic Church, for Christ. Now, the foreign missionary by his mere presence is a standing witness to the truth that the Church, if it is truly the Church, is not a private concern of the Indians. But, apart from his mere presence, he is, if not the only, yet the chief channel through which other interests can flow in and out of the Indian Church. He helps to keep the door open and to prevent the Indian Church from being shut in on itself. And if it were so shut in, what would happen? This brings us to the second great danger—namely, heresy. The Church of India is still very young, and it will not be grown up till it has achieved the gigantic task of absorbing the traditional life and thought of India into its own living and thinking. This is the work, not of a few years, but of a century or more. What a struggle it will be for India, which for centuries and centuries has based all its deepest thought upon a belief in the illusion or evil of matter, to think and live its way through to the fullness of sacramental truth! If it were shut in and left to itself, would it not almost inevitably fall a prey to every kind of Gnostic heresy that was known in the second and third centuries of our era? But so long as the foreign missionary has a natural place in the life of the Church, so long the Church of India will continually be compelled to test its beliefs by the judgment of the Catholic world at large, and will not be in danger of being content if a statement commends itself merely to the majority of Indian minds.

I claim, therefore, that the missionary is to-day the chief safeguard of this young Church against the dangers of nationalism and heresy, and I claim that as such the missionary is the pledge of India's future Catholicity. And if you ask me how long the missionary must act as a safeguard, I reply that I cannot tell; but I have already indicated one factor in determining the *terminus ad quem*— namely, that the Indian Church has to grow up and absorb the traditional life and thought of the nation. I will tell you another, and perhaps a more determining factor. The Indian Church must itself become a missionary Church. When it is sending out missionaries of its own, first to minister to its own people in Africa and elsewhere, and then to follow, perhaps, the route that the Buddhists took centuries ago into Thibet and China, then will the Church of India have made good its standing in the Catholic Church of Christ, and by the vigour of its own life will keep clear the channels of communication with the universal Church. Till then, I say, the foreign missionary has his own indispensable work to perform.

Of less importance, and yet not to be despised, is the help which he can give in the way of handing on and interpreting to the Indian Church the great heritage of Catholic devotion. For we do belong to an older Church; and though it is true enough that India has much to teach us about prayer and meditation and the ascetic life, yet we too have much to teach her; and there are many of her own treasures which she will never discover or know how to use in the Church until she has learnt what we have to give her.

To add one more thing under this heading: the missionary is one who is sent, and he is the earnest of the love and prayers of those who send him. The Indian Church needs the counsel and teaching which the West can give. It needs even more your sympathy and prayers. The most precious and effective contribution we missionaries carry to India is—I say it in all sincerity—your prayer and self-denial.

In writing of what the missionary may do for us in India I have so far assumed that he will be employed in some way which will keep him, so to speak, in the main stream of Indian Church life. But there is room for missionary enterprise which lies rather outside of that main current, and I for one believe that it is one which can be developed to the incalculable profit of the Church. I refer to the Religious Community. When we review the history of the Western Church and see the immensely important part which was played by the Benedictine and other monks both in evangelising Europe and in building it up into Catholic faith and practice, we cannot refrain from asking ourselves whether we have not here an evangelistic agency which has been all too much neglected, and one which is peculiarly adapted to the fulfilment of the needs of the present time. I should like to see much serious thought given to this subject. I have not space to write much about it in this letter; but I will offer three points for consideration.

The first point is that the very fact that such Communities are outside the main stream of the Church's life makes it easier for a young and ardent Church to learn from them during those periodical times of " growing pains " and self-consciousness which are bound to come to it. Here are people manifestly trying to be quiet and live their own life; they are not trying to " run " others. We can study them, question them, and learn of them without compromising ourselves in any way.

Secondly, Religious Communities can be at the same time both more conservative and more innovating than the national Church. They preserve what the Church too hastily throws away, and thus often act as staunch bulwarks against heresy. At the same time new methods of worship can sometimes be " tried out " in them at a time when they would not yet commend themselves to the Church at large.

But, thirdly, and most important of all, the Indian Church itself will not have attained to its full growth until it has many Religious Communities of its own. These the Indians must form for themselves; but English Communities are needed to give them the impulse and to save them, by providing them with patterns, from wasting much precious time in discovering things which they could, if left to themselves, only learn after much costly failure.

I have written of what the missionary might do for us in India both as an individual and as a member of a Religious Community. I have said that the keynote of his work must be the honest endeavour to live the life

Y

of the Indian Church. I feel that what I have said is not complete without some reference to the Church which sends the missionary. In the long run, the attitude of the sending Church towards the younger Church in the mission field must determine the attitude of the missionary. If the missionary is to go out to give himself up to living the life of the young Church abroad, then the older Church which sends him must have a glad and generous confidence in that younger Church. This younger Church is bound to enact canons which would not be suitable to the older Church at home. Some of those canons may seem even to be wrong and scandalous to those at home. But there it is ; the whole social environment is so utterly different ; the Christian of the jungle is a very different creature from the Christian of the semi-detached villa, the back garden, and the wireless installation. There is the question of reunion too. A Church in its youth and period of formative growth can, and ought to, approach and deal with this question in a different way from a Church in a land where sects have grown to maturity and hardened in the growing.

What, then, should be asked of the home Church ? To put it as shortly and bluntly as possible, this—No armchair criticism, and no party catchwords. There are things which we could not abandon in England without being guilty of contumacious indifference to the Catholic tradition ; yet there is no real reason why they should be introduced into India. " Catholic " and " Protestant " may be well-deserved labels in England. They are libels in India, if used as they are used at home, because we are not old enough yet to be truly either the one or the other. Yes, remember our youth ; and, remembering that, realise that no written formulas, not even the Creeds (though we treasure and rejoice in them) can really hold us in or safeguard our Catholicity. We are too young, I say ; we are not old enough yet really to know what the words we use mean to *us*. There is only one safeguard, and we ask you to help to provide it. That safeguard is men and women living the Catholic life as keen and hopeful members of the Indian Church—men and women who, if they have learnt and loved the Catholic life in England, yet are ready to lose it in order to find it again in Indian forms.

Is it too daring of me to suggest that the more the

Church of England will give of its best to India on these terms, the greater reward it will reap ?   Has not Zanzibar already helped England to see more clearly the essentials and the beauty of Catholicism ?   May not India too one day do the same for you ?

I have written at much greater length than I wished on the subject of whether the foreign missionary is wanted in India and, if so, how he is to do his work.   And yet, much as I have already written, there is still something unsaid which I want to say.   I feel great diffidence in trying to say it ; because I shall write of the missionary's calling in a way which it may seem presumptuous in a missionary to write.   But I venture, because I am afraid lest, if I leave it unwritten, I may leave a false impression. I have laid great stress upon the need for the missionary to live the life of the Indian Church.   I want to make it clear that I do not regard this as something that can be achieved by any kind of posturing however adroit, or by any statesmanship however far-seeing.   I have already called it a great spiritual venture, and I mean that.   It is, in fact, the greatest of all ventures, that of losing one's life to find it.   The missionary has to sell all in order to give to the poor and follow Christ.   Now, no doubt, this is true of every form of self-sacrifice, of every kind of true service of Christ and His kingdom.   Our lives must be lost in order to be found in others, or else we cannot be true disciples of the Lord Jesus.   That is true of all self-sacrifice and acceptable service.   But may not the missionary claim that there is an element in his self-sacrifice which does not enter into the self-sacrifice of others ?   It is the element of leaving father and mother, relations and home, for the sake of Christ and His Gospel.   When St. Columba looked westward from Iona and decided to settle there because at length his own native land was no longer in sight, had he not then broken his way through to a form of self-sacrifice which has its own peculiar virtue and power ?   " Always bearing about in the body the dying of Jesus, that the life also of Jesus may be manifested in our body.   For we which live are alway delivered unto death for Jesus' sake, that the life also of Jesus may be manifested in our mortal flesh.   So then death worketh in us, but life in you." Have not those words a meaning for the foreign missionary in a foreign land which they can have for no one else ?

Y 2

May we not claim that the life and experience of any Church is incomplete, unless those words are being interpreted to it and lived into it as only the missionary can do ? May we not justly say that, until the Indian Church has missionaries of its own to fire it and, when necessary, to stir its embers anew by the power of that particular form of self-sacrifice, the foreign missionary must be there to contribute to its life something which it cannot provide of itself ?

But this is a very high claim ; and nothing but the most rigid faithfulness to this lofty calling can save us from the charge of presumption if we make it. The missionary goes abroad to die in order that others may find their true life and live ; and if his whole life is not dominated by this one thought, if he is not able to say with St. Paul " I die daily," if he rests content before he has sold *all* and given to the poorest of the poor, then he is but a sounding brass and a clanging cymbal. The problems of the mission field, to-day as always, need for their solution not so much the skill and wisdom of the missionary, as his utter self-abnegation and fervent love and zeal.

Who knows what God in His love and wisdom has in store for us ?　It may be that the Church of India's deepest need is not men nor money, not counsel and guidance, but simply the blood of martyrs.　We may not pray for persecution ; but if the day should come, then without doubt native Christian and foreign missionary would vie with one another in their joyful witness to the truth of the Gospel, and the missionary would find the crown of his vocation in laying his bones beside his brother Indian in a martyr's grave.　We sometimes dream of such things ; but we soon turn back to the immediate task of learning to die daily, because we know—yes, we have learnt from much shameful and bitter failure—that we are only of any use as missionaries in proportion as we can truly say those other words of St. Paul, " Yet no longer I ; but Christ liveth in me."

B

Jesus Christ is the same yesterday, to-day, and for ever.　Every people will build its true life, realise its full possibilities, only upon the knowledge Jesus gave of the kind of God there is, therefore the kind of men we ought to be. The Church of Christ has but the one message to give at home and overseas, to European and Asiatic and African, in the first century and the twentieth. Both the Church and the message are Catholic, fundamentally the same in all times for all men. But the Church is called upon to be infinitely adaptable : to meet men at the stage to which God has brought them ; to give to each people just what it needs—not merely what " man " needs. Therefore we at home—though it must be with great diffidence that we ever seem to be stating guiding principles for the Churches overseas ; though our opinions of the great non-Christian peoples and of the stage the Church overseas has reached must be very humbly founded on what our workers overseas report to us—yet have the duty of study of the present-day position, in order to help them to meet it. We are not to think for them, but to think with them. The problems of a young Church are far too complex and too vital to be left merely to the unaided solution of the men on the spot, or of the race concerned ; they must have the right to call upon us for intelligent and sympathetic study with them, so that the mind and prayers of the Church as a whole shall be brought to bear everywhere on each necessary local adaptation of the one Faith by the one Church. This must be the justification for the contributions in this book offered by workers who are not themselves overseas. I need hardly add that the Society of which I have the honour to be Secretary is in no sense bound by the personal thoughts that I here put forward.

Christian communities overseas have reached in their development " an end of an age." Everywhere bodies of native Christians are becoming conscious of the call to be a real Church, the Church of their nation, its soul, its guide to the new life that peoples are very hungrily feeling after. As to Abraham of old the call and promise of God is in their ears and hearts to come out " unto a place which they are to receive for an inheritance." For this venture the peoples themselves are conscious that they must find new foundations ; they cannot live the life and build the culture that will satisfy them in the twentieth century merely on the foundations of the past. In these great movements Satan will find his chance, unless the Church of Christ in each nation offers the one foundation on which alone every people can build a satisfying life and culture. Christ must be offered to them by representatives of their own people who share their passionate patriotism towards their own race-future. Behind all the confusions and spasmodic savageries of these tremendous movements there is a hunger, a life-and-death struggle to retain national self-respect and to rebuild national life.

Try to imagine what it means for a handful of Christians to realise that they must be, in this new quest, the soul of their nation. The proclamation of their newly seen responsibility may be tinged with pride and over-confidence, but it is really the acceptance of a colossal and glorious task.

Bodies of native Christians have to-day ceased to be merely clusters of converts gathered round foreign evangelists, and are becoming self-conscious native Churches.

As a consequence of this fact there is one imperative need and longing which has come to Christians everywhere. If Christian communities in non-Christian lands are to undertake this task they must be one body, united into one Church.

No doubt they are rightly impatient that schisms, in which historically they have had no share, should continue to hamper their own development, and may claim that if by the malice of Satan they fall into divisions in the future, those divisions should at least be of indigenous growth and so be capable of being indigenously healed. But behind this impatience there is a more profound desire. It is ludicrous for native Christians to attempt to mould the life of their nation except as one body, and one organic Body in Christ they long to be.

This means that proposals for Christian reunion are and will be a feature of the Christian world of to-day and to-morrow.

In these circumstances what is it that a young Church overseas must demand from an older Church, such as our own ? from a Church that has taken a share in bringing the Good News to them, and may be relied upon to accept the new situation and go on with the work, giving what is needed to-day and in the future ? And what is the duty especially incumbent upon those within the older Churches who rejoice to call themselves children of her Catholic heritage ? Is there, for example, something quite vital which is in real danger of being lost or neglected if the Catholic-minded in our Church here in England do not think clearly and act energetically in missionary enterprise to-day ? Is there anything which they have to give for lack of which the young Churches are likely to go fatally wrong ?

My own opinion is that there is just this contribution : that the one great safeguard which the present situation needs is the setting forth by life and word of the Catholic elements in the Faith, and the inculcation of that catholic spirit which will make Christians have a real horror of breaking the brotherhood or shocking the Christian feelings of the Church in other parts of the world. It is in fact the only safeguard worth talking about.

What support would a truly Catholic bishop from England, presiding over a diocese in India, Africa, China, or Japan, hope to receive from his brothers and sisters in the Home Church ?

He faces (and rejoices in) a determined movement of his people and those of other communions of Christians to unite into one Church. He finds that numerically the Christians of the Free Church denominations greatly predominate ; and that these have a natural tendency to unite by the simple process of taking as a basis what they mostly agree upon. This seems " practical politics," and has already been the basis for the formation of National Christian Councils which, without claiming to be so, yet tend to be looked upon as the real Church of the country, a sort of " super-Church." We need not wonder at this ; it is a natural line of thought. Napoleon, in the course of a conversation at St. Helena, said that if he found all men united in agreeing upon anything, he would regard that union as being the true Church.

But our bishop would feel that he must oppose such a method of reunion as fundamentally wrong. There are inherent in the Christian message principles concerning the Church and Sacraments which if left out or compromised do not merely impoverish her message, but make it cease to be Christian ; the promises of Christ that the Gospel shall prevail no longer attach to such a mutilated message.

The bishop will wish to see what these principles are as clearly as possible, and to proclaim them graciously, positively, and constructively, and that not merely in word and theory, but by the winning witness of lives lived on these principles in the very midst of his people. It is of little use to quote the lives of Christian Kebles in England ; he must have the argument of those who have come to live their lives in the native Church and for the native Church.

The bishop will unfortunately find that the keenest of his native Christians, those who are most conscious that their Church must exist not to save a few native souls but to be the soul and guide of their nation into new life through Christ, tend to wish to claim their individuality in a provocative way. They are so anxious to be themselves that they almost wish to shock the foreigner ; they think of their Church, not primarily as part of one great Catholic Church, but as the very individual Church of their own people and region. The claim of liberty in Christ is often first put as a claim to be just what Christ makes them, starting on their own way, developing entirely on their own lines ; and no one shall say them nay. The signs of this tendency are unmistakable ; there is occasionally a real wish to jar and shock and challenge the older evangelising Churches—a readiness to break off from them absolutely rather than suffer the least check, however friendly, on absolute freedom of development. This is the very reverse of the Catholic spirit. It is a tendency most difficult for the Western missionary to meet without being denounced as " controlling," or as being no friend to the native Church and its rightful freedom.

Our bishop would be terribly handicapped by merely " superior " pronouncements from home about Catholic principles, purposely made downright, and expressed in the provocative language that would " score off " Protestants. He would long for the most gracious and winning expositions of the true value and essence of Catholic principles, very clearly thought out with an obvious wish to understand the native line of thought and a loving and passionate desire to " show a more excellent way." There must surely be a readiness to see the essentials of Catholicity in their biggest, broadest aspects as principles, not as a multitude of details such as Western peoples have quite rightly worked out from these principles for their own use.

For myself, while I can feel certain that some ideas and principles are fundamentally Catholic, so that without them the Church anywhere must go wrong and lose Christ's promises, I feel great reluctance to pronounce ideas or principles to be uncatholic. This may seem like sitting on the fence. It is so much easier to be downright—such things are Catholic ; what departs from them is uncatholic. But after all there is nothing in the world more Catholic than energetic self-sacrificing love for others which expresses itself in missionary work. Where I find such a spirit, for instance, in a body of Nonconformist Indian Christians who show the marks of Christian life and missionary vigour, I would reverence that spirit before I would criticise the framework of its organisation. I would be quite convinced that it is my bounden Christian duty to show them " the more excellent way " ; for instance, to insist that Episcopacy and the Sacraments are of the essence of the Church, and that the argument from " practical politics " simply does not count where these matters are in question ; that the utmost possible friendliness and the most passionate wish to unite with them and the most humble admiration for the Christian virtues they show cannot make it right for me to stir one step towards compromising upon these essential points in framing with them the future constitution of our united Church. But I would hope to do it in such a way as obviously shows that I too hate the breaking of the Catholic brotherhood, the keeping apart of fellow-Christians, and the provocative shocking of the feelings of brethren in Christ.

This, then, is what our Catholic bishop overseas would surely want from the Home Church :

The suppression of the glib arm-chair critic.

The banning of provocative shibboleths.

The longing to find common grounds, in search for which we interpret all that others do in the most favourable catholic sense, often making out a better case for them than they can or care to make out for themselves, and thus show and inculcate the true catholic spirit which we hope in return to find in them.

This will demand the clearest possible thinking out and statement of what are the Catholic fundamentals, especially on questions which affect movements towards the formation of united Churches among native Christians. All have a right to know as clearly as possible where they stand with regard to us. There is no doubt that non-episcopal Christians are showing a most welcome readiness to look towards us for the proclamation of such principles and to accept them for their united Church. It is hardly too much to say that no such Church of the future will be non-episcopal unless we fail them now. If we offer them clear thinking in brotherly love, the Catholic structure, flexible and thoroughly practical as it is, will prevail.

Finally, and above all, the Bishop would say : Do not merely talk about this at home. Send me men and women who show it forth, and the future is ours.

I have been taking for granted that the Church at home is truly Catholic in its burning desire to offer the glorious Gospel of the blessed Christ to all mankind. But we must face facts ; this is not so. Nor can we claim that those most eagerly " Catholic " in our Church are the most missionary section of it. Study of the overseas Church, unless allied to a passionate desire to help, is too liable to become merely critical of other people's shortcomings. So we must contemplate something more than the usual " home base " propaganda. Something far more radical is needed to stir our Church. It is not enough for a Church (still less for a section of a Church) to be interested in other races, or to be stirred by the romance of missionary heroism. It must be aflame with a passion for the glory of God and the Church of the living Christ. Nothing less will suffice. A Catholic revival that will take " Hallowed be Thy Name " as its motto, that cannot rest while God is cheated of the worship He deserves from even the remotest of His peoples—this alone will meet the need of to-day. It is the only propaganda worth relying upon. The Anglican Christian who is keen about the missionary honour of his Church will throw himself heart and soul into every movement that gives new vision of God, new passion for prayer, new thrill in the idea of the Catholic Church. That is the most practical of missionary propaganda.

INDEX

Printed in England at THE BALLANTYNE PRESS
SPOTTISWOODE, BALLANTYNE & CO. LTD.
Colchester, London & Eton